Music and Cyberliberties

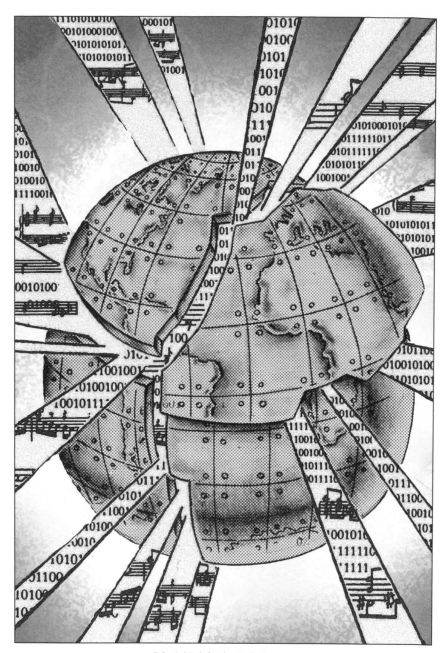

Celestial Jukebox by Rob Sussman

PATRICK BURKART

✳

Music and Cyberliberties

✳

WESLEYAN UNIVERSITY PRESS

Middletown, Connecticut

Published by Wesleyan University Press,
Middletown, CT 06459
www.wesleyan.edu/wespress
© 2010 by Patrick Burkart
Printed in the United States of America
5 4 3 2 1

Library of Congress Cataloging-in-Publication Data

Burkart, Patrick, 1969–
Music and cyberliberties / Patrick Burkart.
p. cm. — (Music/culture)
Includes bibliographical references and index.
ISBN 978-0-8195-6917-2 (cloth : alk. paper) —
ISBN 978-0-8195-6918-9 (pbk. : alk. paper)
1. Music and the Internet. 2. Sound recording
industry. 3. Internet—Social aspects. I. Title.
ML3790.B847 2009
306.4'842–dc22   2009036025

Wesleyan University Press is a member of the Green
Press Initiative. The paper used in this book meets their
minimum requirement for recycled paper.

Contents

✳

Acknowledgments

*

I am grateful to Vinny Mosco, who provided inspiration for this project. Encouragement and considerable assistance came from my friends and colleagues, including Tom McCourt, Eric Rothenbuhler, John Downing, Harris M. Berger, Kembrew McLeod, Jim Aune, Linda Putnam, and Charley Conrad. Joel Schalit, Brock Craft, and Joseph Lopez provided feedback at all stages of this project, and Mike Godwin, Gwen Hinze, Wendy Seltzer, and Fred von Lohmann made themselves accessible for my many questions. Thanks to Kip Keller for preparing my manuscript, and to the Melbern G. Glasscock Center for Humanities Research, the Ford Foundation Program on Media, Arts, and Culture, and the Texas A&M University European Union Center for providing support for this research.

Abbreviations

*

AAC	advanced audio coding
AAIM	American Association of Independent Music
ACLU	American Civil Liberties Union
ACME	Action Coalition for Media Education
ALA	American Library Association
A&R	artist and repertoire
ARPANET	Advanced Research Projects Agency Network
ASCAP	American Society of Composers, Authors, and Publishers
AT&T	American Telephone and Telegraph
A2K	Access to Knowledge
BBS	bulletin board system
BLO	Barbie Liberation Organization
BMI	Broadcast Music Inc.
BMG	Bertelsmann Music Group
CDD	Center for Digital Democracy
CFP	Computers, Freedom, and Privacy
CIMA	Center for International Media Action
CODEC	coder-decoder language
COO	chief operating officer
CPSR	Computer Professionals for Social Responsibility
CRIS	Communication Rights in the Information Society
CRM	customer relationship management
CSS	content-scrambling system
CVS	concurrent versions system
DDoS	distributed denial of service
DIY	do-it-yourself
DMCA	Digital Millenium Copyright Act
DMCRA	Digital Media Consumer Rights Act

DRA	Digital Rights Agency
DRM	digital-rights management
DR-CAFTA	Dominican Republic–Central American Free Trade Agreement
EFF	Electronic Frontier Foundation
EMI	Electrical and Musical Industries (EMI record company)
EPIC	Electronic Privacy Information Clearinghouse
EULA	end user license agreement
EULAAA	End User License Agreement Activist Amendment
FCC	Federal Communications Commission
FFII	Foundation for a Free Information Infrastructure
FOMC	Future of Music Coalition
FOSS	free and open source software
FSF	Free Software Society
FTA	free trade agreement
GLBT	gay, lesbian, bisexual, and transgender
GUI	graphical user interface
ICT	information and communication technology
IFPI	International Federation of the Phonographic Industry
IODA	International Online Distribution Alliance
IP	intellectual property
IPR	intellectual property rights
ISP	Internet service provider
MAIN	Mountain Area Information Network
MOO	MUD object-oriented
MPAA	Motion Picture Association of America
MUD	multi-user dungeon
NCMR	National Conference for Media Reform
NGO	nongovernmental organization
NSM	new social movement
P2P	peer to peer
RAIN	Radio and Internet Newsletter
RIAA	Recording Industry Association of America
RM	resource mobilization
SDMI	Secure Digital Music Initiative
SMS	wireless short message service
TCA	theory of communicative action
TOR	The Onion Router
UCITA	Uniform Computer Information Transactions Act
USCO	the Company of Us (media-art collective)
US-PIRG	U.S. Public interest Research Group

WELL	Whole Earth 'Lectronic Link
WIPO	World Intellectual Property Organization
WMA	Windows Media Audio
WSIS	World Summit on the Information Society
WTO	World Trade Organization
WTO-TRIPS	World Trade Organization–Trade Related Aspects of Intellectual Property Rights

Music and Cyberliberties

Introduction

In the 1990s, as popular-music fans bought CDs and listened to music on FM radio, the entertainment industry in the United States promised congressional leaders the construction and delivery of a "Celestial Jukebox," an always-on entertainment appliance with all possible media selections available on demand, in exchange for wholesale deregulation of the electronic media and telecommunications markets.[1] The Telecommunications Act of 1996 was intended to enable construction of the Jukebox, which could retrieve and deliver any cultural artifact and satisfy all the "pushbutton fantasies" (Mosco 1982) of the digital generation. Of course, the heavenly promise was too good to be true. A proliferation of pay-per-view channels and subscription services notwithstanding, on-demand interactive television and cable radio platforms offered few innovations and only at a high cost. On-demand selection of albums and tracks was not attainable. Today, digital distribution of music through the Internet has the potential to deliver on push-button fantasies, but only recently have the high social costs of the Celestial Jukebox become apparent.[2] This book addresses the risks that accompany the period of transition from digital music products to digital music services, including the ever-shrinking number of gatekeepers, owners, and managers of intellectual property, and their ever-growing market power and political power. In the turn from a permissive policy on the gift economy to a punitive system, millions of people now directly experience new pressures to become consumers or clients of the popular-music industry, mere music "users," and to acquiesce in the pervasiveness of technocracy in everyday life. Because the new cultural landlords in cyberspace enjoy state-sanctioned monopolies, and the policing powers to enforce them, they act as agents of state capitalism and fuse legal authority with market power. The music fans and artists who reject the terms of the new consumption norm are the subjects of this study.

1

Whereas my previous work, with McCourt, focused on the culture industries from the perspective of the economic and legal systems (Burkart and McCourt 2006), this book examines the "place of music" (Leyshon et al. 1998) in the lifeworld and in the context of the theory of communicative action (Habermas 1984, 1987).[3] When McCourt and I presented the technological and economic details of the media lockdown now in progress, we noted the oppositional currents active during the formation of the Celestial Jukebox, but omitted details about the social agents who aim to present alternative places of—and for—music. To paint a more complete picture of the movements converging around saving a place for music, I have selected case studies of groups opposing the completion of the business model of the Celestial Jukebox (Burkart and McCourt 2006). In my perspective, these fans and artists are trying to save a place for music as a zone for reproduction of "free culture," identity formation, and broad participation in making music and music scenes. Musicians and fans are challenging the current business model of digital distribution in four ways: by (1) bypassing copy protections on music files; (2) facilitating anonymous file sharing; (3) developing commercial alternatives to doing business with major labels; and (4) creating software innovations that provide open and multipurpose alternatives to closed systems.

I consider music and cyberliberties to be an incipient social movement opposed to technological lockdowns on music, online surveillance, crackdowns on copy-protection research, restrictions on fair-use rights and their chilling effects on speech. It follows a recognizable history of opposing the insinuation of regulation into private life: "Much social protest today does indeed seem to be provoked by the imposition of inappropriate principles of evaluation and interaction in different social domains. These can be well described as resistance to commodity culture and juridification, and both of these can be plausibly explained as necessitated by capitalist growth and the increased responsibilities of the interventionist state" (Sitton 1998, 78–79). In the desire to preserve personal autonomy over technology for accessing and sharing music, fans who reject the Celestial Jukebox experience a repeating clash of worldviews and viewpoints with the regulationists' Internet and its increasingly juridical composition. "The 'regulators' tend to see the problem of cybercrimes as being an overall lack of effective regulation, so they demand changes in the law to empower or strengthen the existing powers of police and other regulatory organizations" (Wall 2000, 5). The political responses by cyberlibertarians to the regulators lie not exclusively in formal changes to the law and political system, but also "in influencing the behavior of individuals by changing normative behaviors" (Wall 2000, 6). *Music and Cyberliberties* addresses the social agents who pursue changes in normative attitudes and laws and technologies concerning access to music, media, knowledge, and culture.

Until recently, serious music fans traded music and thoughts on music in person, hung out in record stores, and participated in local music scenes. Popular music fans can be passionately and loyally committed to participating in culture and have exerted a democratizing influence on the production and distribution of music (Hesmondhalgh 1998). This book examines the social agency of the fans and artists who have pursued democratization of the music industry through a variety of organizational, technological, and symbolic strategies. Music and cyberliberties activists' roots go back to the "new communalism" movement of the 1960s and 1970s, which adopted a tech-savvy do-it-yourself approach to democratizing cultural and social institutions. The new communalism movement set personal autonomy as a standard for technology practices and linked personal autonomy with public-policy commitments to information rights and innovation.

The Internet accelerates and sharpens the many contradictions and conflicts of capitalism and "techno-capitalism" (Kellner 1989). The communalist or communitarian attributes of the Internet's cultures have been severely depleted as it has become both commercialized and incorporated into institutions of economic and governmental control and coordination, including the resurgent military-industrial complex. The "change of state" (Braman 2007) accommodates information technology used to exert new controls over personal, social, and cultural realms, but also provokes conflicts between state authority and personal autonomy.[4] This study of music and cyberliberties is, in many respects, a study of how people organize politically to maximize their autonomy when powerful and often intrusive information technologies thoroughly change the rituals and rhythms of everyday life. This political organizing occurs in the midst of cultural conflicts over the new consumer and user roles imposed on music fans by the Celestial Jukebox.

Following Jürgen Habermas, I present the lifeworld as the background knowledge, or "worldview knowledge," that provides a "context-forming horizon" in which "participants in communication come to an understanding with one another about something" (Habermas 1984, 337). In the context of music fandom, music making, and music distribution, I shall speak of the "music lifeworld," which is describable using ethnomusicology, music studies, and social-scientific studies of music. I take a sociological, social-systems approach to the music lifeworld, considering its structures and processes, including music scenes and other "places of music" (Leyshon et al. 1998). Habermasian social theory makes it possible to describe the invasion of the music lifeworld by power dynamics that reinforce the roles of "client" and "consumer," which are analogous to but downgraded from those of "employee" and "citizen," and which carry "privatized hopes for self-actual-ization and self-determination" (Sitton 1998, 78). In the transition from sharing music scenes and collecting records to consuming music as a com-mercial service, digital music distribution pulls the rug out from under many of the communal and sharing practices that have enabled local music scenes on and off the Net.

This book would not be relevant if not for the history of the powerful firms that have promoted clientelist and consumerist roles. Four media gi-ants—Sony-BMG, Vivendi-Universal, Warner, and EMI—have consoli-dated the ownership of intellectual property rights to recorded music, and they share some rights to the digital technologies now used to handle it. The control wielded by giant corporations is substantial but not absolute. The recording industry has been particularly inept and uncoordinated at distrib-uting popular music digitally.[5] This criticism emerges within the ranks of the executives themselves. Leyshon and his associates interviewed the chief op-erating officer (COO) of an online music broker who works with major la-bels in digital distribution. When asked why record companies were having so much trouble adapting to MP3 and the Internet, the COO responded:

They get paid way too much money, they're definitely afraid of losing their jobs. Based on those things they are afraid to make decisions, they're afraid to take chances, their Boards of Directors demand instant profits, the days of artist develop-ment are long gone. . . . All the record industry needs to do is go back and copy what it did 25 years ago and the problem is solved. But the problem is that it's going to take two or three years of dreadful profits before they're going to start reaping the rewards of that investment in time, energy and straight thinking . . . they know their jobs generally only last for a short amount of time, so why rattle the cage or rock the boat when they're going to be out of the boat in a few years anyway and who gives a shit, they can take their money and house in Beverly Hills and retire. (Leyshon, Webb et al. 2005, 196)

The short-term thinking, greed, and fear displayed by the Big Four's decision-makers have contributed to a stalled-out business strategy for digital distri-bution. In the United States and worldwide, "digital music spending growth has not offset the decline in music CD revenue" ("Digital music soars" 2008).

Rather than change their organizations to compete in a new arena and win back lost customers, the Big Four have behaved negligently and in ways that have served to emphasize their abuses of market power. Payola settle-ments, renewed antitrust concerns, the use of aggressive legal and business tactics to slow innovators, and attempts to change social norms about shar-ing music by weakening consumer rights—all have contributed to suspi-cions and hostility about the intentions and operation of the major labels. Consequently, however accustomed music fans have become to being treated as consumers, many fans are resisting now being treated as mere music "users." As a colleague of mine, Eric Rothenbuhler, put it, serious music fans who have collected records for decades now draw a distinction "between a time when Warner Brothers could advertise, 'The revolution is on Warner Brothers' and we didn't laugh (even if we should have), and a time when all serious music fans take it for granted that the industry is run by idiots and charlatans."

Online music brokers and other intermediaries now bridge the gap between Internet service providers and artists, having outmaneuvered the Big Four's traditional artists and repertoire (A&R) departments and nibbled away at their other businesses. These nibbles will become bigger bites as the proportion of digital sales grows. More serious challenges to the basic business model of licensing and selling commercial music come from renegade bands seeking to bypass the Big Four altogether, do-it-yourself (DIY) artist collectives, fans themselves, and a resurgence of indie labels and online "Netlabels." These groups were among the earliest to mobilize in response to new networking options and music-industry abuses. Using new technologies and new forms of collective action and organization, they are promoting a grassroots music industry, using alternative and radical methods to promote projects that undermine the Big Four. These efforts represent a restructuring that has inaugurated a new era of entrepreneurial activity in the penumbra of the Big Four and has been organized around the Internet, free and open-source software, and other tools that can "decolonize" or democratize access to music.

Music and cyberliberties activists are drawing attention to an incipient social problem: the attempted takeover of online music and audiovisual cultures by bureaucracies and technocratic systems of control. A sociological systems theory provides the basis, in communicative action, for finding in music studies new examples of oppositional social agency. Music and cyberliberties activists may exhibit more power and political agency than either "ordinary" music fans or active and engaged audiences, and so should be studied in the context of society and culture together.[6] Critical legal studies identifies the "copyright grab" (Samuelson 1996) and the inflation of the power of the intellectual-property-rights regime to unprecedented levels as major factors contributing to ruptures in the lives of artists, fans, and music researchers. The theory of communicative action (Habermas 1984, 1987) makes it possible to link these ruptures to specific processes of "rationalization," or modernization, of society (Habermas 1987, 147) in order to promote policies conducive to deliberation and communicative reason, and to critique the processes that put personal autonomy and the cultural commons at risk.

In the German sociological tradition, rationalization and modernization are associated with a progressive loss of meaning and with increased alienation. The Marxist identification of alienation and "reification" (distorted thinking) with waged capitalism was expounded by the first-generation Frankfurt School of critical theory, particularly by Horkheimer and Adorno. Horkheimer and Adorno expanded the notion of rationalization to include all forms of instrumental reason, but focused on the culture industries because of the intimacy of their products with the lives and consciousness of members of mass societies. Like other Marxisms, their strand of critical theory appeals to the desire of radical thinkers for a complete system that explains the totality of the social world (Jay 1984). However, the exhaustion of the rational social subject in negative dialectics (Horkheimer and Adorno) was challenged by an argument for recognizing a communicative reason standing alongside a functionalist and means-end model of rationality. Habermas presents a dual model of system and lifeworld processes. Updated — or "second-generation"— critical theory seeks to identify and address social injustice, in part to avoid the dead ends of critical theory's first generation. Critical theory can be used to explore how social groups promote a more just social order, and to explore communicative action as a basis for understanding the cultural politics of Internet-based music scenes. I adopt Habermas's "system and lifeworld" framework presented in his *Theory of Communicative Action*, which provides a way to describe and evaluate the music industry as a culture industry creating media effects that include reification, alienation, and loss of free culture on the Internet, but also as a basis for a full-fledged rebellion from within the music lifeworld.

Emblematic of the "linguistic turn" of the social sciences, Habermasian critical theory introduced many disciplines to the foundational role played by language and communication in social life. Communicative action augments labor as an activity for self-realization and achieving political solidarity as aspects of "communicative rationality." Communicative rationality denotes a teleology of action oriented to understanding; it is argumentative and dialogical. It is also incommensurable with instrumental reason and means-ends thinking, or "functionalist reason," although social contexts with mixed purposes are commonplace. In its purest notional form, communicative rationality is a "utopia...to reconstruct an undamaged intersubjectivity that allows for unconstrained mutual understanding among individuals and for the identities of individuals who come to an unconstrained understanding with themselves" (Habermas 1987, 2). So communicative rationality and communicative action are idealized notions designed for evaluating real-world social problems and policy dilemmas; they can serve as a normative basis for critiquing "distorted" communications and contemporary social problems to which culture industries can contribute.

Of special interest here is the "colonization thesis" of Habermas's theory, which updates the Marxist concept of reification[7] by showing how communal social practices and institutions can become "mediatized" by power and money, and further "colonized" or taken over by "mechanisms of system integration" (Habermas 1987, 305). In advanced capitalist societies, as reification takes hold, the state and economy can progressively take over lifeworld structures (Habermas 1987, 173–197, 305). The colonization thesis helps explain how money and power can attach to the music lifeworld and convert it into complex technical systems for exchange and surveillance (see Habermas 1987, 173). I shall use the colonization thesis to illuminate this process at work for music fans. Entertainment-industry giants successfully built an intellectual-property-rights regime around a Celestial Jukebox design that has helped diminish and trivialize the public-good characteristics of culture and immobilize the institutions that depend upon continued access to fair use, public domain, and other areas of access to knowledge and culture.

This book intends to correct an imbalance in critical media studies, which tends to use Habermas's *Theory of Communicative Action* to guide research geared to preserving and expanding the "public sphere"—where democratic cultures carry out their processes of political conflict and conflict resolution. The colonization thesis, however, has been relatively neglected in communication studies generally. *Music and Cyberliberties* criticizes the colonization of cyberspace by intellectual-property law, contract law, digital-rights management, and perpetual surveillance. It highlights sites of reification in the political economy of the music industry and relates these to specific activist responses. It contributes to an understanding of social agency relevant to other approaches to online music cultures, including fandom studies, uses and gratifications theory, audience studies, and legal studies. The colonization thesis exposes the incremental threats to communicative rationality by technologies and institutions of global capitalism in complementary ways to analyses of media and the public sphere.

By using the term "cyberliberties," I mean to circumscribe communicative rationality in the everyday activities of cyberspace, which is a broader concept than the narrowly juridical sense of "liberty" as concerned with free speech and privacy. The right to communicate (Hamelink 2004), equitable access to the "networked public sphere" (Benkler 2006, 240), access to knowledge about technical aspects of copy-protection schemes, and the preservation of open-information architectures, public-domain works, and "free culture" (Lessig 2004) are all updated democratic norms and values that spring from an underlying "communicative rationality" (Habermas 1984). Habermas uses the notion of communicative rationality to add scholarly, artistic, and political language as a zone of research that belongs alongside labor and praxis (theoretically informed politics) as focus areas of Marxist critical theory. In contributing to cyberliberties research and theory, the works of Coombes, Hamelink, Benkler, Lessig, Vaidhyanathan, and others highlight key political and social conflicts occurring over cultural colonization. Collectively, their case studies and diagnoses provide support for the colonization thesis. Many also engage with contemporary cyberliberties politics in addition to contributing to the struggles with their academic work. These thinkers sound an alarm about the eroding ground of the music lifeworld, showing where the system is substituting its own mechanisms and imperatives for lifeworld processes.

Adapting the Theory

The record industry is now bathed in conflictual modes of collective action against it, including direct action such as hacktivism and culture jamming. My basic position is that the theory of communicative action stands to enhance our understandings of and explanations for the varieties of political and cultural conflict that we now observe surrounding digital distribution of music. Moreover, I endorse the claim that this approach provides us "a general framework for comprehending the relationships between citizens, state and economy and, also, a basic moral orientation for a rejuvenated democracy" (Spaul 1995, 321). These are my points of departure. I now address some of the critics of second-generation critical theory and the theory of communicative action (TCA).

No sociological theory of social change fits perfectly with music studies. I acknowledge that Habermas's approach to interpretive social science in the *Theory of Communicative Action* has drawn significant and deserved criticism, particularly in his strict division of system and lifeworld contexts. I shall sketch the primary objections, and then provide a general defense of my use of critical systems theory.

Habermas's English-language translator, Thomas McCarthy (1985), criticizes the system-lifeworld approach as insufficient for describing processes of democratization as they actually occur in social movements. This objection deserves close attention. It calls into question the ability of Habermas's critical systems theory to assist music and cyberliberties (or any incipient social movement) to undertake a collective, democratic project to reclaim music as a shareable public good, and sharing as a legitimate cultural practice. It also challenges the conceptual stability of the dualistic, system-and-lifeworld framework for interpreting modern history.

McCarthy envisions critical theory as a practical aid that helps us decide if interactions within large-scale economic organizations (like those of the recording industry or other culture industries) are, and should be, *solely* guided by administrative power and money, or by something else instead, or by a mix of influences. Likewise, critical theory should illuminate whether market relations are, and should be, steered *solely* by money and power (McCarthy 1985, 50 note 49), or by other influences. The important fact to note is that market and nonmarket relations are negotiable, and have been politically negotiated to begin with. McCarthy intimates that critical theory should advance socialist values, or at least pro-labor values, in the aid of labor-based appeals for collective action, and that Habermas has paid insufficient attention to labor as a source of social value or as a potential collective project.

McCarthy lands a second serious criticism against the theory of communicative action. Democracy and democratization, which are key values for music and cyberliberties, are more robust phenomena than those that functionalist systems theory is able to describe on its own. Yet Habermas relies on systems theory to provide a descriptive model for the public sphere and its historical transformations. The ambiguities of systems theory yield few practical strategies for democratic social movements, and democratization is practically incomprehensible, as it is presented in systems language, as "de-differentiation of the state" (McCarthy 1985, 50).

As it stands, the TCA lacks many of the subtleties needed to handle hybrid and morphing organizations, such as those that characterize music scenes. And, overrelying on an either-or, system-lifeworld choice for understanding and describing social changes introduces some weaknesses into our analyses (McCarthy 1985, 34). "Even if we restrict ourselves to the most bureaucratically hierarchized forms of organization it is not clear that the system integration versus social integration contrast captures what is specific to them. . . .We cannot talk of formal organizations as being systemically *rather than* socially integrated. . . . System integration and social integration . . . seem to be extremes rather than alternatives that exhaust the field of possibilities: The denial of one does not entail the other" (McCarthy 1985, 40–41). Symbolic and material reproduction are interdependent, but their interrelation is not clearly shown (Baxter 1987, 77). "'System' and 'lifeworld' thus do not . . . name different *spheres* of society; rather, they define two different *perspectives* on society" (Baxter 1987, 78). Likewise, Habermas presents a model of clear breaks and ruptures in everyday discourse belonging to separate realms of culture formation, identity formation, and political discourse (Calhoun 1995, 267), although these realms are rarely separated in real life.

McCarthy takes Habermas to task for embracing functionalist systems theory too closely for a critical theorist, which causes second-generation critical theory to inherit some of the recognized risks of systems theory: principally, that such "administrative" social science (to use Lazarsfeld's term) reproduces conditions conducive to the growth of bureaucratic systems. This is the context for McCarthy's addressing the "spectre" of instrumental reason and domination haunting the *Theory of Communicative Action* (McCarthy 1985, 27). As a subdiscipline of administrative social science, systems theory is uncritical, neglecting the inner dynamics of the system and its contradictions (McCarthy 1985, 51), and neglecting relationships between the lifeworld "spheres" and between subsystems.

Calhoun (1995, 273) and Koivisto and Valiverronen (1996) take aim at Habermas's bourgeois public sphere as an Archimedean point of reference for democratic theory. "The problem with this kind of normative critique, based on ideals, is that the critique remains inside the normative categories without posing consistently the question of their social constitution and the limits of these ideals" (Koivisto and Väliverronen 1996, 22). Calhoun puts this criticism another way, that Habermas takes bourgeois liberalism as a democratic standard, and that this model cannot handle political identities that are emergent in political movements (1995, 205). Calhoun (1995) also rejects Habermas's portrayal of the theory of communicative action as a psychoanalytic talking cure for the ills of democratic societies. It is not clear who will play the roles of the psychoanalyst and subject, particularly in international and intercultural contexts. "It is hard to figure out what sort of collective *project* is strictly analogous to psychoanalysis, and especially what sort of project *between different cultures*" (Calhoun 1995, 53; emphases in original). Perhaps formal organizations, political movements, and critical theorists can negotiate a psychoanalytic relationship (Calhoun 1995, 206). But the talking cure for conflicted interests competes with other varieties of social conflict that movements could pursue for the purpose of democratization.

Nancy Fraser criticizes Habermas's idealization of bourgeois family life as patriarchal and oppressive (1992). As Calhoun summarizes the argument for feminist and queer political perspectives, traditional "families are hardly realms of free and uncoerced mutual pursuit of understanding" (1995, 52). Habermas responds to this criticism by saying that "the rights to unrestricted inclusion and equality which are an integral part of the liberal public sphere's self-interpretation" are therefore also shared by feminism (quoted in Koivisto and Valiverronen 1996, 22) and perhaps by extension, queer theory. Although Calhoun critiques the public sphere concept as patriarchal and traditional, à la Fraser, he also argues—confusingly—that Habermas rejects any role for tradition in the intellectual life of a society (Calhoun 1995, 206).

Calhoun (1995), in a well-read evaluation of the theory of communicative action, joins McCarthy (1985) in objecting to the fact that Habermas "virtually abandons class and other fundamental divisions" and "doesn't make conflictual social action part of his account of social change" (206). He notes that macrostructural factors contributing to changing action orientations, such as large-scale demographic and trade-related patterns of globalization (cf. Castells 1996), are not considered at all by Habermas as external factors affecting social life (Calhoun 1995, 206). The same could be said of incipient ecological factors such as climate change. Calhoun (1995) and Baxter (1987) both find it unlikely that "formal organizations in state and economy are [wholly] independent of norms, values, and personal motivations" (Baxter 1987, 72); they thus challenge Habermas's basic claim that system and lifeworld are "uncoupling," such that modern political and social life continues to show a "progressive indifference" (Baxter 1987, 70) to the "structures of the lifeworld" (Schutz and Luckmann 1973). I find evidence to support the uncoupling proposition in the experiences of music fans acquiring access to music in Celestial Jukebox organizations online, and I propose that this kind of evidence updates Habermas's colonization thesis more generally.

My own adaptation of the theory of communicative action is informed by political economy, which tracks changes in commodification, structuration, and spatialization that are associated with neoliberal structural reforms worldwide. These reforms have exerted a colonizing influence upon people's cultures, societies, and personalities—the structures of the lifeworld. I also broaden the consideration of participatory collective action to include a "sphere of publics" (Calhoun 1995) in which "the identities of members...[are] formed and revised partly through the participation in the public sphere, not settled in advance" (Calhoun 1995, 273). My focus in *Music and Cyberliberties* is to illuminate the evidence that exists for political and social agency oriented to preserving and extending civil liberties in cyberspace.

I shall address these critiques, concerns, and modifications of the TCA more fully in the course of this book. Here, though, I shall present the case for using the TCA in the present study. Habermas's theory captures the historical juncture at which we music fans, musicians, and other technologically informed participants in music culture find ourselves: caught up in the formation of the Celestial Jukebox. I argue that among us, there are new social movements, alternative and radical media practitioners, culture jammers, hackers, and critical legal scholars who all share, in different ways, a "hermeneutically enlightened and historically oriented functionalism" (Mc-Carthy 1985, 52) and who can work in-between the system-and-lifeworld framework of ideal types. I shall also argue that these groups demonstrate a sense of social agency in the way that they are beginning to subject forms of state power over culture to continual scrutiny and curtailment. Critical legal studies, for example, is an enlightened professional practice that enables the law to become more "reflexive" and "provide the discursive apparatus out of which new, and better, laws are generated" (Graham 1996, 11).

In spite of the acknowledged weaknesses of its 1980s formulation by Habermas, "the lifeworld and system model provides a reflective framework for those working to integrate emancipatory practices into the efficient functioning of organizations" (Spaul 1995, 330). I use the model to support a model of social agency for new social movements. Music and cyberliberties activists are providing continual, focused, and public debates about public policy and civil liberties centered on music. Specifically, music fans and musicians are recognizing and highlighting the occasions when decision-makers are making political compromises with a shared music culture. I adapt the general framework of the TCA from a "defensive" account of social movement conflicts into a more "offensive" (or proactive) account of social movements theory (Spaul 1995, 328; Cohen and Arato 1992) to account for emerging cyberlibertarian strategies.

Although intellectual property, Internet regulation, and software systems for media distribution are usually boring topics that typically fall outside of everyday discourse, music and cyberliberties activists are identifying, naming, and challenging these encroachments into the music lifeworld in a systematic and exciting fashion. Music and cyberliberties activists show clearly that emergent politics, culture, and identity are commingled in discourse and social action. As the critics of Habermas have made clear, the orthodox position on maintaining strict analytical separation of "spheres" of discourse in the system and lifeworld oversimplifies social reality in separating music scenes from political participation and identity formation. I attempt to pull together these perspectives.

Organization of the Book

Chapter 1 addresses the widespread perception, increasingly supported by evidence, that the music industry is taking liberties with legal rights and expectations about fairness of takings associated with sharing free culture and the cultural commons. It also describes some of the communicative features of rebellions organizing on behalf of projects designed to exit or bypass restrictive communication environments online. The reconfiguration of production, distribution, and consumption roles in new music cultures online is taken for granted by fans, but is also under sustained attack. The theory of communicative action aids the study of music and cyberliberties together as a political movement about access to knowledge and culture. Oppositional politics oriented to enhancing non–property-based rights, and to expressing social conflicts over the music and media lifeworld, also expresses the effects of conflicts within processes of commodification, spatialization, and structuration identified by the political economy of communication (Mosco 1996). Saving a place for music on the Internet requires paying attention to some of the greatest risks to the music lifeworld. Exploitation of opportunities to diverge from established business models for popular music, and the use of technology and independent organizational models, have pushed boundaries on participation and access to music production and distribution. Chapter 1 considers principal players and movement intellectuals, including those associated with the ACLU, EFF, and other professional cyberliberties experts. I also discuss the key implications of online music's entanglement with legal code and institutions. Juridification of the music lifeworld is a basic consequence of its colonization.

Chapter 2 considers the possibility that music and cyberliberties has the making of a social movement, complete with a discernable organization or network, and self-awareness as a movement. Dismantling the Celestial Jukebox and replacing it with an Alternative Jukebox require comprehensive changes in public policy, business norms, and legal norms for the rights of access to knowledge and culture. Who is taking up this radical project? Researchers in communication studies, critical legal studies, critical information studies, cultural studies, and new social movement theory see cyberliberties as an existing—albeit multifaceted and fractured—social force that can exert power, even if only counterhegemonically. Radical and alternative media build upon older rights-based movements, the labor movement, and new social movements. I explore the potentials for transformational social change by radical and alternative media, hacktivism, and culture jamming in the context of popular music making and distribution. I shall consider these cases as politics of symbolic action, which are, in the end, weapons of the weak (Lovink 2002; Scott 1985). I also address some of the specific contexts of colonization of the music lifeworld at which these "tactical" media are targeted. This chapter presents the case that the theory of communicative action can do a better job at addressing the agency and structure of music and cyberliberties than some alternative approaches, including reception-based media theories and media economics.

Chapter 3 considers what is lost or at risk in the transition to the "informational" (Braman 2007) mode of regulation and its attendant colonization pressures on the music lifeworld. The juridical eclipse of fair use by copy-protection technology and supporting policy, extortion of music fans by lawsuit-happy record companies, and abusive end-user license agreements are symptoms of lifeworld loss. The loss accelerated after what I call the "Napster watershed." I compare these real losses to some of the imagined features of the music lifeworld online, some of the "taken for granteds" that most music fans still have, including music sharing. Chapter 3 also introduces the notion of "clientelization" of music fans, a process in which music fans voluntarily give up legal rights and privileges in exchange for whatever conveniences they may find in becoming "users" of a music "service." Music fans' resistance to clientelization takes some creative, amusing, and effective forms inspired by the new communalism and hippie subcultures of the 1960s.

Chapter 4 assesses what may be (or what may become) the roots of an incipient music and cyberliberties movement attempting to restore a basis for the organic decomposition and recomposition of music and audiovisual culture after the transition to digital media and the informational mode of regulation. I consider music and cyberliberties from the perspective of new social movement theory, as a complementary approach to the theory of communicative action. The conflicted dynamics of cyberspace reveal a key challenge to liberal democracies now: deliberating and making "a choice about how to be free, equal, productive human beings under a new set of technological and economic conditions" (Benkler 2006, 27–28). Where an ethos may have united the cyberlibertarians, ideology now divides them. The new communalist roots of the cyberliberties ethos branched into conflicting political philosophies about property rights in relation to other kinds of rights and civil liberties. In this chapter, I explore the contours of the "two cyberlibertarianisms" that remain in conflict. I also compare updated versions of the deliberative approach to new media studies, including the global civil society approach and the "networked public sphere" approach. I also address some of the main objections and skeptical rejoinders to new social movement theory generally, and cyberlibertarianism specifically.

Chapter 5 compares the cyberlibertarian ethical streak to the ethos of the record collector of the days of the 45, LP, cassette, eight-track, and CD. In the race to commodify digital music distribution, music service providers are experimenting with converting record collectors into music service users. I ask which of the record collector's fetishes can be satisfied or partially satisfied by music services, and reflect on the social and cultural roles in music scenes that were once played by record collectors. Chapter 6 concludes with some reflections on theorizing music and cyberliberties together with the aid of the theory of communicative action.

CHAPTER ONE

Saving a Place for Music

✳

The intrusion of technocratic controls into the activities of collecting and enjoying music with friends and family reflects a colonization of the lifeworld. Copyright law has helped to "uncouple" (Habermas 1987, 365) the music lifeworld from other social subsystems to the point that the law is no longer called upon to justify itself with reference to its interventions into the music lifeworld. Rather, the law, together with power, money, and communication networks, works as a "steering medium": it works independently of the lifeworld, colonizes it, and converts its cultural communications into formal, instrumentalist, market-based transactions (Habermas 1987, 365). While the legitimacy and moral authority of intellectual-property (IP) law is lost on both legal subjects and critical-legal scholars alike (Demers 2006), and its de facto holding power is weakened, its de jure regulation of new places of music online is almost perfect.

Illustrating disillusionment over the predicaments of music fans, music studies has taken an activist bent that can be seen in work by Demers (2006), McLeod (2005), and others who explore the "variable and often contradictory relationship between music appropriation and IP law" (Demers 2006, 144). Persistent abuses of the rights of music makers and their fans by a culture industry operating under the protection of IP law are at least partly visible to popular music fans as well. Evidence of collective action calling attention to legalistic (or juridical) colonization appears in the example of the February 24, 2004, "Grey Tuesday," an online "happening" in which protesters posted copies of DJ Danger Mouse's *Grey Album* to the Web, at the risk of prosecution. Grey Tuesday created a precedent for "distributing, as a social protest, a work that potentially violated copyright....The aesthetic integrity of DJ Danger Mouse's artwork alerted the general public to inconsistencies in the copyright regime....The *Grey Album* will probably be seen as a highly visible first step in a public backlash against IP extrem-

ism" (Demers 2006, 141). Grey Tuesday illustrated social resistance to practices of commercial music making, music distributing, and music playing
that have accompanied the compounding financial crises in the popular-
music industry, the disruptive technological innovations that challenge the
industry as a middleman, and increasingly unruly audiences. Something of
a populist revolt has broken out against the music industry, symbolized by
collective action like Grey Tuesday, and the taken-for-grantedness of digital
"piracy" by music fans (Strangelove 2005, 234 n. 17 and 240). Another collective action was the Internet Webcasting "day of silence" on June 26, 2007,
that protested retroactive royalty-rate increases that small and noncommercial Webcasters feared would shut down their streams (Bangeman 2007).
And, of course, the file-sharing rebellion has not ceased since the recording
industry fought pitched battles with peer-to-peer (P2P) sites and the so-
called Darknet, notably Napster and Grokster.

Rather than meeting the challenges of P2P with innovative new business
models, the industry chose to hobble itself with a digital distribution strategy laboring under new "crippleware" (copy protection by digital rights
management [DRM] that disables the copy, edit, and save functions of
music players). The industry selected crippleware as part of a broad, aggressive, and punitive approach to IP-rights enforcement beginning about 1998.
Music and cyberliberties activists who are leading the revolt against crippleware may be shaping the new politics of the "technoculture" (Robins and
Webster 1999) by altering the political economy of the music business:
cracking its DRM, bypassing its expensive and exclusive distribution channels, and avoiding its regulations. The political economy of music production, distribution, and consumption springs from a variety of factors: imbalanced IP-rights laws, unfair wage relationships in the music industry,
marginalized and colonized music fans, and distorted power relationships
between owners of commercial services and fans, relationships inscribed
within the technologies supporting digital distribution. Some of these factors also contribute a basis for a collective identity organized in opposition
to them.

Arguably, music file sharing, online civil disobedience over access to music,
software hacks on copy protections, and other forms of resistance could
have been avoided by the Big Four with some innovations in business models, and through more fan-friendly behaviors. Instead, the Big Four set up
fan-unfriendly digital distribution sites such as MusicNet, while Apple cultivated online communities and flexible sharing policies on iTunes. The Big
Four postponed direct involvement with digital distribution, and embarked
on a protracted phase of damage control from falling CD sales and antitrust
investigations. The Recording Industry Association of America (RIAA) and

its members finally lost control of digital distribution to Apple as they focused their attentions on cost-cutting, defensive legal measures, and encumbering the CD format with copy protection. Apple's iTunes music store and interoperability with the MP3 format drew many file sharers into in its own proprietary DRM format (advanced audio coding, or AAC). They also helped pull in users of Apple's operating systems, music software applications, and hardware players, including the iPod. By 2004, about a year after the opening of the iTunes store, Apple's vertically integrated music-acquisition-and-playback system concentrated the company's market power in digital music distribution, and weakened the ability of the majors to dominate end to end digital distribution. The Big Four have also made strategically poor decisions about digital music formats, favoring those encumbered with strict (rather than flexible or nonexistent) DRM.

The clash between the youthful digital-music culture and the music industry was epitomized when the industry pushed to criminalize any sharing and hoarding activities that circumvented copy protections.[1] Consequently, and despite the cultivation of sharing and hoarding during the "Rip-Mix-Burn" era of iPod marketing, it is becoming more and more difficult for music collectors either to share or to hoard music, even by collecting copy-protected music files, which are frequently "locked" to one music player or to one burned CD copy.

DRM fuses legal realist and positivist IP law with technological control that transforms cyberspace from a social space characterized by freedom, to a zone of controls imposed by social subsystems with few other connections to the music lifeworld. DRM is object-oriented software code, in which the user, the music, and the media player are all objects manipulated by the code. A music fan with a standard CD collection and a standard CD player experiences music as mediated only by the CD and the CD player. There are no extra steps requiring authentication, nor any other transactions requiring a user interface. Introduce a computer, and the instruments for acquiring recorded music become peripherals, subject to new social uses, and abuses. (See the discussion about the Sony-BMG rootkit fiasco in the next chapter)

In cyberspace, music fans have experienced the overriding behavioral controls imposed by their media players, and have seen access to music put at the mercy of hardware and software vendors. As a basic example, if a media player fails to initialize properly, it will be impossible for it to find the music file names necessary to generate a song queue, or playlist. (A record player's tone arm, on the other hand, can usually find the edge of the record, unless there is user error.) Graphical user interfaces (GUIs) can restrict user controls over music files, especially in comparison to the more direct, hands-on access to music through a CD player, cassette player, or record player. A fan playing music from a collection of MP3 or AAC or Windows Media Audio (WMA) files is subject to compliance with antisharing and anti-hoarding policies dictated by the new formats and their software players. The restrictions are tightened in online portals.[2] Besides sidestepping restrictions, music and cyberliberties activists have systematically targeted DRM and its supporting legal infrastructure in the Digital Millennium Copyright Act (DMCA) and other intellectual property legislation (CPSR 2002; EFF n.d.).

On Suing Your Best Customers for Life

Because hubris and privilege informed their response to the first movers of music on the Internet, the Big Four record companies now face the prospect of a protracted battle with a hostile fan base that is engaging the music industry in more and more regular spates of ritual conflict. As one of the oldest of the mass-media industries, the music business is accustomed to conflict, particularly of the legal sort, but not usually with its customers. The recording industry was consolidated through threats, cajoling, and negotiations over patents for technology innovations early in the twentieth century. It perfected the art of hard bargaining in dealings with its stable of best-selling musicians and recording artists through the golden years of its profitability. Yet it began the twenty-first century by devoting increasingly scarce revenues to propaganda, spin, and litigation in a sustained effort to browbeat and threaten young people—still its best customers—into compliance with new copyright laws that favor the industry. Like the Motion Picture Association of America (MPAA), the RIAA makes bogus "labor-related appeals" (Gates 2006, 58) to scrupulous fans, authors, and creators, encouraging them to challenge not only file-sharing practices, but also underlying technologies, like P2P, that have substantive, noninfringing uses: "Unfortunately, the invocations of authors' rights that we come across today are misleading, if not insincere. The true beneficiaries of recent IP law changes are neither authors nor consumers, but rather corporate content providers" (Demers 2006, 12).[3]

The concentrations of young music fans at universities and colleges have put the institutions in defensive legal postures. To avoid future threats or coercive bargaining, some universities have preemptively complied with RIAA requests to personally identify purported file sharers behaving badly and to implement new network-filtering policies. The RIAA patronizes college students in public relations campaigns, presenting town forums and public-service–like programs on the perils of piracy. The music and film industry propaganda is sometimes spun as sponsored messages from gracious corporate citizens for the benefit of at-risk children. These pitches are "systematically distorted communications" in the clearest sense, while representing concerted efforts by the culture industries to socialize fans into the new norms dictated by the DMCA. The refiguring of legal and cultural codes has spread conflicts involving fans and the culture industries at a time when music cultures are changing and technology practices are being transformed. The RIAA and MPAA presumptively assume guilt, treating all music fans as potential criminals, and portray young file-sharing music fans as criminals on par with street-gang members. Below the surface of the public relations is a social conflict between the property interests of concentrated media and telecom firms, on the one hand, and musicians, fans, and a broad swath of social groups organized around music, on the other.

The increased rate at which new technologies have been introduced into musical cultures and industries has intensified direct conflicts with the recording industry and pushed them into broader social, cultural, and technological contexts. A broader participation of musicians and fans in music production and distribution underlies changes within some traditional power relationships. Greene (2005) illustrates this trend on digital platforms:

> Music technology has tended to bring about a blurring (in the sense of a loss of distinction) of the spheres of music production and consumption. Almost as soon as new musical technologies become available and affordable, they are put to service in the local musical cultures. And as quickly as new sounds are engineered in local cultures, they are copied and loaded into the next generation of synthesizers or tone banks to be produced and distributed by music technology factories. In the process, musicians have become not only producers of music but also significant consumers of technology. As musical products become so thoroughly and rapidly recycled, the distinction between production and consumption begins to blur. (6–7)

Music operates as a mode of social and cultural reproduction even before the consumption and production roles blur (or de-differentiate) in the institutions of the technoculture. This de-differentiation is accelerated in the context of lossless and practically free online distribution of music. Blurring also occurs elsewhere in the music industry value chain, including in between the packaging and distribution stages.

Despite the blurring of production, consumption, and distribution promoted by "Mix-Rip-Burn" marketing, the new music practices are purposefully hampered by new limits. Digital copyright, DRM, proprietary software and business models, and other legal monopolies on access to communication and culture are the expressions of the capital-accumulation logic of the system, but also reflect basic failures of the social system to adapt to the changing technoculture. Music fans and artists, if they are cognizant of the blurred "spheres," may tend to recognize the value of blurring in popular music, and find cultural enrichment in the fusion of horizons that the new technologies offer. They respond to the music lifeworld's freedom. The distributors represented by industry "suits" tend to see only missed opportunities to introduce new bottlenecks and points of control. These choke points represent the primary linkages between the market system and the symbolic lifeworld. The suits respond to the system's imperatives and political economy.

The disruptions in music distribution channels caused by broadband Internet diffusion and P2P networking have been documented (Burkart and McCourt 2006; Benkler 2006; Gillespie 2007b). Regressive responses to the disruption have created the social problems. The imposition of scarcity into digital distribution channels where none should exist has created the juridical conversion of music fans and consumers into music "users," who lack property rights to their recordings, and even rights to ordinary consumer protections. The consequences of these changes are both harmful and socially significant for the history of the music lifeworld. The remainder of this chapter addresses the snowballing of bad faith and ill will that overcame the recording industry and mobilized active resistance to the digital distribution strategies of the Big Four. It also identifies some democratic norms of cyberlibertarian literature, and explains how these norms do not at present find much support in formal law.

Democratizing the Celestial Jukebox

The revolt against the recording industry (and the film industry) has snowballed since 1998 — about the time when the recording industry adopted the Celestial Jukebox business model for distributing music digitally. Borrowing heavily from the innovations of the Darknet (a set of unsecured networks used for file sharing), the recording industry and its technology partners have devised a secure, always-on, on-demand, interactive pay-per model of restricted access to music and other kinds of digitized media and culture. The Darknet, however, continually competes with this Celestial Jukebox for usability, quality of service, price, and fan autonomy in their legal affairs and control of technology. Most important, the recording industry and its partners have taken a punitive approach toward a thriving Internet culture, which was marked by free and open flows of digital text, music, and images. The criminalization and subsequent crackdown on "pirates" and hackers are important aspects of the newly punitive Internet regime, comparable to the "hacker crackdown" of the 1980s and 1990s (Sterling 1994). The history of consumer culture provides little to compare to the treatment of file-sharing music fans by the RIAA, which has tried to change the consumption norm of file sharing through brute-force legal intimidation. The entertainment and packaged-software industries have likewise helped smear the hacker culture that participated in delivering the open technologies and libertarian ideology of the Internet, stigmatizing hackers as "miscreants, vandals, criminals, and even terrorists" (Nissenbaum, quoted in Gates 2006, 59). Because hacker culture is oriented to bypassing bottleneck controls over culture and software, the "content industries" have lobbied for, and won, political and "regulatory efforts to control computer-mediated transactions...[and provide] an image of the abnormal against which to define good behavior, while also offering justification for ongoing investments in security measures and new deployments of Internet control strategies" (Gates 2006, 59–60). Some of these smear campaigns against music sharing were waged by the major labels at the same time as the FBI and the U.S. Department of Justice were investigating the Big Four record companies for colluding to fix prices for digital downloads (English 2006), and as Warner and Sony-BMG were working out payola scandal settlements (Ross et al. 2006). The record industry's recent PR history also includes sensationalistic media campaigns linking P2P to child pornography; this bizarre charge became the pretext for the Inducing Infringement of Copyrights Act, or the Induce Act, in the U.S. Senate in 2004 (as reported by Declan McCullagh in a series of CNet News articles). These efforts collectively worked to incite a "moral panic" over copyright (Godwin 2008). The legal defeats of Napster and Grokster were watershed events that disenchanted cyberlibertarians: with these decisions, music fans lost much of the legal grounding for perpetuating the music-sharing rituals that are basic to the survival of digital musical cultures (Jones 2002). Fans also saw that innovations such as P2P technology were themselves threatened.

Attempts to transcend the strictures of the inherited ways of the music business and to inject recognizable democratic values of broader participation and access into online music cultures have been stymied in confrontations with the legal system. Cyberlibertarian appeals to personal autonomy and the right to communicate share a political sensibility with post-punk and DIY music cultures from the 1980s, when indie labels took off as music scenes. A democratic theory of music scenes inspired by that era has since emerged, providing conceptual yardsticks for evaluating creative and expressive freedoms. "It is possible to construct some criteria for assessing the level of democracy in any given form of media production—such as that of popular music. Fundamental to a democratic media system are the notions of *participation* and *access*" (Hesmondhalgh 1998, 255; emphases in original). However, democratization of popular music is, on its face, a social value at odds with the industry's imperative to survive through financial growth on the Celestial Jukebox model. A basic struggle against system logic pervades cyberliberties activism and still thwarts its alternative project.

The dominance of the Big Four is, in large measure, tied to their Hollywood star system approach to financing, A&R, and marketing: to make many small financial commitments to artists and bands as a way to search for the big hits, which will be more heavily financed, and tightly controlled by contract. The economies of scope and scale required to sustain this business model required bureaucratic hierarchies with gatekeepers at every level. Therefore, new artists' access to channels for financing, music production, distribution, and marketing is highly restricted. If the music industry were party politics, its machinelike workings would cultivate privilege and cronyism for a small few, but only exclusion for most. Therefore,

[a] vital corollary to access as democratization would be the *decentralization* of media technologies and organizations....Democratic media production would also involve *collectivism, collaboration and co-operation* amongst media workers....Finally, these changes have aesthetic consequences too—the aims of such systems are not only the self-realization and fair treatment of a wider range of producers, but also the making available of new voices, new experiences and perspectives. *Diverse and innovative forms* of expression need to be found. (Hesmondhalgh 1998, 256, emphases in original)

This conception of democratic media, as we shall see in subsequent chapters, is shared by radical and alternative media, "OurMedia" activists, and libertarian librarians (or "semiotic democrats").

Alternative-music scenes feature unstructured or loosely structured roles for creative expression, performance, and participation by fans. Post-punk alternative-music organizations tried to democratize the popular-music industry, even before the diffusion of the Internet. A variety of activist organizations and lone-wolf operators still exert democratization and decentralization pressures: by using networking channels on the Internet, they have taken advantage of a new set of "political opportunity structures" (Brown 2002) for promoting alternative production and licensing schemes, managing do-it-yourself marketing plans, creating independent record labels, and forging innovative distribution channels. Improved access to production and distribution sites and fans' communications with one another and with artists is a design for more communicative rationality. Music activists, media-reform activists, alternative media, radical media, nonprofits, and a multitude of artists and fans have converged in social action around making—or reclaiming—places online for sharing new music. Despite its chaotic appearance, music and cyberliberties activism resembles social-movement politics. (Chapter 4 addresses the political prospects of collective action aimed at the creation of an Alternative Jukebox, from the perspective of several communication-based social theories.)

Independent record labels, music stores, and other institutions of the music lifeworld also operate in this marketplace that subjects them to pressures for profitability and efficiency like other commercial music firms, but denies them the preferred terms for financing, distribution, retailing, and business activities. Of course, these enterprises are not necessarily operating for high profitability; noneconomic and affective goals and missions are widespread. Alternative-music production and distribution flourishes, and titles produced and distributed independently of the major labels compete with one another and also with the output of the Big Four.[4] In 1999, the market share for independent labels represented 22.5 percent of the global market and 13 percent of the U.S. market. In 2002, the market share for independent labels increased to 25 percent of total music sales globally, and to 16 percent in the United States (Burkart 2005, 492). Independent labels have also used the Internet to reduce the cost of marketing and promotion, and were early in retooling for digital distribution.[5] The success of DJ culture, including rap and hip-hop, has helped revitalize support for indie labels, as have dance-music scenes and Internet communities (Théberge 2005), building on models developed more than twenty years earlier. Alternatives to iTunes and other locked-down services incorporate aspects of open technology (such as DRM-free formats, including MP3, P2P networking, podcasting, Webcasting, and free and open-source software), open organizational structures and memberships, and artist-advocacy support networks, sponsored sharing circles, and collective voluntary licensing.

New Music Scenes Meet Old Activist Players

Hesmondhalgh's principles of access and participation, which he sees in post-punk indie-label enterprises and scenes (1998), also find expression in the lobbying, public education, and litigation of civil libertarian activism. The American Civil Liberties Union (ACLU) is the oldest civil-liberties–based membership organization in the United States. It maintains an active "cyberliberties" program and legal docket, which was developed by Ann Beeson (Strossen 2000, 5) in 1995. Traditional interests of the ACLU in free speech, open communication, the "marketplace of ideas," and the right to personal privacy are reflected in its ongoing litigation of cyberliberties cases. The ACLU tends to take cases with the greatest potentials for judicial impact, precedent setting, and cross-applicability. Those cases address "whether government may restrict our cyberliberties in order to create new crimes, peculiar to cyberspace" and "whether government may restrict our cyberliberties in order to prosecute existing crimes, common to all media, more effectively" (Strossen 2000, 12). The ACLU lawsuits have sought to fight

Internet censorship laws, defend students' privacy and free speech, oppose mandatory blocking and filtering software on public library computers, advocate for data privacy, challenge government surveillance, and restrict legal workplace monitoring (ACLU n.d.). The ACLU filed suit to block an effort by the recording industry to force a university to reveal the name of a student accused of trading music files on her university's network; the suit asserted her constitutional right to anonymity based on her right to privacy (Schwartz 2003). The ACLU has also publicly criticized government-sponsored programs to label rap and rock music with parental warnings ("Popular music," n.d.), and has collaborated with the Electronic Music Defense and Education Fund to fight police "rave raids," which the ACLU calls "music profiling" ("Racine 'Rave Raid,'" 2003). Because the ACLU's organization includes state affiliates and local chapters, it pursues numerous local campaigns of public education, litigation, and lobbying, and hosts many music events of its own, as well.

Like the Electronic Frontier Foundation, the ACLU operates as a network of affiliated nonprofits, using labor from a few paid staff members and unpaid volunteers, including many cooperating attorneys working pro bono, board members, and local activists. Attorneys like Ann Beeson, Chris Hansen, and J. C. Salyer have fought and won Supreme Court cases, including *Ashcroft v. ACLU* (2004), which overturned the Child Online Protection Act. Bruce J. Ennis was counsel of record for the ACLU in the U.S. Supreme Court hearing of *Reno v. ACLU* (1997), which overturned the Communications Decency Act. These court decisions democratized cyberspace by preventing the setup of a nanny state online, the likes of which have been adopted in other countries with much less open societies.

The Electronic Frontier Foundation (EFF) also litigates, lobbies, and provides public education, but focuses primarily on expanding rights for innovative information technologists to access markets, and for computer users to protect their personal privacy. Among the founding members of EFF were countercultural luminaries who shared "new communalist ideals" (Turner 2006, 162); they hoped to disrupt established technology practices and make innovations accessible to mass markets quickly. Other nonprofits pursue technological law and policy projects with cyberlibertarian objectives. The Software Freedom Law Center (SFLC), of which Lawrence Lessig is a director, supports open-source software developers, distributors, and users; as a part of the open-source software movement, it owes much of its inspiration to the work of Richard Stallman. Computer Professionals for Social Responsibility (CPSR) organizes software and information-technology (IT) professionals in campaigns for democratic access and participation in Internet governance, in the workplace, and in global civil society. Many other groups include media and software in broader, community-oriented technology-policy programs such as the Loka Institute.

However well organized these groups may seem, their missions may be conflicted by liberal and communitarian values in a constant tension. Participation and access potentially find satisfaction in both individual and collective practices. Social struggles are built in solidarity, while civil liberties are defined individualistically in the U.S. form of constitutional government. Juridical treatments of cyberliberties, taken alone, have been criticized in communication studies for not addressing collective rights or even "the right to communicate" in a more broadly construed sense than the U.S. style of free speech (Hamelink 2004; Cunningham 2008). The ACLU and the EFF have argued successfully within a legal system based on a liberal political philosophy within which personal autonomy is a legal priority (or has been, before the Global War on Terror) and on case law dealing with private property, contracts, and the U.S. Bill of Rights. These organizations are classically liberal and reformist. While Streeter (1999) and others emphasize the neoliberal individualism of the first wave of cyberlibertarians, contemporary cyberlibertarians tend to think that politics, not the marketplace, protects the vibrancy of cyberspace as a "never-ending worldwide conversation" (ACLU, quoted in Post 2000, 1439).

An interesting critique of Lawrence Lessig, a cyberlibertarian activist luminary, has emerged over the role of politics in protecting and saving cyberspace as this never-ending worldwide conversation as well as a place for music. Lessig perceives the system imperatives of capitalist commodification to be debilitating for oppositional political agency. "Left to itself, cyberspace will become a perfect tool of control. . . . The invisible hand of cyberspace is building an architecture for cyberspace that is quite the opposite of what it was at cyberspace's birth. The invisible hand, through commerce, is constructing an architecture that perfects control" (Lessig 1999, 5–6). To Strangelove (2005), who writes of digital piracy as a social movement, Lessig represents a dystopian visionary who overlooks social resistance to control: "Lessig represents a school of thought that sees digital technology as enabling a new type of totalitarian society before which all other empires pale in comparison. Yet today, within the Internet, content and audiences are out of control" (20).

Lessig, who has clerked for both U.S. Supreme Court Justice Antonin Scalia and Judge Richard Posner of the U.S. Seventh Circuit Court of Appeals, shows himself to be a pragmatist. Lessig's juridical perspective addresses, case by case, the Internet's potential to enhance or undermine "individual freedom and growth" or autonomy (Lessig 2002, xxi). His work on cyberliberties is both theoretical and applied, and he carefully selects his cases to target the worst potentials of abusive power, those in which legal codes are most closely intertwined with lines of software code. Together with Siva Vaidhyanathan and others, Lessig has helped jump-start academic discussions of cyberliberties, placing music at the center of cyberliberties activism. He famously disassembled the RIAA's rhetoric about music "piracy," showing it to be both disingenuous about the music industry's own history of rights obtainment, and harmful in its consequences for creators, innovators, and society at large (Lessig 2004). But as Strangelove intimates, he does not acknowledge collective resistance to online controls; instead, he emphasizes individual examples of cyberlibertarians who stood up to abuses by corporate IP owners. Nor does Lessig offer a very clear picture of the kind of social agency that might channel cyberliberties into an incipient social movement. Typically, Lessig's case studies are people whose work has been frustrated by unjust IP-rights law, especially university researchers, scientists, musicians, and students. Among these aggrieved parties may reside the makings of a movement, but they are presented as individual subjects unified only in their status as casualties of an unjust IP-rights system. No solidarity exists among these alienated geeks.

Strangelove's critique reveals that Lessig's writings leave behind a puzzle about the sources of social and political agency. Other approaches besides the juridical perspective on cyberliberties are needed to solve this puzzle. Jurists writing about cyberliberties tend to adopt a technologically determinist perspective on history in order to show whether the rule of law obtains in certain cases. As a critical thinker and activist, Lessig takes the extra step of critiquing the legislation, legal fictions, and unreasonable precedents in case law that inflict damage on people's civil liberties. But to make the critique come off as a manifesto, and to make the case for preserving and expanding "free culture," Lessig builds up the Internet's capacities and characteristics in such a way that the Net takes on a subjectivity and agency of its own, as an intelligent artifact of enlightened engineering. Lessig finds something like a constitutional "framers' intent" in the "original" Internet's open designs and protocols. This analysis strengthens his normative critique of proprietary and closed standards. His critique of overreaching IP-rights laws, while bold for legal scholarship in the United States, does not criticize IP "rights" (or private property "rights") per se. I shall say more about this later, but online music services can cause private property rights to appear to be natural, whereas they are the byproducts of labor relationships that can be coercive and unjust. And as the Internet's agency grows (from the juridical perspective), the background power relationships introduced by social stratification along lines of class, race, and gender can likewise seem to become further naturalized. In the legal system, legal subjectivity and "rights" exist principally for the individual or the incorporated individual, so rights-based collective action, movement politics, renters' strikes, and other expressions of collective action and solidarity often fight uphill battles for reforms, and are forced to resort to adversarial political practices to promote free culture. Offe and Wiesenthal (1980) have determined the principal dilemma of labor and social movements to be the relative difficulty of organizing people in collective action, as compared with the relative ease of mobilizing capital and force by state and corporate agents.

In arguing for the right of the Internet to be left alone by colonizing forces, Lessig introduces the prospect of a *right* to a free culture. This notion presents cyberliberties activists with a question of first principles. Cyberlibertarians are torn between legally and philosophically "prior" principles, or principles that lie behind the civil libertarian project for a just society. On the one hand, private property rights of artists and fans—their royalties and rights to use and enjoy music, respectively—are routinely violated in the Celestial Jukebox. However, claims to these partially satisfied rights can rest uneasily beside nonproperty rights, including the right to communicate, personal autonomy, freedom of association, free speech, and privacy. EFF lawyers derive innovation and greater access to knowledge and culture from these principles, and use them as program objectives (von Lohmann 2006). In the cyberlibertarian discourses of global civil society, such as the WSIS and CRIS (see chapter 4), the right to communicate informs cyberliberties as a first principle. Professional discourses such as critical information studies prioritize personal autonomy and freedom of expression and association over other liberties.

Siva Vaidhyanathan's work on cyberliberties also addresses questions of first principles directly. He uses anarchism as a political theory to explicate the first concepts of "radical democracy" and to put them into a systematic relationship (2004, xvii). In the fashion of EFF staff attorneys, Vaidhyanathan prizes personal autonomy and innovation as values for high-technology societies. These values support and nurture "the culture of science," which needs to be able to share "music, poetry, data, and rumors" in order to thrive (150).

Vaidhyanathan highlights the changing legal status of technologies that are central to online music production, distribution, and consumption, including blogs, MP3, lyric servers, P2P, broadband networks, decryption, and wireless networking. According to Vaidhyanathan, preserving access to these technologies is a major struggle for music and cyberliberties activists.

Both Lessig and Vaidhyanathan warn about alterations to and redesigns of the Internet's architecture that impinge upon cyberliberties. They share critical insights into how legal codes governing intellectual property interact explicitly and implicitly with software code and technological designs. These insights paint a potentially catastrophic picture for professions and cultures based on sharing information, knowledge, and culture. They also provide important measurements of democratization for alternative-media activists, albeit with the limitations of a juridical perspective that is based on a strictly individualistic reading of civil liberties and cyberliberties.

Vaidhyanathan's literature review of activist "critical information studies" yields something like a "right to communicate" as a manifesto:

Critical Information Studies interrogates the structures, functions, habits, norms, and practices that guide global flows of information and cultural elements. Instead of being concerned merely with one's right to speak (or sing or publish), Critical Information Studies asks questions about access, costs, and chilling effects on, within, and among audiences, citizens, emerging cultural creators, indigenous cultural groups, teachers, and students. Central to these issues is the idea of "semiotic democracy," or the ability of citizens to employ the signs and symbols ubiquitous in their environments in manners that they determine. (2006, 303)

Like Hesmondhalgh and Lessig, Vaidhyanathan focuses on broadening access to media and information and critiquing restrictions on access. Both Hesmondhalgh and Vaidhyanathan also link access to knowledge to democracy: for Hesmondhalgh, post-punk alternative-music scenes inculcated openness, participation, and access; for Vaidhyanathan, critical scholarship in information science supports the same functions and holds the same values.

The works of Lessig and Vaidhyanathan are the reflexive responses of experts to threats posed by power shifts in the linked domains of IP law, telecommunications policy, and media policy. Both scholars are cyberliberties activists residing in university departments, and both enjoy extensive relationships with others in media, research, and nonprofit research units who are investigating problems of access to knowledge. Lessig in particular has been successful at networking groups dedicated to free culture and semiotic democracy. He founded the Center for Internet and Society, chairs the Creative Commons alternative-copyright project, and is a board member of the Free Software Foundation, the EFF, and Public Knowledge.

Music, Juridification, and Cultural Reproduction

Attentive participation in the legal market for digital downloads, with care taken to review all legal documents, is an unpleasant education in the legal minutiae and legal fictions that pervade our technical access to digital culture. Reading the fine print and understanding it require considerable knowledge of law, technology, and certain combined aspects of both. In the legal-realist theory of IP law, music is a "bundle of rights" associated with IP law in developed countries. This is a "system side" perspective on music that is shared by record companies, legal studies, political economists, and media economists. But from the perspective of the lifeworld—a communication-centric perspective—music is also a form of symbolic interaction that stimulates personal growth and cultural identities and carries and reproduces identities through time while also mediating the present moment. Music, in other words, participates in cultural reproduction, and in processes of "mundane reasoning" among members of a "communication community" (Pollner, quoted in Habermas 1984, 13), and both of these aspects make music part of the lifeworld.

That music is also a commodity composed of information regulated by international trade law, civil law, and criminal law is not "natural," per se, but an outcome of power relationships in the contemporary world. Media economics and the political economy of popular music make it clear that the music business obeys a logic of commodification that tends toward globalization and concentration. It also happens that music, like other forms of culture, must increasingly comply with what Max Weber called "juridification"; that is, legalistic rule making, broadly speaking. In the 1980's, "Habermas became convinced that 'juridification'—the expansion of the legal system to comprehend issues formerly decided by authority or deliberation—is the mode of systems-rationalization that most directly attacks the discursive and ultimately democratic life world on which the very possibility of civilization depends" (Kettler and Meja 1996, 326). Excess juridification can cause culture to cease flowing. Overregulation can inhibit the reproduction of the cultural codes and memories that feed individual and social identities. This finding, recurrent in music studies, suggests further that a music lifeworld can help support democratic cultures and open societies, and that its erosion or removal could diminish important resources for democratic culture.

On the other hand, the formalization of existing rights and the creation of new rights require a certain level of juridification. Otherwise, arbitrariness and inherited biases in favor of traditional and abusive routines and practices become perpetuated. Therefore, critical media studies researchers and activists in critical media studies demarcate zones with "too much" or "not enough" juridification to support cyberliberties. IP law provides ample examples. The exercise of tracking the extent of usable "fair use" rights for music studies in cyberspace considers both which uses have been left alone by formal law and what formal protections exist for music instructors and researchers.[6] The unavailability of clear rules for taking advantage of fair use is, in one sense, a problem of not enough juridification, in that it prevents creators, educators, and electronic publishers from taking advantage of explicit fair-use rights. On the other hand, the Sonny Bono Copyright Term Extension Act, which added ninety-five years to copyright terms, is an example of too much juridification, because it put cultural objects that would have entered the public domain sooner out of reach until about the year 2052 — far beyond the life expectancy of most creators whose works were protected by the new law.

Another risk of too much juridification is the "chilling effect" it can produce on the speech of creators who would continue to innovate and build upon the work and ideas of others, but are held back by perceived threats from IP rights holders. Chillingeffects.org, a collaboration between the EFF and law school clinics in the United States, maintains an online database of case studies on problems encountered by authors, speakers, performers, researchers, fans, and others in (1) sharing through fair use, Web linking, derivative works, and fan fiction; (2) maintaining anonymity; and (3) running afoul of e-commerce business patents and commercial trademarks. Most of the cases chronicled on Chillingeffects.org pertain to the unavailability of free culture or semiotic democracy today, illustrating conflicts in cyberspace over the juridification of sensitive lifeworld processes, such as naming, sharing, critiquing and commenting upon, and reappropriating music and affiliated cultural objects. When such communication rituals in the lifeworld as borrowing, sharing, and creating music are stifled and supplanted with what Habermas calls the "communication media" of money and power, cultural reproduction becomes commodified, detached from lifeworld processes of social integration, and attached to commodification processes in the economic system.

Sometimes it is not commodification itself but the legal inability to commodify cultural reproduction that can lead to chilling effects in the music lifeworld. In these cases, too little juridification inhibits communication. For example, Indiana University Press decided not to support the editor of *A Rebecca Clarke Reader*, who claimed fair use in citing quotations from another source. The press "withdrew from circulation advance copies of a book about a relatively obscure, deceased composer, Rebecca Clarke, because the copyright holders of Clarke's compositions intimidated them" into doing so (Striphas and McLeod 2006, 126). In this case, the fear, uncertainty, and doubt that a bogus copyright claim sowed in the Indiana University Press office caused a publisher to self-censor. Risk management dictates avoiding "a costly lawsuit, even if it's clear the university will prevail" (126).[7] At Texas A&M University, my own research program on the digital-rights management built into the major music service providers' software was tied up in legal wrangling that ultimately postponed a "hands-on" comparison of strong and weak DRM policies. In a memo to university president Robert Gates, legal counsel for the university wrote that disseminating the results of the research, rather than conducting the research per se, could violate the DMCA. Notwithstanding these campus-based examples of chilling effects, university presses and academic departments may be among the more aggressive defenders of fair use and resisters of bogus IP claims. If fair use (or "fair dealing," in Canada) could be relied upon by creators and publishers, through formalized guidelines encoded in legal statute, for instance, juridification of the music lifeworld could actually strengthen cyberliberties.

McLeod offers an apt example of juridification outside academe with the tale of the Girl Scouts of America (2001, 55). Upon discovering the practice of campfire singing, the American Society of Composers, Authors, and Producers (ASCAP) wrote a threatening letter to the Girl Scouts:

> A big part of a camping experience is music.... We're not talking about four to five girls sitting around a campfire singing songs. We're talking about several hundred girls sitting around a campfire singing songs. These children are charged a fee for coming to camp, and that fee includes such things as food, housing and arts and crafts. They buy paper, twine and glue for their crafts—they can pay for the music, too. (55)

Another ASCAP official threatened, "We will sue them if necessary" (55). ASCAP's lawyerly letter made it clear that "Ring around the Rosie," "This Land Is Your Land," "God Bless America," "Edelweiss," and "Happy Birthday to You" "could not be sung at the summer camps without paying royalties" (55). Upon learning that the penalties for nonpayment of "performance" royalties for songs sung around campfires could range "from $5,000 and six days in jail to $100,000 and a year in jail for every unauthorized performance," the Girl Scouts' leadership restricted campfire singing to special Girl Scout songs only, while poorer and more cautious camps "stopped singing songs altogether" (55).

This absurd example (reported originally in the *Wall Street Journal* in 1996 by Lisa Bannon, and also cited by Lessig, 2004) would seem to illustrate a serious threat to a sacred place of music with taproots sunk deep in the soil of the lifeworld. It should go without saying that singing campfire songs without paying royalties contributes more to socialization and development of personal identity than it deprives rights holders. It is a victimless "crime." Yet, juridification disrupts commonplace understandings about the music lifeworld. Consequently, music and cyberliberties activists track the risks to democratic institutions in the mutually reinforcing violations of free-speech rights, and notice when over- and under-juridification creates a disruption in people's mundane reasoning about music in the lifeworld. Likewise, they notice when the law works to preserve the music lifeworld, works at cross-purposes with it, or does not operate at all.

The greatest risk to the music lifeworld is that neither eroded nor "distorted" communications there can easily mend themselves. Fortunately, the unbalanced power relationship of the culture industries to free culture shows some signs of being equalized in music fans' gift cultures and in political activism. For example, educators in music, media, and software were among the first to encounter the sharing prohibitions of the new information regime. Film and media instructors were blocked from working around copy protections on DVDs to make sample tapes for in-class instruction, and computer science professors were threatened by software vendors whose copy-protection schemes were found to have flaws. Librarians quickly bumped up against the imposition of DRM when they tried to archive software and media disks. The Digital Millennium Copyright Act's prohibitions on the circumvention of copy protection foreclosed educational guarantees of fair use and the freedom to tinker with computers and digital-recording and playback gadgets until activist instructors succeeded in temporarily amending the DMCA in 2006 to better accommodate educators (Carlson 2006).

This temporary "freedom to tinker" is another example of too little juridification of the rights of researchers, librarians, and instructors who struggle to make music and media more accessible. Tinkering was largely unproblematic legally (except in encryption research and hacking) before the DMCA, but was outlawed by the DMCA. Under the current (and unreformed) law, cyberliberties activists must repetition the U.S. Copyright Office every three years to seek DMCA exemptions (von Lohmann 2005a). Edward Felten, a DRM researcher from Princeton University, has highlighted the fact that the DMCA has overrestricted the freedom to tinker—as illustrated when his legitimate research was put under a legal threat by a copy-protection software company (Lessig 2004; Felten and Appel 2000). EFF provided legal counsel for Felten when he sought to present and publish the findings of his DRM research. Without legal cover for semiotic democracy and free culture, all participants in our shared technoculture are exposed to formal legal sanctions and pressured to self-suppress their rights to free speech and access to knowledge.

Saving a place for music and for music research, as cyberlibertarians see it, is primarily a question of demanding that government and corporations take a more hands-off approach to forms of culture sharing. It has inspired an incipient social movement aimed at decriminalizing file sharing and tinkering, and reinvigorating fair-use rights. Although these sharing tendencies are in tension with the monopolizing tendencies of the culture industries, Benkler (2006) argues that sharing is a basic activity of communication, and one of increasing importance in the information age: "Because of changes in the technology of the industrial base of the most advanced economies, social sharing and exchange is becoming a common modality of production at their very core—in the information, culture, education, computation, and communications sectors" (121). Music and cyberliberties activists want to reclaim sharing as a normatively grounded, legitimate, and culturally protected activity for both democratic culture and the technoculture. Cyberliberties activists "aim to reappropriate society from the state," as Pichardo says of new social movements more generally (1997, 418). Their concern with the place of music in the lifeworld, the sharing practices that make music integral to the reproduction of societies, and the encroachment of state-sanctioned power structures into places of music makes their activism especially relevant to the theory of communicative action.

CHAPTER TWO

Creating the Music Lifeworld Online

*

Do we still have cyberliberties?
—Richard MacKinnon, personal communication, 2007

The music lifeworld that I described in chapter 1 exists both offline and on-line. The theory of communicative action provides distinct advantages over other approaches for understanding the music lifeworld as a key compo-nent of music activists and fans as social agents who combine online and offline activities related to music. Other approaches to the economics of the music industry, including media economics, policy studies, and fan-focused studies, tend to leave the relationships of language, communication, and most media lifeworld considerations out of their discussions. This chapter aims to provide popular music studies with a critical framework for linking changes in IP law and telecom policy to changes in fan behaviors that dis-rupt "business as usual" in the music industry. A communication-centric, social systems approach accesses the symbolic realms of politics and culture to identify expressions of alienation, describe them, and relate them mean-ingfully to system processes identified by political economy. Also, it pro-vides a normative basis for critiquing the dominant system (the Celestial Jukebox), faulting it for producing systematically distorted forms of IP law, abusive markets, and desiccated consumer rights. In this chapter, I take a closer look at how the music lifeworld experiences colonization, and how it is being defended from juridification and clientelization. I address four ideal types of cyberliberties activism that capture most of the cases available for study. I also show how music and cyberliberties activism is a form of resistance to the spatialization of the music commodity in the Celestial Jukebox.

I have selected the theory of communicative action to frame music activ-ism not because it perfectly explains what is occurring, or because it mea-sures participation in a movement politics precisely. It does neither. Rather,

I select this approach because it presents social agency in a form that identifies social conflicts expressed in collective action, solidarity, and political conflict as translatable into communicative action and recognized discourses about civil liberties and human rights. Other schools of thought that have engaged with music studies and cultural studies in the context of activism do not address new social movement (NSM) theory, which, as I shall argue in chapter 3, supports a system-and-lifeworld perspective that offers us some purchase on the appearance of cultural conflicts over music distribution in the political system.

Political economists are more successful than media economists at characterizing conflicts over music production, distribution, and consumption as conflicts involving social agents acting reflectively. The labor theory of value provides political economy with a coherent and historically informed account of transformational social agency, revolutionary change, human rights, and justice, while media economics dispenses with practically all normative concerns as externalities, utilizes a rational choice model of agency, and does not consider historical conjunctures in its models. Political economy is not altogether sufficient, however, to address music and cyberliberties in its complexity. It retains a productivist bias that overemphasizes the powerful social agency of firms with dominant economic and political influences (such as the major labels) achieved through their role in the market as producers of commodities. The bias comes at the expense of attention paid to smaller producers, and to the players "downstream" in the markets for distribution: retailers and the music fans themselves. In the age of digital-music distribution, the productivist bias leads to a neglect of networking dynamics and the appearance of new social agents influencing people's choices of access to music. Apart from advertising and marketing researchers, media economists tend to neglect music fans as well, except when analyzing music pricing and sales trends. Nonetheless, these fans are presumed to be rational choosers and consumers who greet each day in search of gratifying their personal needs and improving their marginal utility through their informed consumer choices. Nothing else in media economics informs us about the communicative action of fans.

In music studies, fandom research has rescued audience studies from these brain-clamping discourses of economizing and performing the economic minimax. It also provides a new set of grounded subjects of study for a cultural studies of music that has spent a decade or more in the abstracted world of global media "flows." Fandom studies run the gamut of theoretical and atheoretical perspectives on social agency; even so, they favor the "active audiences" approach to media studies. Fandom studies tend to portray social conflicts as background conditions of race, class, and gender disparities against which battles over textual interpretations occur. Whereas in-formed and passionate consumption of texts distinguishes the fan from the mere consumer, fandom studies has not yet connected the music fan's social agency to ongoing access to the music lifeworld, nor political conflicts around fandom to disturbances in the music lifeworld.

Elsewhere in communication studies, there is a push for recognition of the right to communicate by people who fall across the entire spectrum of access to media and telecommunications; this push includes fans, of course, but focuses especially on less intensive media consumers. The notion of the technologically empowered Netizen, in particular, still animates debates about copyright reforms, free culture, and the availability of "civil society" and "global civil society" as imagined refuges from colonizing pressures. These debates about civil society have displaced much attention formerly paid to the state, political parties, and cultural policymakers, and have pri-oritized the cultural sphere and lifeworld processes as zones of high-intensity conflict. International communication researchers have focused on activism and movement-style collective action aimed at the mass media and new media, often in solidarity with other movements (Hadl 2004; Hintz and Hadl 2008). Media reform activism and radical media activism are, from this perspective, "tools for de-colonization" of the lifeworld (Hadl 2004). Marxist cultural studies has also recognized the resurgence of clashes over culture as expressions of the politics of race, class, and gender (Aronowitz 1993), but has not worked out a communication-centric theory of social conflict over cultural production or distribution. In the next section, I look at some of the ways by which critics of DRM have documented commercial exploitations of consumers' rights to communicate online and control the technical means of access to musical culture. Despite a general recognition that legal forms of DRM are abusive, in the sense of being nonconsensual exercises of corporate power imposed capriciously, and that music sharing remains a victimless crime, the critiques of DRM have not touched the core problems giving rise to DRM. Music and cyberliberties activism reveals these problems in lifeworld colonization.

DRM and Social Conflicts over Juridification

Before digital distribution, the mobility and portability of music was free of technological forms of surveillance; CDs could be physically moved around or "ripped" for mobile MP3 players without going online or getting per-missions.[1] Leaving aside car radios and portable transistor radios for the moment, "music that moves" has been a format design concern since cas-settes and eight-track tapes proliferated before the advent of CDs (Jones

2002). The MP3 format expresses the social and economic value of massively mobile music (Sterne 2006). The Sony Walkmans and Discmans and their copycat competitors predated MP3 players long enough to help establish portability as an expectation among most music fans.

The growing centrality of computers, peripherals, and the Internet to media access, along with a succession of "disruptive" technologies developed for the Internet, has stimulated music and cyberliberties activism, but principally in the clashes over control over the technical bases for distribution and consumption. These clashes grew more frequent as disruptive networking technologies increased the access to culture and knowledge, bypassing many old restrictions. E-mail, listservs, blogs, P2P networks, and social networking sites are supplanting older communication networks among music fans and bands, including fanzines, fan letters, and home tape mixing and sharing that endured through the 1990s. Web publishing facilitated a proliferation of independent labels operating on shoestring budgets. P2P networking reduced costs even further by removing the need to own or lease space on a server and create and maintain Web pages. Napster so disrupted the major labels' business model for distribution that it inspired a regulatory backlash in the form of the architectural designs of the Celestial Jukebox, designs still used by the major online music service providers. Not all disruptions are so severe as those of Napster. Commercial Web services for handling music online disrupt the music-service providers, and include the major social networking sites like MySpace and Facebook. Google, which began as a Web search-engine company, has even made exploratory forays into coordinating markets for broadcast radio advertising as well as online music sales. These various disruptions to the old business models greatly enhanced communicative rationality in cyberspace, and show that technological innovations have worked together to democratize access to channels for music and communication about music. Most important, the alternative, indie, and noncommercial channels now have a distribution and marketing platform available at a marginal cost. These songwriters, musicians, and recording artists are poised to offer alternatives to the Celestial Jukebox to fans anxious to exit. Together with cyberlibertarian activists, they occupy the music lifeworld and slow or forestall the corporate media colonizers.

Music was one of the first digital media formats (after packaged software) to be sold in mass markets and to experience lockdown by copy protection. Since then, music fans using digital formats are always being required to give an accounting for all sorts of new things, such as software registrations, service fees, authentications, agreement to terms of service, end user license agreements (EULAs), and so forth. DRM has hurt paying customers, become an annoyance for nonpaying customers, eroded or destroyed fair-use rights, and has rendered some customers' investments in intangible music libraries worthless (Granneman n.d.). DRM changes the power relationships among fans, labels, artists, and frequently unknown or anonymous software companies to the extent that fans are continually giving up rights in exchange for access.

Music studies' interest in DRM grew from legal studies with a juridical approach to IP law, and has made a property-rights–based case against legal DRM by focusing on the loss of use and possession of recorded music, rather than on the communicative impacts of this loss. But because no theory of social action stands behind a normative theory of cyberliberties law, the injunctions and warnings of music and media studies do not yet connect with a framework for explaining or understanding how the work of change and reform in the culture industries can begin or end. Critical social systems theory provides a robust framework for describing and critiquing the social structures supporting the technological lockdown of culture, and for understanding the social sources of political and cultural resistance.[2] The theory of communicative action allows for the critique of DRM to be expanded to question the moral authority of the regulationist, legal realist, and "copyright maximalist" (Samuelson 1996) views of copyright, telecommunications, and information law and policy. These dominant views have brought us to a basic political conflict between keeping or rejecting civil libertarian values for the Internet.

People who experience this conflict directly in everyday life often experience it as a cultural disconnect or expectancy violation that can come as a shock. Wirtén (2006) confides, that, in confronting increasingly routine cyberliberties violations, "Most of the time I am unsure whether to laugh or to cry. The hair-raising absurdities of an ever-expanding intellectual property regime documented by David Bollier, Kembrew McLeod, and others appear to have no boundaries, moral or otherwise" (282). As moral law is what presumably guides modern systems of jurisprudence and provides legitimation for the rule of law, this failure of IP law to find normative grounding poses a problem for the ongoing maintenance of the Celestial Jukebox. Wirtén is responding to the deformation of music lifeworld practices and structures with routines and "forms alien to everyday practice" (J. Berger 1991, 175). Power and money are the "steering mechanisms" that coordinate colonization. They transfer socialization, cultural reproduction, and social integration to system-integration processes that typically handle material reproduction: "Pathologies result only at the *battle front* between 'system' and 'lifeworld,' and even there only in *one* direction, namely the switch of the 'system' over into the 'lifeworld'" (175, emphasis in original).

McCarthy (1985) and others who have critiqued the rigid system and lifeworld dualism have offered possibilities for thinking of it in different ways, including thinking of it as different standpoints with respect to the phenomenon of complex communication processes between and among formal and informal organizations (Koivisto and Väliverroen 1996; Calhoun 1995). "System integration and social integration...seem to be extremes rather than alternatives that exhaust the field of possibilities: The denial of one does not entail the other" (McCarthy 1985, 41). These standpoints facilitate for observation the "uncoupling" of system and lifeworld processes which Habermas describes. Uncoupling is more visible in Celestial Jukebox than in previous modes of music production, distribution, and consumption. Users are, indeed, integrated into formalized systems logic when they join the Celestial Jukebox: they join "a strongly hierarchical, formally organized setting in which the actors have no clear idea of why they are ordered to do what they do" (McCarthy 1985, 41). Systems theory talk about "uncoupling" seemed more far-fetched before the Internet became a mass medium with panoptic capabilities. Today, online portals can create airtight, hierarchical, formalized, organizational enclosures enforcing norm-free compliance through contract law and technology.

New music distribution systems create pressures in society to "clientelize" and juridify private life and cultural life, while technocratic controls substitute for interpersonal and negotiated transactions in acquiring music. Fans are already to a large extent beholden to the consumerism, clientelization, and juridification of social rationalization that occured as the consumer role became subject to management and protection by the welfare state. Yet "clients" of music companies must accept rights that are increasingly juridically restricted. Juridification "seals the deal" for the system. It formally legitimates online legal relationships, but does so without using normatively sanctioned communication. Instead, juridification allows money and power to help replace meaningful social practices with cybernetic routines. Copyright policymaking stands out as an example of clientelization in the online music lifeworld. The foisting of exorbitant licensing fees in 2007 by the U.S. Copyright Royalty Board upon commercial and noncommercial Webcasters alike drove many independent online "channels" off the Web, consolidating the advantages enjoyed by the major online music service providers.[3] In the process, Web radio listeners have been shunted off to more commercialized music portals featuring user registrations, ads, and copy-protected streams.

Music fans increasingly give up a wide variety of individual rights to acquire access to music. Clientelization and juridification push colonization to new corners of the music lifeworld, and in converting shared and social aspects of life into "privatized" spaces, fans are communicatively sealed off from others. These spaces are built using copy protections and access controls, in architectures designed for digital distribution for the Celestial Jukebox (Burkart and McCourt 2006). Access regulations have oozed into other categories of audiovisual products as well, including Web services, DVDs, video games, and, almost, digital television programming.[4] When music fans must click through numerous lengthy, complex contracts to open a media client that will access or play a music file, for example, they are required to become enmeshed in legalistic systems simply in order to enjoy music. The process begins before this, in fact. Upon installing any operating system, a user accepts a license. Users also agree to terms of use imposed by Internet service providers (ISPs) (Braman and Roberts 2003). Music delivered as a service is neither purchased nor sold, but licensed for temporary and highly conditional access. Acquiescence in these technical means of coordination is not grounded in communicative action. The nonnegotiable terms imposed by DRM on behalf of system technologists are protected by law, but have not been grounded in "moral consciousness" (Habermas 1987, 174), which is willful, deliberative, and discursive. The impositions of the technocratic controls on music fans in exchange for access to culture cannot be a relationship that develops into "socially recognized norms of action" (Habermas 1987, 175), because they detach music acquisition and distribution from the legitimating lifeworld. In other words, the legalistic terms of the Celestial Jukebox are not legitimate from the standpoint of record collectors (see chapter 5).

Famously, Apple's Steve Jobs himself appealed publicly to record labels to remove DRM as a condition for distribution of music through iTunes and other clearinghouses (Jobs 2007). Jobs offered a realist's justification: "because DRMs haven't worked, and may never work, to halt music piracy" (Jobs 2007, n.p.) Yet Apple's FairPlay, Microsoft's Windows Media DRM, and RealNetworks' RealMedia formats all still impose rules or policies on users that are enforceable by contract law, statutory law, and through the operation of software code in supported media players. The nonnegotiable policies are changeable at the sole discretion of the IP rights holders. The "DRM free" releases on iTunes are still in the proprietary AAC format, although they are not encrypted. These formats impose controls on their users automatically and without exception and program out of social life any appeals or exceptions to their restrictions on file sharing. Of course, discussions and debates about the unjust terms of DRMs flourish in music and cyberliberties discussion groups online, such as the Pirate Bay, Engadget, BoingBoing, the Pho Listserv, and Slashdot's "Your Rights Online" page.

After nearly a decade of delays, and Apple's cajoling, the music industry is now experimenting with DRM-free online distributions of digital music. But the Big Four still nurture ecstatic visions of "ubiquitous" DRM that locks down all users into reliably leakproof digital enclosures. Ubiquitous DRM may seem undesirable and implausible to most music fans, but it remains the current objective of the culture industries. Ubiquitous DRM would use legal and software controls to fully automate the Celestial Jukebox. Cory Doctorow, who was director of European affairs for the EFF, presents the dystopian endpoint of ubiquitous DRM (Doctorow 2005):

- Every copy of the song circulated, from the recording studio to the record store, has strong DRM on it;
- No analog to digital converters are available to anyone, anywhere in the world, who might have an interest in breaking the DRM;
- Peer-to-peer networks cease to exist;
- Search engines cease to index file-sharing sites; and
- No "small worlds" file-sharing tools are in circulation[5]

What seems dystopian to a cyberlibertarian is Xanadu for the Internet regulationists.

Ubiquitous DRM would make it possible for the culture industries to bypass any remaining checks and balances on IP law completely by automating the coordination of money and access power across all music players. Assuming for a moment that it were technically feasible, ubiquitous DRM would introduce what Habermas calls a "second nature" in a music lifeworld that is currently sustained in cultural reproduction and social integration. A technocratically constructed second nature would provide a "norm-free sociality that can appear . . . as an *objectified* context of life" (Habermas 1987, 173; emphasis in original). Andrejevic (2003) describes similar conditions that currently obtain in digital enclosures. As technically encoded power and money transactions increasingly transform negotiated agreements into automated exchanges between buyers and sellers of music and cultural objects, and people are habituated to participate in clientelistic transactions, expressions of communicative rationality can become "secularly threatened" (J. Berger 1991, 168). In other words, even though ubiquitous DRM depends upon institutions of the musical lifeworld for demand and for legitimacy as a new technology practice, it can erode the lifeworld enough to threaten it as a future resource for juridification and legitimation. Samuelson (2003) expresses the concern that the "main purpose of DRM is not to prevent copyright infringement but to change consumer expectations about what they are entitled to do with digital content" (41). Touraine

(1988) describes changes to the lived experiences of individuals in the "programmed society" as creating the conditions for future participation in an oppositional new social movement.

> In a large modern city, it is literally impossible to take one step without receiving some command, without being exposed to advertising or propaganda, without being confronted with social scales in which one can indicate one's level by oneself. This is why there is a search for nonsocial relations, for interpersonal ones, or such a desire to erect communities conceived as a refuge within an increasingly thicker social network. Marginality, considered for so long a failure of integration, becomes thus the hallmark of an opposition, a laboratory in which a new culture and a social counterproject are being elaborated. (106)

"The lived experience of the programmed society," for Touraine, demonstrated "the growing disjunction between social relations and civil society and the State" (113). For me, the same phenomena demonstrate a separation of system and lifeworld. Marginality has become a feature of the Celestial Jukebox that could sponsor a "new culture and a social counterproject" under favorable conditions. I shall address these prospects in the chapters that follow.

As I proposed in the introduction, one of the benefits of the theory of communicative action is that it can render instances of the system-lifeworld dialectic observable in processes of rationalization and colonization.[6] The clash between the norm-free capitalist economy and the "independent communication structures" of the lifeworld that support political participation, identity formation, and cultural integration (Habermas 1987, 391) is clearly visible in the operation of the Darknet, CopyLeft musicians, hacker communities, and indie labels outside the Celestial Jukebox. So too, the "rebellious communication and social movements" (Downing 2001, 10) of alternative and radical media activists render the margin of the system and the lifeworld visible. Habermasian critical theory considers these examples of opposition to be evidence of the survival and struggle of "communicative rationality" under conditions of colonization. They are not, however, evidence of a flourishing of revolutionary political agency. The radical roots of communication-oriented media activists are present, but they are not expressions of anything like class consciousness or movement consciousness. Music and cyberliberties activists are engaged in a process of identifying risks to existing communication practices of the technoculture and the online music lifeworld that are worth keeping, singling out corporate strategies or trends in industry and policy that are worth challenging or rejecting. They see colonizing encroachments into the music lifeworld and counter them with symbolic politics and "tools for de-colonization" (Hadl 2004), often in solidarity with affinity groups.

The Social Agency of Alternative Media and Radical Media

In the United States, organized litigation, lobbying, and public education are time-tested methods for activists operating from a liberal-pluralist philosophy—such as those in the media reform movement of the 1960s, who were disillusioned with the failure of commercial radio and television in the United States to provide quality programming. Public-access cable TV, children's programming, public television, and public radio were policy-making accomplishments of alternative-media activists before becoming targets, in turn, of media deregulators in the 1980s under the Fowler-led FCC in the Reagan administration. Mosco calls the rehabilitated "public interest media reform movement" (1996, 241) a social movement that has helped influence "the development of the means and content of communication" (240) by promoting "universal access to the information infrastructure, freedom to communicate, democratic policy-making, and privacy protection" (241). These reformers drew considerable participation from media professionals and civil society institutions that worked within state agencies to win policy reforms. Ironically, alternative media in the United States often work to attain objectives that may already be formally enshrined in federal communication policy, but are dead or at risk of extinction as existing practices.

Radical media, on the other hand, exhibit counterhegemonic attributes insofar as they resist or challenge existing power structures, empower diverse communities and classes, and enable communities of interest to speak to one another (Downing 2001). Radical media have captured the attention of media scholars with a Gramscian perspective on non-state–based forms of resistance that begin in rebellious countercultures and social movements in civil society.

Popular case studies of alternative media include Paper Tiger TV, carried via satellite to public-access cable channels; the Prometheus community radio project; microbroadcasters on FM radio; and the IndyMedia news portal. The Future of Music Coalition, Downhill Battle, and online "eLabels" (Edgecliffe-Johnson 2005) or "Netlabels" (Gumiela 2007) are alternative media efforts by independent musicians and fans to decolonize the music lifeworld on the model of alternative- and radical-media activism. Decidedly capitalistic in nature, these alternative distribution networks have an entrepreneurial spirit and innovativeness that have gone lacking in the music business for decades. Lessig (1999) and Benkler (2006) both acclaim the interplays between entrepreneurs and social movement constituencies as generators of media diversity and innovative business models and technologies.

In many cases, innovation among new music labels offers artists alternatives to major label contracts. The creator of Elektra records, Jac Holzman, launched Cordless Recordings to publish "clusters" of three or more songs online from new artists. Artists with Cordless Recordings sign simple contracts that exchange exclusive distribution rights for twenty-one months for the retention of all masters and copyrights by the artists. "This looks very much like the way records were made in the 50s, 60s and early 70s, when record companies played a pivotal role in the evolution of the artist and in helping the artist to bring out the best they had," says Holzman (quoted in Edgecliffe-Johnson 2005). The invention hearkens back to the early days of the business model, when many recording artists and songwriters enjoyed more autonomy.

The alternative-radical distinction bedevils media studies. Although there is a basic conceptual problem with the notion of "alternative media" that Downing (2001) points out—namely, "Everything, at some point, is alternative to something else" (ix)—I hold that the concept is sufficiently parsimonious to qualify alternative-media activism as a set of social and technical demands promoted as challenging or contrary to the Celestial Jukebox and business as usual. These demands are consistent with Hesmondhalgh's criteria for access and participation, Lessig's free culture, and Vaidhyanathan and Benkler's radically democratic political philosophies. They all support the preservation and expansion of civil liberties and civil society in cyberspace. Whereas Paper Tiger TV, Prometheus Radio, pirate radio, and microradio programmers labored to eke out access and carriage for a small number of analog channels in regulated media markets, cyberliberties activists labor to exploit locked-up music and make music more broadly available on the Internet. Conflicts in the music and cyberliberties domain are principally related to IP claims, and disclose a politics of symbolic action that resembles social movement politics in its potentials for "resistance and transformation" (Carroll and Hackett 2006, 83) in the industry, in local music scenes, and in other places for music.

Alternative-media activism loosens the hold of the culture industries on the music lifeworld by promoting alternatives to the existing copyright regime. Examples of formal organizations devoted to copyright activism include the Creative Commons and the Free Software Society (FSF). As alternatives to industry IP practices, the Creative Commons and FSF's CopyLeft scheme promote creativity (Demers 2006) and serve to establish a creative commons that pools volunteered resources. Alternative-media theorists locate these alternative practices in civil societies of countries and identify global constituencies that are forming around them and nearby them. The World Summit on the Information Society (WSIS) claims to incorporate constituencies from "global civil society" (Burkart 2009) into a global resistance to the worldwide IP regime. Specifically, the WTO–TRIPS (World Trade Organization–Trade Related Aspects of Intellectual Property Rights) Agreement, which formalized a global system for "harmonizing" the IP systems of signatory countries, is being targeted by the free and open-source software movement for reforms and circumvention (Schweidler and Costanza-Chock 2009). Besides copyright, patent law (as it relates to computer software), business methods, and genetics combine into a zone of conflict over the cultural impacts of local obligations under globalized ownership of IP rights. In addition to IP rights, music and cyberliberties activists monitor and influence policy debates in telecommunications, media, and information policy through research, public education, lobbying, and litigation. The Swedish Pirate Party began working in these areas in 2006.

Although the alternative-media label risks becoming a grab bag of leftovers unsuitable for other categories, continuing empirical research and theoretical refinements to the "alternative" category are yielding valuable studies of public-sphere institution building and practices of global civil society (Downing 2001; Benkler 2006; Kidd, Rodriguez, and Stein 2009). In something of an update of *Radical Media*, the contributors to the *Our-Media* volumes (Kidd, Rodriguez, and Stein 2009) provide international examples of cyberliberties activism, including opposition to copyright reform, censorship, and privacy violations (especially Lee 2009 and Schweidler and Costanza-Chock 2009). Public-sphere research in communication, sociology, and political science finds examples of social institutions and media systems that can gather a plurality of groups and interests into a common forum for debating and deliberating the weightiest social problems of the day. Alternative communication channels can challenge or undermine those of dominant, legitimated, and "official" media systems.

Alternative-media groups represent their own work and missions to one another at conferences and conventions. The National Conference for Media Reform (NCMR) is a joint project of the nonprofit advocacy group Free Press and media scholar Robert McChesney, with a mission to thwart the further consolidation of big media and to enable the creation and maintenance of alternative-media systems. The NCMR is a hybrid organization of "old line" media reform activists and cyberlibertarians working with music and new media. NCMR lectures and panels focus on how to attain or regain local control over media, particularly for independent and noncommercial sources of news, music, and arts. NCMR sponsors promote the conference as a message to grassroots activists that structural reforms, such as the replacement of ownership caps on big media conglomerates, should be prioritized as an urgent political objective of its members, ahead of any other political or cultural agendas, in order to make use of the well-known framing and agenda-setting functions of media later. Besides policy-oriented activism, the NCMR also supports promoters of community WiFi networking, community radio, cable-access TV, and indie music labels.

The following list (collected from personal notes) is a nonrandom sample of organizations participating in the 2005 NCMR conference, St. Louis, Missouri:

Action Coalition for Media Education (ACME) (public education and media literacy education)

Champaign-Urbana Community Wireless Network (nonprofit community infrastructure networking)

Center for International Media Action (CIMA) (public-interest advocacy for media reform)

The Free Press (progressive news and commentary, and national nonpartisan media reform organization)

Future of Music Coalition (see appendix)

Grass Roots Cable Coalition (Comcast consumers' union)

Hear Us Now ("Consumer voice for communications choice")

Media Tank (public education and lobbying for media reform)

Mountain Area Information Network, North Carolina (MAIN) (nonprofit community networking)

New America Foundation (nonprofit public-policy institute)

Project Censored (indie journalism advocate)

Public Media Center (nonprofit strategic marketing and advocacy)

U.S. Public Interest Research Group (US-PIRG) (public interest advocacy)

Radio Free Brattleboro, Vermont (unlicensed radio station shut down by the FCC in June 2006)

Texas Media Empowerment Project (community media advocacy and training)

WPVM (Asheville, North Carolina) (broadcaster and MAIN member)

For the most part, the entities presenting at the NCMR conference are not-for-profit organizations, NGOs (nongovernmental organizations), and charities that use volunteer labor to operate media platforms, produce noncommercial media messages, or support the broader diffusion of noncommercial media. The NCMR claimed a victory in 2003 for mobilizing the opposition that rebuffed an FCC attempt to lift media-ownership caps.[7]

Working beside the ACLU, EFF, and Software Freedom Law Center, which I discussed earlier, are complementary groups with links to nonprofit research and advocacy teams. These groups include Consumers Union, Public Knowledge, the Ford Foundation, the Social Science Research Council, the Center for Digital Democracy, the American Library Association, the Electronic Privacy Information Clearinghouse (EPIC), Computer Professionals for Social Responsibility, the Nieman Foundation for Journalism (Harvard), the Brennan Center for Justice (New York University School of Law), the American Library Association (ALA), and the Glushko-Samuelson Intellectual Property Law Clinic (American University's Washington College of Law). This list of peers in the network of alternative-media and cyberliberties activists is hardly exhaustive. Each group contributes to a broader project of preserving and expanding a place for music, digital culture, and knowledge in their many formats and expressions.

Globally, media activists were drawn to the World Summit on the Information Society (WSIS) meetings (2003–2005), which reenacted long-standing disputes over ideological purity and pragmatic compromise as divergent ways of democratizing media institutions. The most pointed disagreements arose over matters of movement identity (for example, libertarian, communitarian, or anarchist political theory; counterhegemonic or liberal-democratic mission; alternative or radical self-presentation) and over strategy. The alternative-radical dialectic manifested itself time and again as activists articulated rationales for pursuing ideological purity and exclusivity, for pragmatism and alliance building, or for a blend of both. The diverse nature of the grievances and agendas reflected broad differences in identity among the participants (Cunningham 2008; Hamelink 2004; Hintz and Hadl 2008).

Entrepreneurial and "idealistic business ventures" (Schmidt, in Rappeport 2006) are for-profit firms operating alongside alternative media, commercial businesses, and noncommercial civil-society organizations promoting access to cyberculture. For example, Rappeport (2006) describes Internet service providers (ISPs) who operate proxy servers that permit Web surfers on restricted networks to break through most restrictions: in a "cat-and-mouse-war with government censors the world over...scores of small companies...have made it part of their mission to defy censors, unlike Google, Yahoo and Microsoft, which recently succumbed to demands to filter the Internet in China." Unipeak, Peacefire, Your Freedom, Cloak, and Proxify are other for-profit examples. By providing anonymizing services and anticensorship platforms, these ISPs meet needs in the markets for Internet access services that otherwise go unmet. The OpenNet Initiative, a joint project of, among others, the University of Toronto, Harvard Law School, and Cambridge University, is an entrepreneurial nonprofit example of a company reducing the impacts of state-sanctioned Internet censorship.[8]

BitTorrent's innovative software for delivering media content through P2P has won awards from technology industry groups and enjoys a wide user base. These commercial firms provide access to cultural and political information to individuals and groups otherwise denied it, even though they are enmeshed in the new economy of "digital capitalism" (Schiller 1999).

Whereas alternative-media activists are frequently content to adapt to existing power structures, and may even personally or collectively benefit from them, radical-media activists want to subvert or overturn the conventional system. They "have very often experienced state repression—execution, jailing, torture, fascist assaults, the bombing of radical radio stations, threats, police surveillance, and intimidation tactics" (Downing 2001, 19). A significant contribution of *Radical Media* (Downing 2001) is its search for the distinctive characteristics of radical (versus merely alternative) media activists worldwide, particularly those struggling to propagate messages under conditions of extreme social repression, political and social revolution, and other social conditions marked by crisis, rapid change, and suffering. Radical media are identifiable in historical studies of international communication that focus on periods of violent political conflict and suppression. Radical media are more likely than alternative media to try to mobilize resources that are not otherwise under their direct ownership or control and to participate in direct action, sometimes using counterhegemonic force. There are fewer examples of radical-media activism among the music and cyberliberties projects than there are in the larger universe of audiovisual media producers, but pirate radio, Internet Zapatismo, and cable-access TV programming by labor and gay, lesbian, bisexual, and transgender (GLBT) groups exemplify radical media that encounter continual bias and resistance from nearly all corners of society. Radical media take many forms: "Dance, street theater, cartoons, posters, parody, satire, performance art, graffiti, murals, and popular songs or instrumental music are...only some of the most obvious forms of radical media whose communicative thrust depends not on clearly argued logic but on their aesthetically conceived and concentrated force" (Downing 2001, 52).

Culture Jamming

Part political thespians, part cultural studies mavens, culture jammers appropriate symbolic—and primarily pop-culture—resources from mainstream institutions and turn the resources against those institutions and their operating logics. In the process, culture jammers rupture the suspension of disbelief required to maintain the ongoing commercial advertising spectacles of consumer society (Baudrillard 1998; Klein 2000; Kellner 2005). Culture jammers deflate the proudest corporate images and subvert their branding, hijack established communication channels, and cast seeds of doubt among audiences, where trust was once presumed to operate. In the process of disruption, opportunities for critical thinking among audience members and media consumers arise, and can stimulate reflection about the function of media in everyday thinking as well as about background expectations that are part of the media lifeworld.

The new communalist spirit of anarchistic, spontaneous, unplanned, and experimental "happenings" inhabits culture-jamming endeavors. Culture jammers tend to use humor to disarm establishment targets. Examples from the contemporary audio world include Plunderphonics, Negativland, DJ Dangermouse, and Brother Russell Ministries. Each enterprise is performative, creates musical and discursive "situations," and, in its own way, purposefully and playfully flouts or skirts the fringes of legality of telecommunications law or the legality of copyright. In the case of each artist or band, sampling and remixing is de rigueur. In the case of Negativland, in 2002 the band conducted pirate FM performances and a pirate radio teach-in in the close physical proximity of the National Association of Broadcasters meeting in Seattle (Holdorf 2002). Brother Russell remixes ludicrous prank telephone calls to live call-in conservative talk radio programs. The legal defense of these artistic activities can become challenging if the jammers are caught and confronted by hostile opponents; Negativland encountered such a situation when it was sued by Island Records for its U2 spoof album. Some, but not all, culture-jamming artifacts are varieties of "illegal art" by dint of their civil disobedience aimed at IP laws. However, popular-music scholar Kembrew McLeod's "Freedom of Expression" trademark earned him notoriety among culture jammers and academics alike for a prank that entailed a legalistic gesture that splendidly gilded the lily. After trademarking "Freedom of Expression," McLeod sued AT&T for trademark violations after AT&T launched its "Freedom of Expression" ad campaign.

Other examples of musical culture-jamming geniuses include the numerous projects loosely associated with the SubGenius Foundation and its long-running radio shows. The SubGenius media machine promoted a faux-fundamentalist Christian church, and produced volumes of humorous, anti-authoritarian, and anarchistic cartoons, books, radio shows, newsletters, and Web epistles. *RE/Search Magazine*'s "Pranks" edition featured case studies of intertwined music and culture-jamming cultures since the Yippies movement (RE/Search 1986). Ever increasing in sophistication and slickness, some full-blown integrated marketing campaigns have emerged around the culture-jamming activities of the Yes Men and the Barbie Liberation Organization (the BLO).

Culture jamming is among the most performative varieties of media activism, incorporating ironic attitudes from situationism and a predilection for *détournement*, hijacking, and diversion (Downing 2001, 140). Culture jamming has been mobilized in antiglobalization demonstrations, in campaigns against media consolidation, and against the Religious Right in the United States. Practically all culture jamming uses a dose of humor and some "social engineering" work to break into mainstream-media discourses and conversations and hijack the message, if not the communication channel. Culture jamming needs cyberliberties to flourish. Personal identities are purposefully obscured to cultivate needed anonymity and obscurity. Many culture jammers depend upon viral modes of communicating news and artifacts; in retro fashion, they also send physical recordings, zines, and home-taped videocassettes, audiocassettes, and disks through the mail. The Yes Men use established public relations firms and media production and distribution companies to launch radical messages through mainstream channels. The Yes Men also receive financial sponsorship from philanthropic patrons. Legendary musician and record producer Herb Alpert donated funds to the work of the Yes Men (Curiel 2004). Other groups mobilize resources by hijacking mainstream cultural objects and communication channels and by dropping conceptual "mind bombs" (Downing 2001, 140) that may take awhile to explode into the mediascape. Culture jammers play cultural jujitsu, taking the force and momentum of the opponent and reflexively turning it back.

Lovink (2002) considers radical media activism to be not a social movement with any single strategy or consciousness, but rather a collection of autonomously constituted "tactical media" responding organically to practical, local needs. Individualism, rather than collectivism, marks the activist ethic for Lovink. Lovink presents a nearly Nietzschean picture of the radical media activist-hero as a happy warrior:

Tactical media are opposition channels, finding their way to break out of the subcultural ghetto.... Typical heroes are the nomadic media warrior, prankster, hacker, rapper, jammer and camcorder kamikaze. They are the happy negatives, always in search of ways to deter the foe. Once the enemy has been named and vanquished it is the tactical practitioner whose turn it is to fall into a state of crisis and depression (264).

At the end of the day, Lovink suggests, the activist is a loner who continually moves within and between virtual and nonvirtual movements and contexts (Lovink 2002, 266–267). While this portrait of the lone-wolf activist holds a certain romantic appeal, it does not capture the sense of community or solidarity that has permeated social movement politics surrounding the evolution of cyberliberties (see chapter 3). Nor does it explain the cases in which cyberliberties activism has achieved results.

Hacktivism

Antiauthoritarianism and rebellious communications also characterize the efforts of software hackers to empower music fans who rely on software for access to their music. The hacker's allure in critical cultural studies is his or her identity as a code manipulator. Female hackers have played an important, though rare, role in hacker culture (Newitz 2001). Hacker culture is anarchistic, and oriented to autonomy and independence. It is also skills-based, reflecting the needs of the technoculture for knowledge work.

While there are professional hacktivists who have work arrangements that allow them to contribute to free software full-time (for example, Linus Torvalds and Richard Stallman), there are also examples of famous full-time hackers who have contributed their labor to commercial enterprise. These include such diverse luminaries as Mitch Kapor, Steve Wosniak, Kevin Mitnick, Napster's Shawn Fanning, BitTorrent's Bram Cohen, and, arguably, Bill Gates. While the social agency of hacktivists is a potentially powerful form of opposition to the Celestial Jukebox, hacktivism is unlikely to pose a dire threat to the economy, law and order, or even complacency about the erosion of cyberliberties. In chapter 4, I address hacking in greater detail, and consider it to be a generalized ethos of the technoculture, with roots in the phone-phreaking and computer-hobbyist subcultures that flourished among early programmers and microcomputer users (Turner 2006).

Jordan and Taylor (2004) distinguish political and cultural activism accomplished through hacking (hence, "hacktivism") from hacking as a merely self-gratifying ego boost for geeks. Hacktivists are individually and collectively producing software code for noninfringing, nondestructive enjoyment of cyberliberties, including online band jamming, sharing music, copublishing, doing research, demonstrating a grievance, performing a prank, or drawing attention to a social problem.[9] Jordan and Taylor organize case studies of hacktivism by ideological intent, from disruptive antiglobalization "mass" demonstrations to the activities of the "digitally correct," whose actions consistently send the message that "digital rights are also human rights" (2004, 91). Jordan and Taylor argue that hacktivists' abilities to bypass and disrupt the Celestial Jukebox have grown meaningfully as software code, cultural codes, and legal code converge around communications online, and as regulationist practices spread.

The Napster shutdown created the precedent for "contributory infringement of copyright."[10] The moment between the judicial shutdown of Napster and Napster's reemergence as a "straight" business in cahoots with the major labels was a sign to music communities on the Internet that communal music-sharing practices were under siege. Guerrilla tactics were adopted to resist the industry's attempts to criminalize P2P and set up ubiquitous DRM. Hacktivists developed a variety of Napster alternatives, including AIMster, Freenet, Fasttrack, and Gnutella (Burkart and McCourt 2006, 63–68). For music file sharing to survive as a noncommercial practice, it had to become anonymized and further decentralized. Reformed hackers Fanning (of Napster) and Russo (of Grokster) have promoted P2P software development for commercial purposes, which lands them in the entrepreneurial capitalistic category of cyberliberties activism. The ideologically "pure" and "elite" hackers (or "digitally correct hacktivists") serve projects that tend to be aligned with fair use, broader access, and participation in the digital domain. Copy-protection removal and other work-arounds on locked-down music files, anonymous surfing and file sharing, and the development of free software applications are therefore prominent projects. Act-lab.tv, anonymous computing based on Freenet, and peer-to-peer gaming engines are examples of hacktivism projects undertaken in teams with Freenet developer Brandon Wiley.

Hacktivism may well be yet another "weapon of the weak" (Lovink 2002), but its oppositional activities force confrontations with mainstream media systems and politicize unchallenged and "natural" power relationships in the technoculture. Hacktivist projects can resemble radical media activism, which also uses communication technology to chisel away at the influence of the big media distribution channels. For ethical and even aesthetic reasons, hacktivists may prefer a subversive mode of oppositional engagement with media and online monopolies. Software hackers have helped create the music lifeworld, from the underlying Internet protocols to MP3 players and encoders, to P2P, to the myriad music library managers, file taggers, and so forth, with the intention of enjoying greater freedom to hear, share, and enjoy music.

As hackers tend to see it, saving a place for music need not be highly organized, but should take direct approaches to injecting speech (or software code) into disputes or potential disputes over access to knowledge, music, and culture that would otherwise be beyond the influence of other fans. The "hacker ethic" considers software to be reasoned speech that can be utilized as a means to a principled end (enhanced freedom and autonomy). The hacker ethic is inspired by anarchism (Jordan and Taylor 2004), a political theory that prizes individual autonomy over communitarian ideals (Wolff 1976). Ian Clarke explicitly places his hacktivist P2P project, Freenet, which anonymizes P2P traffic on the Internet, within an "ideology of free communication" (Clarke n.d.) steeped in the hacker ethic. Clarke's contributions to music and cyberliberties activism create access, opportunities for dialogue among music fans, deliberation about our technology practices, and negotiation leverage for fans with their technology providers.

They can partially satisfy the political desire for personal autonomy characteristic of most new social movements (see chapter 4). Jordan and Taylor might consider Clarke's Freenet a variety of "digitally correct" or do-gooder hacking (2004). Yet in the popular press, hackers have trouble earning recognition as creative intellects, much less as ethical activists. Hackers' media portrayals have gone from "'heroes to hooligans' over a period of four decades"; whereas hackers were once represented as beneficent technical wizards, "today, hackers are conceived as 'miscreants, vandals, criminals, and even terrorists'" (Nissenbaum, quoted in Gates 2006, 59).

Hacktivists were instrumental in raising public awareness about the widespread deployment of two kinds of malicious software by Sony-BMG products onto the computer hard drives of thousands of unsuspecting music fans.[11] As discussed, major labels have experimented with copy protection placed on intangible music files as well as on physical CD-like discs. Sony-BMG released up to 1 million disks with "rootkit" software designed to hijack the administrative controls of users' computers in order to prevent users from "ripping" copies of tracks from the CD. A historic hack exploited the Sony-BMG rootkit "fix" that the company distributed, belatedly, after its music disks were shown to be infected with spyware and copy protection. The software hack of the rootkit "fix" took advantage of Sony-BMG's incompetent response to a serious mistake that left between 100,000 and 1,000,000 music fans unknowing victims of a computer security breach (Marson 2006). The hack impishly caused PCs to shut down and restart; althought no damage was done, the hack drew attention to the experience of thousands of computer users who were unwitting victims of Sony-BMG's rootkit and even more dangerous "fix." The cumulative effect of these events was to show the world that Sony-BMG not only had harmed users' computers, but also had undermined what little trust may have existed for "trusted computing" and DRM. Sony-BMG settled with at least fifteen parties who sued the company for damages, and reached separate agreements with attorneys general of U.S. states in a deal worth at least $5.75 million (McMillan 2006).

Hacktivism challenges emerging or extant information regimes that are perceived to be antidemocratic or imposed by bureaucrats or police. The TOR Project, supported by EFF, is a nonprofit organization that responds to the loss of anonymity on the Internet with a new model of networking software. The juridification and colonization of the Internet, not only by corporate players but also by state bureaucrats and police, have created the need to evade online surveillance and preserve anonymous surfing and online speech. The TOR developers have explained the rationale and method of their system:

Tor aims to defend against traffic analysis, a form of network surveillance that threatens personal anonymity and privacy, confidential business activities and relationships, and state security. Communications are bounced around a distributed network of servers called onion routers, protecting you from websites that build profiles of your interests, local eavesdroppers that read your data or learn what sites you visit, and even the onion routers themselves. Tor's security is improved as its user base grows and as more people volunteer to run servers (TOR 2007a).

TOR was developed as an open-source application for which other programs, patches, and hacks have emerged. TOR claims to provide anonymity for publishing and browsing by people with sensitive communications, including journalists, whistleblowers, dissidents, NGOs operating in repressive countries, illness survivors, and abuse victims (TOR 2007b). To that list could be added illegal artists, TOR researchers,[12] RIAA lawsuit targets, DRM researchers, P2P technologists, cryptographers, and political activists out of favor with the executive branch of government in the United States and elsewhere.

Hackers have repeatedly targeted the dominant commercial-software technology supplier to the world. Creating a work-around for the tricky Microsoft Windows music DRM scheme inspired the anonymously released unfuck.exe WMA hack, which emerged practically as soon as Microsoft released that DRM. Viodentia's FairUse4WM crack of the Microsoft PlaysForSure DRM (which is used on Zune players) provoked a lawsuit, but as Thomas Ricker reported on Engadget in 2007, Microsoft had to drop it after the company could not find the hacker. The BackOrifice hack of Microsoft's Back Office server software stands out among innumerable Microsoft hacks because it targeted one of the earlier e-commerce platforms offered by Microsoft as the PC operating system monopolist first tried to dominate the market for Web business software. The hacker group called Cult of the Dead Cow claimed successes both in its Microsoft BackOffice hack and in its management of the negative media attention that subsequently engulfed Microsoft (Knight 1999) as it once again faced numerous security problems with its software. Other operating systems, of course, also attract hackers. Hackers have forcibly opened up proprietary media formats that were previously restricted to Apple users, including Jon Johansen's iTunes Fairplay AAC hack. The DeCSS DVD hack by Johansen and others enabled Linux users using free and open-source software to view DVDs, bypassing copy restrictions based on CSS (content-scrambling system), which were protected by the DMCA. Code for the hack of the HD-DVD format was mass-published on Digg.com and spread virally to other media when there was an attempt to quash its publication.[13]

Moving to the higher level of network hacking, FloodNet software created by the Electronic Disturbance Theatre was designed to flood targeted servers with Internet traffic, when instructed. FloodNet has been called a tool for cyberterrorists, and was used extensively in antiglobalization and "Internet Zapatismo" activism (Jordan and Taylor 2004, 72, 84, 87, 88). FloodNet exploits the Internet's dispersed network architecture in ways that render undefended sites vulnerable to attack.[14]

Hacker culture uses software code to assert free speech rights in cyberspace. Software code has technical effects and can also have the effect of being a speech act in itself.[15] The DMCA has been used to silence research and reporting on DRM by computer scientists such as Edward Felten at Princeton, who (as mentioned previously) researches music copy protection. Dmitry Sklyarov, a Russian Ph.D. student, was arrested at the behest of Adobe Systems for violating the DMCA's prohibitions on sharing anti-DRM software, *before* he presented an academic paper on ebook readers at a computer science conference. Other publishers have been silenced. *2600* magazine publishes technical articles on telephony and Internet signaling and regularly asserts a freedom to tinker with technology. *2600* lost a court battle waged by Universal City Studios for publishing DeCSS source code on its Web site, and by extension of a peculiar line of legal reasoning, also created the legal precedent that "circumventing CSS to make fair use of a DVD movie" violates the DMCA (Samuelson 2003, 43). The illegal code became illegal speech, and an instant cause célèbre. The code has subsequently appeared in numerous and novel places, including an online art museum curated by David Touretzky (Knowles 2003):

Examples range from T-shirts and ties bearing the DeCSS code, to MP3s of complete songs whose performers sing the code as lyrics. One anonymous [poet]...wrote a lengthy series of haiku that, Touretzky observes, is "both a commentary on the DeCSS situation and a correct and complete description of the descrambling algorithm":

Reader, see how yet technical communicants deserve free speech rights;

see how numbers, rules, patterns, languages you don't yourself speak yet,

still should in law be protected from suppression, called valuable speech!

Hacktivists make use of anonymous and pseudonymous speech in cyberspace to make or communicate about technology that can disrupt the plans of monopolist gatekeepers, play pranks on the political and legal establishment, and promote tools for sharing culture. Organizationally, they are informally connected to one another. They can employ collaborative software tools, such as the open-source CVS (concurrent versions system) code-management system and Internet Relay Chat, to compile code contributed by hackers working across far-flung international networks. Yet in creating new approaches to sharing music and relevant information, either where none exist or where there are unjust prohibitions on tinkering and sharing, hacktivists make themselves targets of the criminal justice systems of most countries. In this respect, they can be said to engage in forms of civil disobedience.

The Social Agency of Marginalized Groups

In the next chapter, I shall address the ideological dimensions of hacktivism, culture jamming, and radical media activism. This section prepares the way for an ideological analysis of cyberliberties. I consider how communication theorists have addressed media-based movements as political agents with broadly transformative social potentials. Carroll and Hackett (2006) describe democratic media activism as "emergent movement praxis" (85), while Downing (2001), writing of radical media movements, describes participation as a variety of political praxis or social struggle with rational, just, and broadly transformative political goals. Mosco (1996) describes new social movements as opening a window for researchers into communication processes underlying structuration in late-capitalist society. As counterhegemonic expressions of power, they work against social stratification by class, race, and gender while also offering alternative ideologies to consumer capitalism. Downing and Mosco both see new social movements, and particularly media movements, as containing enough collective agency to intervene in the cultural sphere with messages and institutional reforms that can shake up the seemingly natural and inevitable mainstream. Although *Radical Media* echoes sentiments offered from sociological research (Pichardo 1997) that not all social movements are progressive, or even rational, Downing wants to illustrate examples of communicatively collective action and political solidarity around socially progressive goals—and, in the process, to criticize the contemporary social systems that cultivate atomized, passive, conformist, and quiescent couch potatoes. These three perspectives are in tacit agreement that radical media activism and even alternative media do visibly assert resistance of the lifeworld to colonization by the system.

There are aspects of new social movements among all four categories of music and cyberliberties activism. All are symptomatic of a colonized music lifeworld that is shrinking like the polar ice cap. Some argue that in the process of fighting in the margin between big media and music lifeworld, cyberlibertarian activists are forging a coherent, cohesive, and oppositional collective identity. Strangelove's (2005) "uncontrollable public sphere" and Hardt and Negri's (2004) "multitude" are glimpses of this radical vision, and of a different magnitude of political opposition from the mere "interest group anarchy" of which Mosco speaks.

From a critical social systems perspective, such as the theory of communicative action, hackers and hacktivists, culture jammers and radical media activists all work at the margins of the lifeworld and the system, and make periodic incursions into it, with some visible effects. The networked media environment in which they work inform their activities in basic ways, but the social agency of the political actors resides in their speech acts, manipulation of symbolic politics, and control of material resources. The perspective I am offering on cyberliberties activism is different from other perspectives that attribute social agency to the networked environment itself. For example, Strangelove (2005) adopts Hardt and Negri's (2000) postmodern interpretation of imperialism,[16] and proposes that hackers and hacktivism are part of a social movement that poses a severe threat to the integrity of capitalism. Strangelove sees causal relationships between the emergence of the Internet, its commercialization, and the development of oppositional hacktivism.

Capitalism's power structure is embedded in a symbolic economy that is under assault within cyberspace....Globalizing capitalism uses the Internet to extend its domain, but even as it does so it decreases its ability to control the foundation of any empire—the hearts and minds of its subjects. It may be the ultimate irony of globalization that it inadvertently created an uncontrollable public sphere, which in any empire is a dire threat. (210–211)

Strangelove (2005) argues that hacktivism, like labor, seems to be in a dialectical relationship with globalizing capitalism and its network infrastructures. In this account, capitalism's undoing is built into the ability of its own network-based technology to put capitalist enterprises and state capitalism at serious risk. But Strangelove does not characterize any further the characteristics of the coming cataclysm (economic depression? revolutionary overthrows? failed states?). Nor does he explain why it is this technology, the Internet, and not a prior technology, like the telegraph, that induces crisis. The political and economic dimensions of the "crisis" extend only as far as the emergence of computer hacking as an identifiable technology practice in opposition to certain moneyed interests. But hacktivism does not really precipitate a crisis, as it turns out, as it may also help work out social conflicts in communicative action in a "public sphere" (however "uncontrollable").

Hacktivists are rebellious *and* communicatively rational. They seek and rely on lifeworld resources like other fans, and perceive risks of alienation from the clientelization of their relationships and the juridification. They respond tactically by challenging the perceived threats, and can demonstrate political solidarity in doing so. Cyberliberties politics is but another politics of symbolic action (M. Edelman 1971) that can with speech acts point to, name, and address the sources of the affronts to music culture, democratic culture, and technoculture.

The next section argues that colonization is a useful and relevant way to explore music and cyberliberties activism, media activism, and NSMs together in a critical theoretical project for media and communication studies. Colonization joins commodification, spatialization, and structuration as an observable process of media rationalization in late capitalism.

The Colonization of the Music Lifeworld

The "colonization of the lifeworld" is the theory of communicative action's interpretation of the reification thesis as introduced by Marx. Reification was later adapted by the Frankfurt School of critical theorists and by Georg Lukács. Colonization is detectable in visible processes of bureaucratization and commercialization of media cultures, and the cutting off of flows of music and other media. From my perspective, the colonization thesis describes processes that contribute to the conversion of the Internet into a mass-media distribution platform for the entertainment industry. Principally, the strategic use of law and technology by the major music labels, and the responses of typically passive consumers and regulators to juridification and reification, have led to (1) the desiccation of music scenes organized around practices of collecting and sharing recorded music in physical places; (2) the emergence of music as a commercial service provided online in private and atomized streams; (3) the insinuation of DRM into music-listening experiences; (4) the erosion of fair use as a public-interest exception to copyright; and (5) the invasion of contract law and lawsuits into the everyday lives of music fans. These effects are all symptoms of the colonization of the music lifeworld. I have already addressed some of the ways in which economic and bureaucratic forces can affect groups, organizations, and society as a whole through the "mediatization" and "internal colonization" of the lifeworld (Fairtlough 1991, 557).

In music scenes, and within virtual music communities, socialization, cultural reproduction, and social integration are symbolically reproduced communications that constantly come under pressure to "monetize" (to borrow a word from e-business that means turning nonpayers into payers in an online community) music and fandom more efficiently. Willing participation by fans in the industry, or complicity in the process, can render colonization effects invisible, which in turn serves to support the growth and expansion of the system. Updating the colonization thesis, Mosco (1996) refers to "cybernetic commodification," or market making for information-based products and services. He does not explore some implications of the process for cyberliberties, however. Insofar as audiences are both constituted and marketed online, the users of media software and services become cybernetic commodities, partly through their "work of being watched" (Andrejevic 2002, 230). The laboring relationship of the user for the provider is actually acquired and paid for by the user. Paying to labor in a portal is the juridical basis for the negative privacy consequences to the user. Popular music portals, like iTunes, that distribute DRMed music also commodify users' profiles and personal information through contractual relationships that give the portals nearly complete control over users' access, activity logs, personally identifying information, and terms of service. A music fan's extra value to a music-service provider consists in his or her "digital shadow" or "second self," in Andrejevic's terms (137). The second self appears as a surplus value to the provider and benefits the firm in addition to the first self, or user, who is the purchaser or renter of music, watcher of advertisements, and a generator of site content. The surveillance may continue even after the music fan leaves the digital enclosure of a place like iTunes. The fan can in fact remain a user subject to surveillance by the presence of a "persistent" cookie or a system service (for example, the Apple "iPodService Module"), even if he or she is no longer paying to use any other aspect of the service.

The value of the work of being watched online increases as more people switch from CDs to digital downloads. Contract law has expanded into digital music by forcing users to enter into legal contracts for each transaction required to access music; these juridifications occur in online work. Logins, authentications, digital signatures, click-wrap agreements, terms of service, EULAs, and purchase agreements bury the music fan with the real work of demonstrating, over and over, who he or she really is, and swearing, repeatedly, to not having criminal intents with respect to IP law. The juridification process requires consumers to make allegiances and overcommitments of their own rights and money to corporate entities. The new regime of legal-economic transactions for basic access to culture exposes the lifeworld to system pressures by converting undisturbed lifeworld experiences into contractually obligating, technologically mediated legal agreements. The coercive power of the service-client relationship, forged in contract law, resembles the wage relationship insofar as it is individually arranged, unavoidable, and nonnegotiable, with all-or-nothing terms. In the process of digitally "signing" all those agreements, music fans turn over old and new rights and freedoms to the entertainment industry while participating in a broader privatization of the music lifeworld.

Try as they might, however, the culture industries have not yet been successful in getting people to shed basic expectations about music as a part of the cultural commons. When the Celestial Jukebox eventually becomes the consumption norm for media delivery, it will for most music fans become a natural and ordinary way of doing things; as with the other structures of the lifeworld, it will become "the result of the emergence of a 'second nature', in which we habitually orient ourselves in a changing 'space of reasons'" (Honneth 2002, 500) .

It is possible to opt out of the Celestial Jukebox as a music fan. Music fans who seek the least intrusive, most participatory, most accessible, and most rights-retaining formats find that vinyl and CDs still offer consumers the most rights (and highest copy quality) retained for their money spent, while DRMed music formats streamed or downloaded from music portals offer the fewest (and lowest copy quality). The site eMusic.com was among the earliest of the music service providers with catalogs from each of the Big Four labels to distribute MP3s, which are un-DRMed. Apple has negotiated with one major label (EMI) to release unencrypted advanced audio coding (AAC) files through iTunes, and Amazon.com began offering MP3 downloads from all four major labels in 2007.[17] CopyLeft music is also widely available from independent artists on such Netlabels such as Magnatunes, Netlabels.org, Phlow.de, and Goingware. CopyLeft radio guides, such as http://actlab.tv/radio_guide.htm, are flourishing. With online search options provided by RIAA Radar, "music consumers can . . . easily and instantly distinguish whether an album was released by a member of the Recording Industry Association of America (RIAA)" (RIAARadar.com 2008), and boycott it if the RIAA Radar deems it tainted. The Darknet remains an option for obtaining music of both infringing and noninfringing legal status.[18]

Of course, music fans need not be earnest cyberlibertarians to prefer some kinds of music delivered from an Alternative Jukebox. Nor are they any more likely to be grizzled high-fidelity hobbyists who refuse to let go of their vinyl record collections. Consumers who actively seek out independently produced and distributed recordings, may also accept DRMed distribution through music portals, however grudgingly. Most fans make choices about obtaining and listening to music for idiosyncratic reasons, including reasons of personal taste, and also for nonnormative and "unenlightened" reasons, including the sheer utility of unencumbered digital downloads. Nonetheless, these fans contribute to aggregate demand for uncrippled music, adding inertia to the lingering "second nature" in the lifeworld that still supports sharing and communicating about music as a vital part of one's culture.

In the final section of this chapter, I look at changes to the music lifeworld from the perspective of the spatialization of the music industry since the Napster Watershed. The spatialization concept relates financial, organizational, and operational aspects of global music production, distribution, and consumption, from the perspective of the economic system.

The Spatialization of Conflicts over Popular Music

"Colonization" is a concept that can be disambiguated by the political economy of communication, which holds that commodification, spatialization, and structuration are interrelated logics of growth that are visible in capitalism's modern history. The transposition of local and independent music scenes from physical and face-to-face spaces of interaction into cyberspace discloses some basic processes of "spatialization" of the capitalist commodity form (Mosco 1996, 173–211). Spatialization is "the process of overcoming the constraints of space and time in social life" (173) in technical and administrative relationships and routines. The spatialization of the music industry—and of the disputes over the way the music industry currently does business—is occurring at five levels simultaneously.

First, it occurs in the ownership structures of the Big Four major labels, which still account for between 72 and 87 percent of commercial music market share globally.[19] The transnationalization of the corporations publishing and distributing music has proceeded apace: the Sony-BMG merger created the Big Four from a "Big Five," and the "little giants" EMI and Warner have repeatedly tried to merge since then. But rather than forming a more and more tightly integrated market for popular music, the popular-music cartel exhibits aspects of "loose integration": a network of partnerships, coventures, and affiliates outside the cartel more flexible toward other parts of the entertainment industry than it was under the Big Five (Burkart 2005). In concentrating, it also differentiated into two ownership classes. An affiliated-unaffiliated distinction emerged among the four members of the cartel, which is an effect of spatialization in the popular-music industry. The affiliated members, Sony-BMG and UMG, are integrated into media conglomerates, and compete head-to-head for market share with stand-alone music companies EMI and Warner, which do not have entertainment conglomerates as parent companies (Burkart 2005, 492–493). The importance of industry restructuring into a looser federation of corporate music companies is that digital distribution and the new business models for music sales—including social networking, subscription, and ring tones—are creating a broader music-industry base involving more non–major-label organizations and creating a porous environment that could more easily absorb influences from the creative environment than stand-alone, vertically integrated companies have been able to do so far.

Second, the spatialization of the distribution and marketing of popular music has been essential to the creation of markets for "cybernetic com-modities" (Mosco 1996), beginning with the differentiation of the role of the music fan. The role of music fan or consumer splits, adding the role of the user to the existing role of customer. On the one hand, music fans be-come users of one of many information services and thereby become sub-ject to the terms of whatever contracts they sign digitally with an operating-system vendor (usually Microsoft or Apple), a Web-browser vendor such as Microsoft, a music-player vendor such as Winamp, a music-service provider such as iTunes or MusicNet, and a broadband ISP such as Time Warner or Comcast. Users become highly juridified legal subjects who exchange rights and money for access to a growing part of their musical culture. Before the music fans became music users, they may have been "netizens," or online-community members, home tapers, anonymous or pseudonymous satirists or hackers, hobbyist tinkerers, or any permutation of these roles. Regarding the music they purchased on CD or LP, they enjoyed more property rights: for example, the right of first sale (the right to buy or sell used music) and fair-use rights (the right to make a noninfringing copy for certain noncom-mercial purposes). These rights enhanced accessibility and participation with-out blocking or undue surveillance or the insinuation of a power relation-ship by the Big Four record labels. By turning music fans into users, the marketplace has squeezed new economic value out of consumers at the ex-pense of important rights and, with shrunken consumer rights, a smaller place for music in cyberspace.

Third, spatialization occurs in the work of being watched. Users who are "authenticated" are subjected to continual online surveillance and relin-quish rights to anything of value that they generate in the "digital enclo-sure" (Andrejevic 2002). Surveillance can become internalized, so that users willingly perform the "work of being watched" and willingly contribute to the value of their own user profiles as cybercommodities (Andrejevic 2003). Something like this occurs in virtual-community user ratings, and other loyalty-building programs. The wage relationship created by music fans participating in online digital "enclosures" introduces a new power dynamic related to music fandom, and to the activity of listening to music, where one did not previously exist. In joining a digital enclosure like a music-service provider, a music fan not only concedes to give up a personal right to prop-erty (a musical recording, a product), but also accedes to innumerable legal terms and conditions that typically do not expire.

Fourth, spatialization effects are visible in the digital divide that persists between rich and poor countries, and also within these countries. Even at the local level—for example, in "global cities" (Sassen 2000), along national borders, and at rural-urban borderlines—disparities persist between populations on and off the network. The digital divide increasingly reflects the accumulation of prejudices of markets and regulatory systems against communities of rural, inner-urban, minority, and impoverished citizens (Rojas et al. 2001). It also reflects discrepancies between communication needs and infrastructure availability, which in turn reflect the limits of individual network topographies. Because the digital divide removes access to potential Celestial Jukebox users, this aspect of spatialization can work at cross-purposes with the broader and deeper commodification of music across all markets and social strata. Mitigating these losses are lobbying against universal service policies, price tiering, windowing, and personalization strategies used by culture industries to maximize revenues from paying customers.

Fifth, in the division of the fan's role into the consumer-user roles, there has been a coevolution of the role of the collector in the music industry. I shall devote chapter 5 to this aspect of spatialization. In the decades of vinyl record history, record collectors performed such roles as public archivist, fan scenester, promoter, financier, and commentator, to name but a few. Record collectors contributed materially to the reproduction of music cultures. Today DJs, dance clubs, blogs, and other online spaces are filling in the areas of fan culture that have been eroded in the migration to digital distribution (Théberge 2005). As the CD format continues its decline, music fans will deliberate about the implications of making the turn to an archive of all-digital files.

New Action Domains for Music

The variety of music and cyberliberties activism (alternative and radical media, culture jamming, and hacktivism) demonstrates the influence of lifeworld-based politics on music cultures, cybercultures, and democratic culture. The variety of oppositional struggles also reflects the layered and crosscutting aspects of spatialization. Oppositional and rebellious actors' aims oscillate between the redistributive justice characteristic of collective and class-based politics and the right to be recognized in society as citizens with autonomy (fans, musicians, legal persons with rights, and identity-based countercultures). In both modes, the activism targets the client and consumer roles into which music fans are being pushed by the system. Music and cyberliberties activism is expressed in the politics of symbolic action, in which identities are presented to others and self-presented in layered, conflicted, or even confrontational symbolic speech acts.

This chapter has presented four varieties of music and cyberliberties activists: alternative-media activists, radical media activists, culture jammers, and hacktivist-cyberwarriors. Privacy, free speech, and access are three norms around which all three types of activism have oriented their tactical speech acts. These norms underpin a diverse set of grievances and claims against business and legal institutions that fail to recognize an interest in protecting fair use in the digital domain, many forms of cultural production and sharing, and privacy threats. I have shown that antiglobalization and, to some extent, anticapitalist identifications are identifiable in some music and cyberliberties activism; even so, for-profit enterprise and entrepreneurialism also make up part of the political agency and identification. I have also presented an expanded view of the effects of capitalist spatialization on the music lifeworld, indicating the field of social spaces for communicative action around music. That will be the subject of the next chapter.

CHAPTER THREE

Culture Clashes on the Internet

✳

The net, the very network itself, is merely a means to an end. The end is to reverse
engineer government, to hack Politics down to its component parts and fix it.
—Joshua Quittner of *Wired* (quoted in Turner 2006, 219)

In the last chapter, I laid some groundwork for addressing the social agency
of music fans with reference to communication theory and critical theory
rather than to theories of fandom, audience studies, media economics, or
reception theory. Critical theory that uses the theory of communicative action as a sociological systems theory discloses the power relationships operating in the confluence of music industry economics and digital distribution
on the Internet, and links cyberliberties activism to circumventing, confronting, and "hacking" some of those exercises of power.

In this chapter, I address some of the conflicting ideals and ideologies of
the "regulationists" (Godwin 2003) and of the music and cyberliberties activists. I use the critical social-systems perspective to address social change
from a systems perspective and a lifeworld perspective together. I address
cyberliberties activism as disturbances emanating from the music lifeworld
and arising in the transition of law and policymaking from a bureaucratic-
welfare mode to a deregulatory and informational mode (Braman 2007).

At the heart of the culture clashes on the Internet, P2P file sharing has
come to symbolize a contested social order and a challenge to authority to
such an extent that a cultural politics has emerged around file sharing. The
deployment of technological power, capital, and punitive crackdowns against
sharing practices has led to an incomplete colonization of the music lifeworld, however concerted the efforts of the RIAA. That is to say, even as
power and money have switched over lifeworld institutions into system
functions, there is still resistance to adopting the new digital distribution
models of the Celestial Jukebox.

First, I examine two specific zones of continual clashes over Internet culture: the decay of the fair-use doctrine, and the clientelization of the fans' roles in the popular music lifeworld. The shrinkage of the scope of the fair use of digital media has accelerated since the DMCA, and has been met with civil disobedience, including file sharing and the hacking of copy protections. Music fans' recognition of diminishing rights, and defensive responses to becoming corporate clients or service users of music, can transform them from couch potatoes into cyberliberties activists. On the other hand, their acquiescence in the Celestial Jukebox can convert them into more mere users for the content industries to add to their user bases.

Next, I address the historical moment of the Napster Watershed, when file sharing went from being a suspicious activity to an activity banished from legitimate social life online. A progressive politics of cyberculture that emerged around the time of the Napster Watershed updates the concepts of democratic citizenship to include free culture, the cultural commons, expanded fair use, and enhanced privacy protections. I review the influences of countercultural movements, youth movements, and new music of the 1960s on the ideology of cyberlibertarianism.

I then address emerging conflicts over the labors of artists and fans, which have become key zones of contestation in cyberspace, particularly since the Napster Watershed. As the norms of free culture abruptly gave way to regulationist legal norms, some important cultural expectations about openness and sharing were violated. These expectations still persist, however, in the technoculture. I conclude with some international examples of media activism and cyberliberties activism that demonstrate the interconnectedness of media activism, the technoculture, and the international contexts for policy affecting cyberliberties.

Rather than developing innovative responses to P2P challenges, the music industry rushed out services laden with DRM and set about laying traps for noncompliant music fans in lawsuits. In the midst of this frenzy, Lessig observed that "the architecture of . . . [cyberspace] is changing, interfering with the features that made innovation so rich. And the consequence again will be a decrease in this value that we thought defined the original Net" (2001, 140).

The colonization and reification effects that Lessig's academic work describes represent the combined effects of money and power organized by music-service providers, the major labels, the entertainment industry, and the hardware and software sectors. The end-to-end user experience in the Celestial Jukebox is dominated by corporate giants of interconnected industries. As Deetz (1992) argues, the modern corporation is the form of organizational communication that is most highly adapted to managing the combinations of power and money that institutionalize capitalism and help keep its wheels greased. Corporations are legal entities, which is to say that they are expressions and implementations of power relationships that enjoy the legitimacy of social norms as well as the protection of the capitalist state: "In the long history of IPRs [intellectual-property rights], it has mainly been companies and their representatives that have demanded the commodification of knowledge and information" (May 2006a, 48). Economic and bureaucratic growth gives impetus to colonization and, as colonization expands into the lifeworld, conflicts happen in which "socially integrated contexts of life are redefined around the roles of consumer and client and assimilated to systemically-integrated domains of action" (Sitton 1998, 70).

The theory of communicative action takes concepts and terminology from both systems sociology (Parsons) and *Verstehen* or interpretive sociology (Weber) to explain and understand social changes accompanying cultural changes. In the metanarrative that Habermas provides social science researchers, foundational forms of social integration, rooted in communicative action, are becoming uprooted and replaced with "steering media" and processes of system integration. Culture ("cultural reproduction" processes), society ("social integration" processes), and identity ("socialization processes") are all at risk of being colonized, or taken over by economic-steering media (Sitton 1998, 70), together with the communicative-rationality potential in these lifeworld processes. These steering media— money and power—operate in "delinguistified" social processes (73), which can foreclose the opportunity for people to accept or dispute these parts of their normal lives with music.

The Internet is still a deeply contested social order, and the music lifeworld is incompletely colonized. However, the lifeworld cedes more and more grounds for contestation every day.

The Juridical Eclipse of Fair Use

Cyberlibertarians are making an accounting of the disappearing act of fair-use rights. As Benkler (2006) notes, "Fair use in copyright was always a judicially created concept with a large degree of uncertainty in its application. This uncertainty, coupled with a broader interpretation of what counts as a commercial use, a restrictive judicial view of what counts as fair, and increased criminalization have narrowed its practical scope" (440). Godwin (2003) notes that much of the current uncertainty surrounding fair use was created during the DMCA negotiations during the Clinton administration. That administration relied upon an IP attorney from the software industry, Bruce Lehman, to recommend changes in copyright law to accommodate the interests of the entertainment and software industries. In its "Green Paper," Lehman's working group on IP characterized every loading of a copyrighted work into computer memory as a new "copy" deserving copyright protection, and asserted the rights of digital copyright holders to use lockdown technology to prevent unlicensed copying. The "Green Paper" transmogrified into the "White Paper," which was sent to Congress for ratification in 1996, but failed because of opposition from computer professionals who recognized that fair-use rights were under attack. Nonetheless, Lehmann incorporated the White Paper's main features into the language of the World Intellectual Property Organization (WIPO) treaty, which was later ratified by Congress. The DMCA, which contains anticircumvention provisions for copy protection, was then delivered to an approving Congress by lobbyists for the recording and motion-picture industries (Godwin 2003).

Liberal political theorists envisioned a balance between a rights owner's property interest and the interests of society and consumers, but by imposing software-facilitated contracts on software and digital-media users, IP rights owners have turned the balance into a legal fiction (Lucchi 2007). The DMCA created a copyright regime in which even the smallest copy-protection measure—an "eyedropper's worth," according to the EFF's Fred von Lohmann (personal communication)—added to a piece of music or software creates a federal protection for the IP rights owner from harm from circumvention (under section 1201 of the DMCA).

The DMCA originally gave the RIAA special power not enjoyed by other industries, "allow[ing] copyright holders to issue subpoenas to Internet service providers (ISPs) demanding the name, address and telephone numbers of ISP subscribers suspected of illegally downloading copyrighted material. Unlike usual subpoenas, DMCA subpoenas...[could] be filed prior to any charges of infringement, are not subject to a review by a judge, and requires no notice to, or opportunity to be heard by, the alleged infringer" (Mark 2003). In *Verizon v. RIAA*, a major victory for music and cyberliberties activism, the D.C. Circuit Court of Appeals rejected the subpoena power as it was originally drafted for the DMCA (D.C. Court of Appeals 2003). More than forty civil-liberties organizations, professional organizations, civil-society groups, and telecom carriers filed an amicus brief in defense of Verizon, which wanted not to have to disclose the personal identities of customers accused by the RIAA of file sharing (Alliance for Public Technology et al. 2003).

Cyberlibertarian groups such as the EFF hold that despite a court victory for privacy in the *Verizon* case, the anticircumvention clause of the DMCA (section 1201) remains more than merely a burden on software and music users. It is an abridgement of the public's right to access knowledge: "The

DMCA has become a serious threat that jeopardizes fair use, impedes competition and innovation, chills free expression and scientific research, and interferes with computer intrusion laws. If you circumvent DRM locks for noninfringing fair uses or create the tools to do so, you might be on the receiving end of a lawsuit" (EFF, n.d.a). Within the legal framework of the IP rights with which U.S. citizens and residents are saddled, using music and software with DRM creates power imbalances within the political economy of music and information. With DRM,

content owners can unilaterally determine and dictate terms and conditions limiting consumers' behaviors. Furthermore, in the digital marketplace, consumers are increasingly obliged to deal with unfair and obscure licensing agreements, misuse of personal data, device and digital content which are not designed to communicate together and, above all, with lack [of] or insufficient information about products and services. (Lucchi 2007, 21)

The United States further projects its asymmetrical economic power into the international political economy of communications by requiring trading partners to accept the DMCA and DRM into their music lifeworlds. WIPO provides for stringent anticircumvention penalties for digital media. Because, or in spite of, the fact that many trading partners with the United States—including Canada, Russia, China, the United Kingdom, France, Germany, and Australia (McCullagh 2005)—have opted out of the WIPO framework for managing their IP rights, the United States has pressed for DMCA-style anticircumvention laws to be created in hold-out countries through bilateral trade agreements (free trade agreements, or FTAs). These require foreign IP-rights regimes to model the DMCA through the creation of new information policies. Jordan, Singapore, Chile, Morocco, and Australia have signed these trade treaties with the United States at the time of this printing, and more are in line to do so with passage of the FTA known as the Dominican Republic–Central American Free Trade Agreement (DR-CAFTA) (EFF, n.d.c). Thus, the new orthodoxy of Internet regulation is extended more and more broadly throughout the world.

Reform efforts to limit the DMCA—for instance, by expanding digital fair-use rights and by limiting the scope of its anticircumvention clause—repeatedly fell short. According to Congressman Rick Boucher:

Several members of Congress made the effort in 1998 to limit the new crime under Section 1201 to circumvention for the purpose of infringing the copyright, but the momentum to enact the measure essentially unamended was too strong, and our effort fell short. With a growing realization on the part of the education community and supporters of libraries of the threat to fair use rights which Section 1201 poses, perhaps the time will soon come for a Congressional re-examination of this provision and for the assemblage of a national effort of sufficient size and intensity to enable a much needed modification of the provisions of Section 1201 (a) to occur. (Boucher, n.d.)

The "Digital Media Consumers' Rights Act ('DMCRA') has been reintroduced into Congress three times without success" (Lucchi 2007, 28).

The legal system has some potential for rationality inside itself that could be exploited to reform a broken IP-rights regime, but such an emending is unlikely to be realized. Copyright law contains some important consumer rights that have enabled music fans to share their music cultures without undue anxiety, fear, and doubt. The fair-use tradition in the United States is paramount among them.[1] However, DRM, which is unregulated, overrides these rights, and IP rights owners are not required to provide citizens a means with which to exercise their rights: "Users are not allowed to eliminate the legal protection to validate these privileges. Even when consumers have the exception to make private copies, technological protection measures can effectively hinder consumers in exercising this 'right'" (Lucchi 2007, 40).

These conditions still leave room for legal norms informed by cyberliberties to be imposed. U.S. courts have recourse to a "doctrine of unconscionability" in controlling unfair contracts and their terms. Courts acting on unconscionability find "an absence of meaningful choice on the part of one of the parties together with contract terms that are unreasonably favorable to the other party" (Lucchi 2007, 49–50). Although there is no tradition of reliance on this doctrine in commercial law in the United States (50), a Norwegian consumer court has found Apple's iTunes terms of use to contain unfair terms and conditions (12).

The popular press has responded mildly to what might seem unconscionable harassment and even extortion of ordinary music fans by the record industry. The takedown of the original Napster index server preceded a legal blitzkrieg waged by the RIAA to track down P2P file sharers, to identify them personally to sue in court, or, when falling short of identification, to file claims against "John Does" in court. Combined with protracted radio, TV, Web, and movie-trailer campaigns, the RIAA's lawsuits were designed to change online music-consumption norms from a music-sharing culture to a pay-per-play culture. Thousands of music fans, many of them college students, who were used to "tasting," "snacking," or "grazing" on downloaded songs or clips began receiving nasty letters from industry lawyers. An excerpt from one (RIAA's student extortion letter 2007; emphasis in original):

We represent a number of large record companies, including EMI Recorded Music, SONY BMG MUSIC ENTERTAINMENT, Universal Music Group and Warner Music Group, as well as all of their subsidiaries and affiliates ("Record Companies"), in pursuing claims of copyright infringement against individuals who have illegally uploaded and downloaded sound recordings on peer-to-peer networks. . . .

We have gathered evidence that you have been infringing copyrights owned by the Record Companies . . .

IF WE DO NOT HEAR FROM YOU WITHIN TWENTY (20) CALEN-DAR DAYS FROM THE DATE OF THIS LETTER, THEN WE WILL FILE SUIT AGAINST YOU IN FEDERAL COURT.

Tens of thousands of U.S. residents, including many who were falsely fingered by the RIAA and its private detectives, received some variant of this letter. A Web site dedicated to the legal efforts of those targeted by the RIAA's legal onslaught enumerates countersuits by plaintiffs who accuse the RIAA of extortion, conspiracy, deceptive and unfair trade practices, trespass, and computer fraud and abuse (Recording Industry vs *The People* 2007).

The RIAA's mass-litigation strategy is complemented by a legislative strategy to extend the gains made since the DMCA: the No Electronic Theft Act, and the Sonny Bono Copyright Term Extension Act. The DMCA criminalized the circumvention of copy protection. The No Electronic Theft Act of 1997 expresses "the will of Congress to prosecute filesharers [with] . . . a penalty of up to $250,000 and a prison term of as long as three years [for] . . . 'reproduction or distribution' of copyrighted material via electronic networks" (Vaidhyanathan 2004, 59). The Copyright Term Extension Act of 1998 extended copyright terms in the United States by twenty years. Peter Jaszi , faculty director of the Glushko-Samuelson Intellectual Property Law Clinic at American University, calls this the granting of "permanent copyright on the installment plan" (McChesney 2004, 233). Other forms of "corrupt" copyright policy make it more "obvious that copyright rules no longer have any connection to the desire to balance the needs of authors with the needs of the public domain" (232–233). The rapid consolidation of these new privileges from about 1990 to about 2000 occurred with little public oversight, and therefore little public opposition. The subsequent crackdown by the RIAA, the MPAA, and other mass-media IP rights owners has become warfare, according to Lessig (2004, 17).

The record industry continues to push for a so-called Pirate Act that would increase civil and criminal penalties and force the Justice Department to undertake litigation of tens of thousands of cases on behalf of the RIAA. Senator Orrin Hatch used a military metaphor to justify the proposed act: "Tens of thousands of continuing civil enforcement actions might be needed to generate the necessary deterrence" against file sharing (McCullagh 2004).[2] George W. Bush signed the "PRO-IP Act" in 2008, which increased penalties for infringement and created an executive branch "copyright czar" position.

PC technology platforms are changing to incorporate more, not less, support for DRM. For example, the Windows Vista operating system contains complex DRM schemes that presume every computer user is guilty of copyright infractions before he or she even turns on the computer. Critics of the new operating system object that "the user should manage the PC, the PC shouldn't manage the user" (Schneier 2007). The sentiment that PC users deserve more, not fewer, rights and freedoms in their technology practices expresses a classic cyberliberties identification of freedom with innovation, creativity, and self-determination.

Clients Become Citizens: A Politics of Cyberculture

Artists who are signed to major labels and who are top sellers have a financial interest in snuffing out illicit music file sharing, but their numbers are minute. Far more artists are unaffiliated with the majors, or are affiliated but not making money, or work with indie labels, or self-release. Two-thirds of the musicians surveyed for the Pew Internet and American Life Project in 2004 responded that they were not significantly worried about the effects of file sharing on their income (Burkart and McCourt 2006, 131). Seventy-two percent of musicians responded that the Internet helps them bring in more money from their recorded music (Rodman and Vanderdonckt 2006, 253).

Music fans who object to the new technocratic controls over music and cultural objects on the Internet appeal to the way things used to be, before the crackdowns on file sharing. Siva Vaidhyanathan (2004) argues that the Napster Watershed disclosed certain "embedded cultural assumptions" about music sharing that, together, constitute an existing "ideology" in North America:

Napster revealed the following embedded cultural assumptions: Culture is shared; obscurity mimics anonymity; private, individual transactions can't harm large, powerful institutions; local behaviors and actions seem justifiable at a greater scale and greater distance; [and] large, widespread, uncoordinated actions can't be policed easily, precisely, or moderately. (20)

Vaidhyanathan describes personal music-buying and music-sharing habits followed since his childhood, which include audiocassette trading with friends, and buying and replacing cassettes and LPs whenever disposable income was available.

Was I a thief all along? If I cared less about music, I would have recorded fewer cassettes, but I would also have purchased fewer albums. Before the rise of peer-to-peer music distribution, I don't remember anyone asking these questions. I certainly never asked them about myself. I lived with music however I could get it. Sometimes I paid, sometimes I didn't. No one seemed to care one way or the other (2004, 42).

Napster's user base did not recognize the normative validity of victimless copy crimes. The revolt occurred as a new politics and economics of culture and a new orthodoxy finally brought in new technologies and a punitive legal system to assert: (1) culture is private property; (2) no one is anonymous on the Net; (3) powerful institutions pursue remedies against individuals for huge claims to harm; (4) corporate propaganda attacks sharing cultures; and (5) ubiquitous network security and "trusted systems" may ensnare the merely absentminded, imposing upon them monetary penalties or even jail time.

The economic and legal categories of users and consumers overtook the social agency of the engaged music fan and the culturally sensitive netizen around 1998, when the DMCA altered the music-distribution function. The music lifeworld, likewise, was transformed as contract law suffused digital-music transactions. The consequences were a newly unbalanced power relationship between IP rights owners and IP rights renters. This result was consistent with critical theory's finding of a trend toward both clientelization and consumerism, which are two social side effects of the growth of capitalist bureaucracies (Sitton 1998, 78). Clientelization refers to the subordination of rights and freedoms of creative, participatory citizens to administrative and contractual controls by state or corporate regimes. In the theory of communicative action, state-led capitalism provides political legitimation for policies promoting economic growth.[3] The client role assigned to individuals denotes a prestructured citizen relationship with state bureaucracies and secures tax revenues and mass political loyalty. This role is mirrored by the individual's consumer role in the private sector. Client and consumer roles reinforce the economy, a "subsystem" existing alongside the political system (the state) and reproducing the material conditions of society. Clientelization is an important aspect of colonization.

Deregulation of media and telecom markets, and the implementation of "market based" reforms wherever possible, turns over citizens' social and cultural needs to firms — or does not address them at all. A great deal of public-interest regulation gave way to ostensibly norm-free market decisions after the passage of the Telecommunications Act of 1996 (Aufderheide 1999), even before music became an online service. Being a client of a music-service provider is therefore a relatively new kind of role for consumers in privatized media markets. The changes are hard for people to get used to, particularly when the new terms governing their interactions with corporations are based on unilateralist contracts created by the service provider. As an example of unilateralism, Lucchi cites the Apple iTunes store's contract, which gives Apple the right to change the terms of use for downloaded music files without notice (2007, 9).

Client-consumers are "constituted by formal law"; while "free to act in a strategic instrumental fashion," they are "oriented only to the consequences of action, because the situation is already legally defined, eliminating other normative considerations" (Sitton, 1998, 68). Consumerism cultivates passivity, quiescence, and conformity, which are reinforced as music fans accept ever-changing terms, including the contractual waiver of their few formal rights. Similarly, "The colonization of the public sphere by market imperatives leads to a peculiar paralysis of civil society" (Habermas 2006, 422).

Resistance to clientelization and consumerism occurs through all types of music and cyberliberties activism. Zines, blogs, and networking groups provide public education about pending legislation designed to expand the classes of "copy criminals." They also spread the word about the music industry's corruption, anticompetitiveness, and abusive business relationships with artists, providing illumination of what it is "really like" inside the Big Four–dominated music industry. The manifesto of the Future of Music Coalition "encourage[s] the development of innovative Internet music business models to guard the value of musicians' labor and ensure that artists will continue to be paid for their compositions and performances despite drastic changes in methods of distribution" (FOMC 2000). The FOMC promotes more equitable revenue-sharing arrangements between musicians and online music stores, and provides artists with resources for producing and distributing music independently of the major labels (see appendix).

Collaborative research and documentation geared toward promoting cyberliberties abounds. A popular cyberliberties listserv is the Pho List, with an international membership that sends and receives daily updates on DRM, IP rights policies and proposals, legal cases involving the music industry, and similar topics. A frequent participant on the Pho List, Seth Johnson, contributes research to New Yorkers for Fair Use, an active music and cyberliberties group that publishes articles from artists around the world who reject public claims of representation by the RIAA on issues related to file sharing. University researchers, students, and scholars are compiling documentary evidence of the value of fair use for music and digital media in diverse projects; these collaborations include the fair-use resource page of American University's Center for Social Media, Stanford University's Fair Use Project, and the International Association for the Study of Popular Music's Fair Use Survey. These researchers highlight the abusive terms of the Celestial Jukebox.

Subscribers to digital-music services lease access time to catalogs of recorded music and retain no access rights when their access time ends. The Electronic Frontier Foundation is warning consumers to inspect the restrictions and limitations on their freedom to use computers for music downloading, playback, storage, and sharing. The Apple iTunes Store demands that its users agree to a seven-page single-spaced terms of service agreement that begins this way:

THIS IS A LEGAL AGREEMENT BETWEEN YOU AND APPLE INC. ("APPLE") STATING THE TERMS THAT GOVERN YOUR USE OF THE ITUNES STORE SERVICE. THIS AGREEMENT—TOGETHER WITH ALL UPDATES, ADDITIONAL TERMS, SOFTWARE LICENSES, AND ALL OF APPLE'S RULES AND POLICIES—COLLECTIVELY CONSTITUTE THE "AGREEMENT" BETWEEN YOU AND APPLE. TO AGREE TO THESE TERMS, CLICK "AGREE." IF YOU DO NOT AGREE TO THESE TERMS, DO NOT CLICK "AGREE," AND DO NOT USE THE SERVICE. YOU MUST ACCEPT AND ABIDE BY THESE TERMS AS PRESENTED TO YOU: CHANGES, ADDITIONS, OR DELETIONS ARE NOT ACCEPTABLE, AND APPLE MAY REFUSE ACCESS TO THE ITUNES STORE FOR NONCOMPLIANCE WITH ANY PART OF THIS AGREEMENT. (Apple iTunes Store 2008)

Similarly, the Rhapsody music service grants access on the condition that the user agree to a software license, and then access music only through that software (for RealPlayer). Music accessed is considered merely to be licensed, not purchased, and the company has the power to revoke the license. As Rhapsody's Terms of Service document explains: "Regardless of the use of the word 'purchase,' all tracks offered for download or burning are offered for license, not purchase or sale, and are subject to this Agreement and any other license terms and conditions applicable to the track, including limitations imposed by the use of digital rights management technology" (Rhapsody 2006b). In an explicit admonition against sharing music, Rhapsody says, "the track may not be used, sold, rented, transferred, licensed or otherwise provided to any other user" (Rhapsody 2006b). In this clause, the Rhapsody contract removes the possibility that a music user retains any right to first sale, which had been the legal basis for creating and keeping a record collection, library, or music store before the era of digital distribution of music. Prospective licensees who are fans of sampling or mashups are also notified that the Rhapsody license terms "do not include the right to create a derivative work, to make copies other than for your own personal use, or to use the track in any commercial manner" (Rhapsody 2006b).

Music and cyberliberties activists object to the unilateralism of contracts like this one. Buried under legal jargon and many pages of details, iTunes' restrictions are probably not apparent or obvious to subscribers. A "lack of information can induce consumers to take buying decisions which they would not have taken had they been better informed" (Lucchi 2007, 22–23). Important information that is bound to be lost in the music-service providers' contracts frequently includes the fact that the provider is offering a license, not a sale: "Vendors, usually, prefer license agreements because they allow [them] to avoid the first sale or the exhaustion right, imposing terms and limitations on consumer's use" (26–27).

As mentioned earlier, a Norwegian consumer agency, in a social-democratic policy turnabout, found that iTunes violated consumer-rights laws (Singstad 2007). The nonnegotiable and English-only consent agreement, as well as the waiver of liability for potential damage caused by Apple software, was found to be "unreasonable" (Singstad 2007). A spokesman for the Norwegian Consumer Council said, "A trade agreement with a consumer must be balanced, also in the digital sphere. The Consumer Council has seen a trend where terms of agreement, technical blocks and their legal protection have led to a reduction in the rights of consumers and their opportunities to use cultural material. The digital rights of consumers have been dictated by the industry for a long time. This decision marks the start of a struggle to recover them" (Singstad 2007). Norway's Consumer Council itemized a list of newly negotiable aspects of the iTunes store, including a "cooling off" period for consumers and the functionalities of the DRM that Apple uses (Singstad 2007).

EULAs are another kind of "shrinkwrap" or "clickwrap" or "clickthrough" agreement that typically constrains consumers' freedoms to use, share, and dispose of software. As Newitz puts it, "Frequently, you aren't even able to see a EULA until after you've purchased the item it covers," adding,

These dubious "contracts" are, in theory, one-on-one agreements between manufacturers and each of their customers. Yet because almost every computer user in the world has been subjected to the same take-it-or-leave-it terms at one time or another, EULAs are more like legal mandates than consumer choices. They are, in effect, changing laws without going through any kind of legislative process. And the results are dangerous for consumers and innovators alike. (Newitz 2005)

Examples of pernicious EULAs include agreements on database and middleware software that "forbid the consumer from comparing his or her product with another and publicly criticizing the product"; the Microsoft XP requirement that users permit it to download content "revocation" software onto their computers, agreements that forbid users from using interoperable programs that have been reverse-engineered, and EULAs subject to change without notice (Newitz 2005).

Unlike ordinary CDs, which are owned, not licensed, by music fans and do not come with EULAs, the rootkit-infected CDs that Sony-BMG distributed—before it was forced to remove them from the market and pay damages for side effects from its spyware—contained a 3,000-word EULA with the following terms; the commentary after each point is by EFF senior staff attorney Fred von Lohmann (2005):

1. **If your house gets burgled, you have to delete all your music from your laptop when you get home.** That's because the EULA says that your rights to any copies terminate as soon as you no longer possess the original CD.

2. **You can't keep your music on any computers at work.** The EULA only gives you the right to put copies on a "personal home computer system owned by you."
3. **If you move out of the country, you have to delete all your music.** The EULA specifically forbids "export" outside the country where you reside.
4. **You must install any and all updates, or else lose the music on your computer.** The EULA immediately terminates if you fail to install any update. No more holding out on those hobble-ware downgrades masquerading as updates.
5. **Sony-BMG can install and use backdoors in the copy protection software or media player to "enforce their rights" against you, at any time, without notice.** And Sony-BMG disclaims any liability if this "self help" crashes your computer, exposes you to security risks, or any other harm.
6. **The EULA says Sony-BMG will never be liable to you for more than $5.00.** That's right, no matter what happens, you can't even get back what you paid for the CD.
7. **If you file for bankruptcy, you have to delete all the music on your computer.** Seriously.
8. **You have no right to transfer the music on your computer, even along with the original CD.**
9. **Forget about using the music as a soundtrack for your latest family photo slideshow, or mash-ups, or sampling.** The EULA forbids changing, altering, or make[ing] derivative works from the music on your computer.

In energetic judicial exercises of proconsumer advocacy, the Texas attorney general filed suit against Sony-BMG under Texas's Consumer Protection Against Computer Spyware Act of 2005 and defective-product law; California followed a similar path. According to Lucchi (2007): "Many of these class-action lawsuits were filed in California by Electronic Frontier Foundation asserting the violation [of] California's Consumer Protection Against Computer Spyware Act.... [T]o my knowledge, these are some of the first cases based on consumer law as an instrument of defense against DRM technologies" (16).

Hacking the legal code that regulates software in commercial markets is, arguably, another form of hacktivism, although software activism also shares characteristics with radical media. Reasonableagreement.org has an innovative approach to the EULA problem: adhesive stickers "for to stick it to The Man wot's stickin' it to you."

Call 'em End User License Agreement Activist Amendments, or EULAAAs (for dramatic effect, best pronounced like Stanley Kowalski hollering up at the balcony). Each sticker contains its own tightly crafted anti-nonsense to insulate you from Kafkaesque memos from the Castle, and includes the reasonableagreement.org URL to help recruit others for the cause. . . .

We've got 25-packs of 2″ × 1″ "receipt stickers" for you to: 1). Paste over the paperwork the counter jockey hands you the next time you make a purchase and, 2). hand back to the jockey, thereby nullifying any obnoxious and intrusive agreements. Hey, if a corporation can slip you a scrap that says "These are the rules," why can't you say "Nope, *these* are"? (Reasonableagreement.org; emphasis in original)

The Reasonable Agreement stickers, developed to be attached over the paper receipts generated at the checkout counters of retail stores, read:

READ CAREFULLY. By accepting this material you agree, on behalf of your employer, to release me from all obligations and waivers arising from any and all NON NEGOTI-ATED agreements, licenses, terms of service, shrinkwrap, clickwrap, browsewrap, confidentiality, non-disclosure, non-compete and acceptable use policies ("BOGUS AGREEMENTS") that I have entered into with your employer, its partners, licensors, agents and assigns, in perpetuity, without prejudice to my ongoing rights and privileges. You further represent that you have the authority to release me from any BOGUS AGREEMENTS on behalf of your employer (Reasonableagreement.org, n.d.).

Reasonable Agreement is the collaborative effort of the Bumperactive sticker company and Cory Doctorow's Boing Boing blog. The group has a revenue-sharing agreement with the EFF for proceeds taken from sales of the EULAAA stickers. In some respects, Reasonable Agreement is undertaking a form of culture jamming, or legally informed performance art. In other respects, they are decolonizing the lifeworld by redrawing the lines of music juridification.

Hacktivists who have also taken more direct action against the RIAA include the anonymous creator of a 2004 computer virus released to attack RIAA and Microsoft Web servers: "MyDoom.F . . . deletes several different types of files stored on an infected computer and aims to attack the Web sites of Microsoft and the Recording Industry Association of America with a flood of data" (Lemos 2004). Consumers have used boycotts and write-in campaigns to change over restrictive EULAs (as with Yahoo-Geocities); as Newitz writes optimistically, by "bringing together the organizational potential of consumer activist groups, blogs, and online communities with legal and legislative challenges, consumers can regain the rights they lost the first time they clicked 'I Agree'" (2005).

These examples illustrate how music and cyberliberties activism occurs across a spectrum of social organizations, from organized interest groups to more indistinct and mutable mobilizations of identities, material resources, and messages. It is driven by multiple interests and ideologies, most of which converge around the social uses of (and restrictions on) media and technology. Artists, whether contractually independent of or dependent on major labels, music fans and their opinion leaders, and Internet devotees and "digerati" from the precolonized Internet are directing collective action at legislators and regulators, at the gatekeepers of information in the private sector, at multilateral agencies, and at friendly groups in civil society.

Laboring in the Walled Garden

Labor is the locus of political disputes over class status in social life. Most music fans are probably not aware of the unbalanced relationships of major record labels to band members and other work-for-hire employees in the music business. Alternative and indie-music fans are much more likely to acknowledge the unfairness of the major-label work relationship and to seek out music from artists who exercise more autonomy over their creative work. Many of these fans are rewarded with opportunities to communicate more directly with the artists, especially online.

In the corporate digital-music distribution business today, labor remains a disputed territory for musicians, who must fight repeatedly to recoup royalties and other payments on digital downloads. These royalties may be significantly below the royalties earned from CD sales.[4]

Digital distribution royalties are shared with major label artists inconsistently if at all. The dominant pay-per music service, iTunes, is the target of Downhill Battle, which advocates boycotting the Big Four music companies and establishing a voluntary collective licensing system for P2P music downloads. Downhill Battle, which represents both independent artists and artists on major labels, hosts a Web page called iTunesIsBogus, which enumerates the complaints of artists who are uncompensated or undercompensated by labels doing business with iTunes. The Web page critiques the iTunes music store as a "facelift for a corrupt industry," and denounces the propagandistic entreaties that appeal to consumers' desires to compensate artists by asking them to use pay services for music downloads. The offerings on iTunes are too expensive, inferior to MP3s, and unfair to artists (Downhillbattle.org, n.d.).[5]

I shall argue that the automation of fandom is another abusive labor relationship that has been insufficiently scrutinized (McCourt and Burkart 2007). Corporately controlled online spaces are set up to create and house new IP rights built up around online fan clubs and affinity groups. Fan clubs, blogging, and other online communications among fans have displaced some of the music scenes that clubs, DJs, record stores, cafés, and house parties continue to support (Stahl 2003). User-generated content or online communities have existed as a business model since instantiations such as the WELL's electronic BBS (bulletin board system). However, these communities have become increasingly commodified as e-commerce business models continue to suffuse the Web. Message boards and chat rooms operated by commercial portals like Excite, Yahoo, and AOL did not make it easy to share music during the first wave of huge virtual-community building. The earliest commercial music service providers, such as MusicNet, Pressplay, and eMusic, atomized their users to the point that playlist access became the only tradable asset among users. Social-networking sites now distribute music more selectively than did first-generation Web music portals. MySpace and Facebook, corporate sites that share the bulk of social-networking traffic, offer music streams and downloads supported by advertising revenues. In these systems, users are more explicitly acknowledged as player-participants in online music scenes, and free music is more mobile and accessible.

Organizationally, these virtual communities reproduce systematically distorted communications by being organized in hierarchical administrative-bureaucratic power relationships. Users are not given any administrative control over the sites; thus they are denied opportunities for democratic access and participation. Surveillance by customer-relationship-management (CRM) software is now a part of the basic business model for digital-music distribution (Burkart and McCourt 2006). As mentioned previously, Andrejevic (2002) describes consumer surveillance as an online labor market in which users perform "the work of being watched" by corporate marketers. In a Foucauldian analysis, Andrejevic (2003) groups together activities of "consumers and workers as they conduct their activities within a monitored, mobile, virtual enclosure" (137), and explains how working under surveillance creates "cybernetic commodities" (Mosco 1996) of their selves. As fan-workers' consciousnesses become reified, surveillance becomes internalized as a good work ethic. According to Warwick Mules (2001), who takes inspiration from Deleuze's concept of the atomized "dividual": "In the control society there is no need for this kind of panoptic control, since the embodiment of the panoptic principle, anticipated by Foucault and responsible for the individuation of the subject in disciplinary societies, has itself become a resource for extracting surplus value. In effect, *dividualized* workers survey themselves, not as a form of self-discipline, but as an investment for capitalization" (25, my emphasis). Examples of self-surveillance for self-enhancement and social capital include virtual communities' hosts and other online leaders as well as users who consciously abide by online community standards and even expressly cultivate their own obedience.

Volunteer community hosts police themed message boards and chat rooms for off-topic and inappropriate conversation. Community moderators, who are exemplary participants and who may be volunteers (but infrequently are paid employees of the portal), use administrative controls to shape online conversations (for example, by deleting, moving, or even altering posted messages, all with the implicit consent that community members grant when they sign a terms of service contract with the portal). These instruments program out dissent and other kinds of discussions that are not instrumental for the firm. These factors can limit the individual autonomy of participants by restricting opportunities for collaborating and debating as well as for calling out objections to censorship and other power relationships built into the community. To be sure, editors of fanzines and other publications exercise their official roles all the time; however, they are only infrequently working for or on the behalf of the owners of the music discussed.

Fan participation in the commercial virtual communities that are organized to supplant real places of music discloses that the ideology of Internet regulationism has set in. Participation in the digital enclosure suggests strongly that the reification of the "user" role has been normalized, along with the client-tenant IP relationship of the Celestial Jukebox. The results include acquiescence to (1) imposed routines, (2) cultural frames of reference detached from the music lifeworld, (3) surveillance, and (4) altered legal terms of access to the online places of music. Habermas refers to the "norm free sociality" that pervades bureaucratic and formalized environments. Calhoun (1995) and Baxter (1987) dispute the claim that social life can truly be norm-free and utterly detached from the lifeworld. I propose that the institutions of the Celestial Jukebox promote—if not fully attain— norm-free sociality. iTunes and other music portals introduce routines and procedures for accessing music that are "oriented only to the consequences of action" (Sitton 1998, 68) and that supplant the most important fan rituals of the music lifeworld, such as sharing music and trading free labor.

How musicians and other artists will fight the exploitations of their labor remains to be seen. The Writers Guild of America strike in 2007–2008 demonstrated unusual solidarity among frequently antagonistic groups in the culture industries, including the Directors Guild of America, the Screen Actors Guild, the American Federation of Television and Radio Artists, and the Alliance of Motion Picture and Television Producers. Collective bargaining among recording artists is historically rare, however. Even so, individual artists can negotiate with a Netlabel and iTunes (for example), contributing as needed to their own production, marketing, and distribution. Artists can continue to release new work using P2P distribution and use alternatives to the standard copyright system, such as Creative Commons or even CopyLeft.

Because music fans also perform cultural work when they participate as consumers in online media systems, fans will continue to be able to "strike" by rejecting portals and the "work of being watched" through avoidance, and "rent strike" by circumventing DRM. Or, music fans may change the terms of their work relationships and choose to work for "free" music by watching ads.[6]

Historical Bases of Cyberliberties

The changing relationships of musicians to their work, and of fans to their music, have sparked cyberlibertarianism as an ethos. But it is a conflicted ethos. It is caught between political anarchism and communitarianism. It is also caught between antisystemic and anticapitalist tendencies on the one hand, and merely antiestablishmentarian and reformist approaches on the other hand. Commitments oscillate between autonomy and solidarity as foundational norms. Among the autonomy-driven, some cyberlibertarians prize innovation and free speech; others hold privacy paramount. The communitarian emphasis on the cultural commons clashes with the individualism of claims to personal property rights and free speech rights, which are often conflated rhetorically. Although an entrepreneurial streak runs through cyberlibertarians, they hold disparate positions on the desirability of letting market capitalism exploit the Internet's openness only to close it down. What cyberlibertarians share, though, is a psychological, social, and, especially, political orientation to the Internet: as an aspect of their lifeworld, it is basic to their sense of personal identity, culture, and society. To the extent that their expectations for free culture and openness are counterfactual, they are now considered idealists. But to the extent that their expectations are grounded in personal experience of the history of the Internet before its DMCA turn, they are also realists for whom cyberliberties are a second nature. They share a commitment to preserving aspects of the Internet that they see as critical to the autonomous development of people and communities, free of unwanted intrusion and legal interference by the state, and free of state-sanctioned economic monopolies.

As an ideology, cyberlibertarianism has grown up in and around U.S. political culture, although it also flourishes in British, Dutch, Argentine (Finquelievich 2000), and Korean (Lee 2008) societies, among many others. Turner (2006) describes an early vision of cyberliberties that is reminiscent of John Stuart Mill's political society in *On Liberty*. In this idealization, society is a place for personal exploration and self-realization as long as the rights of none are harmed. In remapping this place of exploration from human geography to cyberspace, cyberlibertarians envision the Internet as a social space with a particular political culture: forms of "authority [are] distributed, hierarchies [are] leveled, and citizens [are] linked by invisible energies. The Internet became both a metaphor for such a system and a means to bring it into being" (Turner 2006, 219).

Turner (2006) describes the broad-based social need for increased openness that arose in the United States in the 1960s, as countercultural and student movement politics suffused the country: "the urge to 'hack' politics by bringing governance down to a manageable local level and by basing social integration on technologically facilitated forms of consciousness" (219). Although he fully recognizes the conflicted political philosophy of cyberlibertarians, Turner ultimately places cyberliberties within a broader history of the "New Communalist movement ... [which] joined the cultural legitimacy of the counterculture to the technological and economic legitimacy of the computer industry" (219). As the *Whole Earth Catalog* reminded its readers, "you don't have to leave industrial society, but you don't have to accept it the way it is" (Turner 2006, 114). New Communalism is distinct from New Left politics in its individualistic orientation and anarchic resistance to party politics and establishmentarianism. New Communalists typically participated in the communitarian practices of the counterculture and youth movements of the 1960s (Turner 2006, 33–34), including musical and artistic "happenings," and worked to re-create communities based on non-hierarchical, spontaneous, and creative collaboration, such as the Whole Earth 'Lectronic Link (WELL). A contemporary New Communalist, Howard Rheingold expresses the ideal of cybernetic self-organization in his book (2002) that unveiled the phenomenon of "smart mobs," or spontaneous happenings organized through social affinity groups connected via SMS [wireless short message service] and wireless e-mail.

New Communalism grew up in and around places of music, and most especially, with music that challenged, and even ridiculed, a U.S. culture suffused with consumerism, bureaucracy, and militarism. Garofalo (1987) uses the "Woodstock Nation" metaphor to denote the coalescence of antiwar and counterculture "energies" in the United States in and around popular music scenes. He argues that the work of music fans transformed popular music into a movement of its own in the 1960s and 1970s countercultures:

Popular music was re-appropriated in the service of an alternative vision of social organization and relations. Again, it was irrelevant whether the music was intentionally political, or whether it was produced by a major or an independent label. What mattered was that the music had broken out of the common-sensical definitions of leisure and had created its own new spaces for pleasure. In subverting the discipline of the work ethic, it was a threat to the organization of hegemony. (90)

Places of music could provide a way out of the cultural dead end presented by culture industries that were stuck in a conventional mind set. Influential music of this era came from John Cage's work in the 1940s and 1950s, and from the Grateful Dead by the 1960s (Turner 2006).

Turner distinguishes New Communalism from the broader countercultural movement by emphasizing its commitments to volunteerism, nonprofits, do-it-yourself projects, and organizations independent of the state and giant bureaucracies and corporations. For the New Communalists, music could be like computer technology: it could forge new varieties of social relationships based on intentional communities, affinity groups, and even enlightened business relationships.

The brain trust of the New Communalist ethos has comprised overlapping networks of publishers, tech entrepreneurs, cyberlawyers, and countercultural visionaries—all "married to a libertarian longing for the reduction of government" and propounding "an idealized political sphere in the image of the forms of organization pursued by the Merry Pranksters, USCO [the Company of Us, a media-art collective], and many communes" (Turner 2006, 219). The earliest cyberlibertarian ethos linked "enthusiasm for electronically mediated forms of living with libertarian ideas on freedom, society and markets" (Murray 2005). This linking stemmed in large part from their being among the first to create the burgeoning personal-computer and networking industries and to exploit them commercially. Low barriers to entry by newcomers, a deregulated business environment, and start-up capital available for "blue sky" business models attracted innovators to personal computing, software development, early online services, and BBSes. The world "online" until the 1980s was small, fragmentary, and inhabited almost universally by geeks and hackers. The Internet, in particular, was an esoteric domain dominated by technical elites, mostly males, working in the penumbra of military and corporate research and development and research universities. The insularity and rarefied atmosphere of the early Internet, and its promotion in the cold war as a global networking strategy, were two reasons why cyberlibertarians "like Mitch Kapor and John Perry Barlow . . . believed that many fundamental freedoms were *inherently* protected in cyberspace: that the inherent design features of the Internet would render any attempts at state intervention futile" (Murray 2005; my emphasis).

Some have tried to show a strong undercurrent of conservative, reactionary, and anticountercultural influences on cyberliberties, but most cyberlibertarians disavow the association. During the high-tech boom of the 1990s, grandstanding neoliberal U.S. politicians like Newt Gingrich adopted cyberlibertarian rhetoric to propound the free-market values of the "Republican Revolution" and its "Contract with America." During Gingrich's courtship of Silicon Valley, most cyberlibertarians there quickly suspected that his civil-libertarian credentials were bogus, and rejected them. Nonetheless, a few identified with his libertarian appeals to decentralization of authority, personal autonomy, and innovation for social problem solving (Dyson 1995). *Reason* magazine's Virginia Postrel and the EFF's Esther Dyson and John Perry Barlow have promoted these values in their careers. Chapter 4 will address the "two cyberliberties" phenomenon in more detail.

The Napster Watershed

Innovations often take us by surprise. Yet seen from an historical vantage point, Napster's disruptive impact on the music industry was a long time coming. According to Turner: "The concept of building a peer-to-peer information system and the idea that individuals needed to gain control over information and information systems had been features of both the New Communalist movement and the New Left for some time" (2006, 115). Napster solved certain social problems that required peer networking to fix. Napster demonstrated that P2P allowed people to form virtual communities online free of regulationism. The uncontested operation of the Napster network lasted from about mid-1999 to July 2001, when the company's owners shut down the index servers in the midst of the noted court battle with the RIAA.

In 2000, in the case *A&M Records v. Napster*, a consortium of music companies sued the P2P file-sharing company for contributing to copyright infringement by its users. A federal district judge ruled against Napster, and the Ninth Circuit Court of Appeals upheld the ruling. The latter decision, which I demarcate as the Napster Watershed, effectively ended anonymous P2P file sharing using the Napster index server and created liabilities for Napster and any other firm releasing Napster-ish P2P software.

The Napster Watershed was the first legal victory by the content industries against a P2P software maker on the basis of contributory infringement and vicarious infringement (von Lohmann, n.d., 4). Napster's defeat in court at the height of its growth was a pivotal moment in the history of the Internet, affecting everyday life for millions of people globally and dividing Internet culture and norms into those from before and after the decision. P2P users who continued to share music became, juridically, copyright criminals.[7] Napster's innovation in P2P software development was to make available a cultural commons in the form of a publicly searchable index of MP3 files; this index pointed to files on individual members' shared directories on personal computers. By providing pointers to these files, Napster coordinated a vast always-on library of materials that most users thought were obtainable because of fair-use traditions and innovative technology. Napster's cultural commons become a basic resource to the music lifeworld. It was set up for sharing music and enabling debate, exchange, and deliberation in an online virtual community where participants made decisions about their participation in the system, and exercised real autonomy in decision-making. Napster became a fixture of the music lifeworld, and a basic part of the set of processes of social reproduction that also included e-mail and Web surfing. It was the proof of concept for an Alternative Jukebox.

Napster's First Amendment defense failed at court. Once the legal precedent of the Napster Watershed had been set, the place of music (and the time of music) in cyberspace was considered differently. Fostering the realization that the regulationist model of the Internet had trumped the people's use of the Internet became, and is still, an ongoing PR project for the RIAA and MPAA. The court decision against Napster may have removed the formal, juridical legitimacy of file-sharing practices, but the practice continued unabated. People concerned about free culture may or may not have still traded files with P2P, but they began to talk about the times "of Napster" and "after Napster" mythically. Napster's longevity was about two years; the Paris Communes lasted two months.

The myth is sustained. The gift economy of music and culture inspired by the Internet is still in tension with (Leyshon 2003), or even "corrosive" for (Strangelove 2005, 20), capitalist ideology. Because the file-sharing cultures that grew up around MP3 and P2P technologies, and the technologies themselves, have come under legal attack by the RIAA, music and cyberliberties activists may be among the most political, and politicized, of any of the "active audiences" examined by cultural studies in many years. Music fans' politics, culture, and identity were all bound up with the experience of losing Napster from the music lifeworld. The loss has informed the rationale for music fans to pursue cyberlibertarian political objectives.

Even in the wake of the RIAA's various assaults on university networks and college-age file sharers, and after all the propaganda campaigns and DRMed music portals, the persistence of file sharing seems to reasonable people to be a reasonable response to the Celestial Jukebox. Wark (2006) even calls file sharing "a social movement in all but name" (175).

Some high-minded juridical justifications for preserving P2P for cultural reproduction have thrived since the Napster Watershed. Noting how mobile music that travels freely among friends, family, and affiliates can contribute to "semiotic democracy," Vaidhyanathan has embraced "a rational revolt of passionate fans...rebelling against the inflexible price structure, limited consumer choices, irresponsible gatekeeping, and technological oligopolies of the music industry" (2004, 60). A dedication to the ideals of semiotic democracy also "unites computer scientists who are concerned with the ability to use computer code freely with cultural scholars who celebrate culture jamming" (303–304).

When Wark (2006) calls file sharing a social movement "in all but name," she qualifies the claim by stating that file sharing "rarely announces itself as a social movement." Contemporaries of Wark have gone ahead and made the announcement. In making DVD compilations for in-class instruction, Striphas and McLeod acknowledge that such fair use was not recognized by the DMCA, and they "advocate a form of digital civil disobedience in which we find ways (and share with our colleagues how) to continue doing our jobs as teachers, even if it means violating a federal statute" (2006, 126).[8] Coombe notes that, besides radicalizing academics whose livelihoods depend upon combining and sharing ideas, information, music, and communication, "the growing role of copyright in the field of music has...turned an increasing number of artists into intellectual property activists, just as it has spawned an alternative, more democratic regulatory regime—the Creative Commons, in which creators and users bypass corporate middlemen to ensure that music is available for shared use" (2006, xi).

Copy Leftists "assert their right to fair use through bold appropriations and borrowings" in "legal but risky" music and text (Demers 2006, 119–120): "Many independent, self-distributed artists sample illegally, knowing that their risk of getting sued is minimal because of their relative economic inconsequence within the music industry" (121). To use Vaidhyanathan's language, they may think that their obscurity aids their anonymity. Some artists always work on the brink of running afoul of copyright law, motivated by a blend of activism and playfulness characteristic of the culture jammers within underground and independent music scenes. Vaidhyanathan writes of commercial popular music, "The death of tricky, playful, transgressive sampling occurred because courts and the industry misapplied stale, blunt, ethnocentric, and simplistic standards to fresh new methods of expression" (2001, 144).

Together, illegal artistry, file sharing, critical technology scholarship, lobbying and litigation for reforms, hacktivism, Netlabel and indie-label operations, and culture jamming join other established roles in a mosaic of activism that collectively resolves to make and maintain a place for music in cyberspace. Equity, autonomy, and cultural change are central concerns in the wake of the Napster Watershed.

Wark's assertion to the contrary, neither file sharing nor the politics of culture sharing really demonstrates that it can reach from the lifeworld into the political system and actually seize political power in a bureaucratic-administrative fashion. So far, incursions from the music lifeworld into the system have not institutionalized into anything like reverse colonization, reverse juridification, or decommodification. "Actual movements are thoroughly political, concerned not only with winning reforms but also with gaining and employing power" (Plotke 1990, 100). Gaining and employing power will require radical reforms to the existing IP regime worldwide. While the politics of the free-culture movement were energized by the Napster Watershed, the legal standing for its prominent sharing practices were debilitated. The Napster Watershed was a further articulation of cybernetic commodification (Mosco), which is the extrapolation of money from labor markets organized around digitized information, knowledge, and culture.

The Napster Watershed as a Historical Marker for the Music Lifeworld

The Celestial Jukebox is vulnerable in its normative underpinnings. The Napster precedent altered legal norms but not other social norms, such that something similar to a legitimation crisis of the music industry has taken place.[9] The legitimation crisis may have shown itself even earlier, in the post-punk Do-It-Yourself music cultures that thrived in the 1980s (Hesmondhalgh 1998). The failure of system pressures to shape the contours of the music lifeworld must be better understood. Why has there been a political resistance to the "change of state" that Braman describes (2007)? And yet, at the same time, there has been such a discernable encroachment of regulationist thinking and juridification into the music lifeworld that the contested terrain may shrink as conflicts subside. Contemporary culture clashes on the Internet can be muted in the silent operation of lifeworld colonization and not because of any newfound consensus about cyberliberties. Because the business of media (and especially music) is becoming ever more manipulative, intrusive, and abusive as traditional distribution channels are supplanted by the Celestial Jukebox, these social harms are becoming less and less recognizable as forms of abusive behavior that can be named, challenged, and halted.

Colonization reflects "the ways in which commodity relations create certain contours of consciousness in capitalist society" (Sitton 1998, 66). The "contours of consciousness" shape our experiences of music and sharing in the lifeworld. Repeated exposure to colonization can create a kind of trauma for lifeworld structures and places of music. The die-off of live-music scenes, fanzines, record stores, and other places of music occurred as computers and networking began to mediate personal music consumption. A subsequent disengagement from sociality and the trafficking in tangible formats occurred as the digital distribution of music supplanted many aspects of physical packaging, retailing, publishing, and performance.

Research on music and cyberliberties activism points out that the colonization of the lifeworld is not yet complete and that there are still multiple modes and bases of resistance to the legitimacy of the Celestial Jukebox and its underlying "change of state." The incompleteness of juridification, reification, and commodification, despite the existence of formal constraints on file sharing and other forms of gift exchange on the Internet, is seen in the fact that gift cultures persist and thrive on the Internet. The very resistance of the music gift culture in particular to evolving DRM campaigns, university lockdowns, anti–file-sharing propaganda, barrages of RIAA lawsuits, and other attacks suggests that a cyberliberties movement could become a potential source of effective collective action for communication policy reforms, political power sharing, and democratization.

In the long process of commodifying digital music, formal policies to diminish civil liberties and the cultural commons has been required. There have been defensive and offensive strategies for promoting music and cyberliberties together. Scholars working in the tradition of critical legal studies have developed civil-libertarian defenses of different areas of the cultural commons, including the public domain (David Lange, Jessica Litman), software copyright (Pamela Samuelson), fair use (William Fischer), and free speech (Mike Godwin). Telecommunications policy scholarship has tracked how cybernetic commodification in the United States has proceeded with public grants of property rights to private-sector players. In telecommunications policy, "[t]he passage of the Telecommunications Act of 1996 constituted a major restructuring of property rights" in the United States (Garcia 2004, 139). Information policy has proceeded toward a similar objective. Although legal scholars have expressed "skepticism regarding the growth of exclusive rights" (Benkler 2006, 487–488 n. 2), cultural enclosure grows as corporate colonization of the Internet lifeworld pushes into online communities and the computer tools for participating in them nonetheless, and "once established, property rights are likely to get locked in" (Garcia 2004, 151). Uncertainties pervade the global IP-rights regime, and "many more actors [lobby] on behalf of increasingly diverse interests and competing agendas" besides the culture industries (Garcia 2004, 151).

The Napster Watershed set legal precedents for ascribing private property rights to cultural objects in cyberspace, so that the benefits of digital distribution accrue only to IP owners, and not to anyone else, with DRM and global anticircumvention legislation (such as the DMCA in the United States; in the E.U., the European Directive 2001/29/EC on the Harmonization of Certain Aspects of Copyright and Related Rights in the Information Society of 2001).[10] The transposition of copyright law into contract law (Lucchi 2007, 21) compromises a fan's "capacity to exercise legitimate rights or exceptions" (21), such as the right to fair use, which is also a copyright exemption in Europe, Canada, and Mexico.

The locking-in of private property rights also occurs in a person's thinking processes. Reification is the mental act of abstracting an exercise of power, including a private property relationship or a wage relationship, into an ahistorical, naturalized, and unpolitical event (May 2006a, 34). Property relations, such as the wage-labor relationship, tenancy, and now the systems for digital distribution and music "use," are concepts in the minds of music fans that are now ripe for reification. The embedded labor relationships of the music industry find expression in all the Celestial Jukebox's systems for commodifying and distributing music, including DRM, distribution agreements, and virtual communities, and every time we either ignore these technical systems, or else take them for granted.[11]

Internationalizing the Colonization Thesis

Corporate colonization through IP rights may meet its match at the global level of capitalism, however. As May (2006) explains, even if the policy reforms ushering in WIPO-style legislation are accomplished by technocrats, public acquiescence is needed to provide normative legitimacy:

The WIPO has recognized the importance of socially embedding the governance of intellectual property in the policy elite of the developing countries, as well as the need for a more general normative reorientation. However, this project has not been as successful as supporters of IPRs might have hoped. In the recent debates around the proposed WIPO Development Agenda...the problem of intellectual property has become increasingly contentious to the dismay of the WIPO's senior officers, and a number of the most powerful members (most obviously the USA, Japan, and a number of European states). (440)

WIPO's Cooperation for Development Program has been challenged by the WIPO Development Agenda, which was introduced by Argentina and Brazil in 2004 (440). The "development dimension" of the agenda pressed for national autonomy and the right to create and maintain policy alternatives to the WIPO orthodoxy. The Access to Knowledge group pursues a reform agenda at WIPO that loosens IP-rights restrictions on poor countries (A2K n.d.).

In countries that have experienced something like a Napster Watershed, fans and activists have responded variously to newly imposed reforms. For example, the Republic of Korea joined the WIPO treaty on trademark in 2003 and the treaty on copyright in 2004, when the country's cybercultures were flourishing. Restrictions on Korean Web publishers provoked impassioned opposition by Korea's netizens. ISPs and other gatekeepers clamped down on protected content in Korea's freewheeling blogs and fan sites, provoking opposition from Internet publishers of "criticism, commentary, news reporting, teaching, scholarship, and research" (Lee 2008). Before the implementation of the Korean Copyright Act of 2004, South Korean netizens published freely on an exploding Korean Web. Through borrowing and sharing freely on the Web, netizens had become acclimated to an unprecedented freedom of speech about politics and culture. They took digital fair-use rights for granted, but the reformist South Korean Parliament ended fair use and imposed other burdens on netizens, and did so covertly, without hearings and with suspicious authority. The overnight creation of broad new categories of illegal communication practices, together with associated criminal sanctions, sparked something of an online rebellion (Lee 2008). Perhaps the greatest feelings of outrage came when South Koreans discovered that private property protections for the national anthem prevented many patriotic performances.

The civil disobedience and cyberactivism that followed in the wake of the online enclosures of free culture in Korea are in keeping with that country's modern history of student protests, strikes, and other varieties of collective action in support of democratization. Efforts to reclaim the rights and privileges that were lost in 2004 have not yet been successful.

Global mobilization over IP rights is linked to conflicts over other exercises of power in the lifeworld. Schweidler and Costanza-Chock (2008) describe interwoven varieties of political and social opposition to overbroad IP-rights claims that extend from transnational corporations to dozens of countries and multiple industries, and impose inequitable terms on communicators and consumers. These mobilizations mainly address conflicts that are wracking knowledge-based industries whose outputs are commonly identified with public goods, such as culture, communication, health, and available food and water supplies. As global capitalism seeks to reap ever-greater value from the knowledge-based economy, the enhancement and enforcement of IP-rights regimes grows in urgency in geographically core countries, as these countries stand to gain the most financially from the regimes. Schweidler and Costanza-Chock (2008) enumerate the spheres of productive and creative life upon which IP-rights regimes are beginning to encroach with harmful effects on citizens' rights. In addition to the media and culture industries, agricultural, health, and software products also contain increasing amounts of tradable IP rights and so fall under enhanced protection and enforcement schemes associated with international trade laws. These laws tend to create structural disadvantages for the majority of the world's people, who are forced to surrender control over locally developed knowledge and even to repurchase access to it.

Resistance to the encroachment of IP rights into zones of everyday life, work life, and private life includes ignoring the new rules, developing and using alternative technologies, cultivating countervailing technologies (such as hacking, reverse engineering, and subversive techniques), engaging in national policymaking to reassert national sovereignty and open standards, pursuing direct action and the public flouting of global IP rights in consciousness-raising campaigns, and mobilizing to change international policies and develop counterprojects that preserve and enhance local access to cultural and scientific knowledge.

Alternative IP-rights regimes such as Copy Left and Creative Commons licensing are a global counterproject to privatization of the digital commons, although they bootstrap from existing IP-rights laws and therefore cannot make a clean break from the system. Free and open-source software development is a counterproject that can benefit developing countries tremendously through both local skills building and savings from software-license remittances. Yet this unfinished counterproject remains vulnerable to further encroachments of IP rights through the extension of software patent protections. Schweidler and Costanza-Chock (2008) describe recurring patterns of resistance to the new orthodoxy at the level of "daily practice," including fair-use exercises, file sharing, use of Copy Left and Creative Commons materials, remix culture, and piracy. As goal-oriented activities that mobilize resources against IP rights, such resistance keeps the culture clash going. Resistant technologies include DeCSS, hacking, encryption bypassing and cracking, and P2P. Internationally, resisters use various rhetorical frames to characterize their opposition, including piracy, free culture, cultural sovereignty, the commons, and indigenous and traditional knowledge. Forms of protest and direct action worldwide include file sharing, Web retransmission of broadcasts, "civil disobedience screenings," remix culture, Wiki, and online-collaboration software (Schweidler and Costanza-Chock 2008, 295).

The recording industry's clumsy power grabs and legal disputes with rivals and customers have highlighted rather than buried the fact that gift cultures organized around music sharing were the norm only a few years before the industry institutionalized copyright warfare. Subsequently, core principles of economic liberalism and private-property law that extended modest protections to music consumers—private property rights, the right of fair use, and the principle of first sale—were eviscerated in the institutionalization of the Celestial Jukebox. The music lifeworld still reasserts itself even from beneath the rubble of its near destruction, but the foreclosure of the rights of consumer-citizens has accompanied the colonization of the music lifeworld by corporations and represents a rollback of certain freedoms enjoyed by previous generations of music fans. The Napster Watershed shows the duality of colonization: on the one hand, it was an accomplishment of exploitative lifeworld colonization. But on the other, it created new social movement activists out of music fans by putting them on notice that their legal access to music on the Internet would be on the exclusive terms of the catalog owners. Unfortunately for activist music fans, juridification and reification depoliticize the effects of copyright grabs, the "grotesquely" imbalanced artist-label relationship (Lovering 1998, 41), the carpet-bomb–style file-sharing litigation, and other kinds of exploitation that the music industry has perpetrated during its rapid consolidation of network power.

Regulationist ideology is taking hold on the technoculture. Nevertheless, as some examples have shown, forms of resistance to colonization and reification are growing, and their complementary and interconnected projects could coalesce at various points. Alternative variants of the Celestial Jukebox, while still not institutionalized, have a chance to flourish by interconnecting independent or unaffiliated artists, alternative IP-rights schemes like Copy Left and Creative Commons, P2P networking, and other innovative frameworks for sharing music cultures.

As Vaidhyanathan has argued, "The act of saying 'Why can't we share music with millions of people around the world?' or 'Why can't we coordinate mass demonstrations with thousands of people we have never met?' or 'Why can't we generate a free and open and customizable collection of software?' has had profound consequences. These shifting expectations have allowed everyday people . . . to consider new ways of relating and communicating with one another" (2004, 14). In the next chapter, I shall compare suitable models of agency for the conflicts over music and cyberliberties. Activism, citizenship, fandom, labor, and new social movements are invoked in various ways to attribute social agency to cyberlibertarians fighting to make comfortable places online for music sharing.

CHAPTER FOUR

Projects and Prospects

❋

Jefferson laid the foundations for a typically American tradition
of radical criticism of the megalopolis, based on nostalgia for
humanity's original relationship with the land—the virgin wilderness
that characterized the heroic age of the pioneers. The tradition was
carried on by Ralph Waldo Emerson..., in the form of a conception of
democracy that exalted the ideal of individuals free from all constraints
and able to do as they pleased. In 1865, Emerson described his disciples
as "fanatics in freedom" who "cannot tolerate any form of mediation."
At the dawn of the third millennium, the technolibertarians of
cyberspace, those fierce adversaries of the very idea of the
nation-state, would draw on this tradition to justify their
planetary project of "virtual communities."
—Armard Mattelart

The previous chapter examined the tendency of a cultural politics of music
file sharing to sustain itself in popular-technology practices, even under conditions of copyright warfare and cultural reification. The cultural politics of
music file sharing discloses an ideology and goals that are centered on autonomy and identity. It joins post-punk, indie-label, and culture-jamming
projects that have been expanding participation and access to channels of
music production and distribution since the early 1990s, and they join a
broad resistance to the corporate commercialization of public spaces.

In this chapter, I explore whether it makes sense to discuss music and
cyberliberties activism as a type of social movement—one that is perhaps in
an early stage of development as well informed by popular-music fans and
creators who want to participate in the democratization of the music industry. I also highlight and compare perspectives on the political agency of
social movements (alternately, "new social movements"); that is, "public
sphere" interest-group activism that can apply to music and cyberliberties
activism. I critique the habit of some cultural-studies researchers to infer the
existence of a social movement, without any evidence of collective action or
coordination among sympathetic groups, from the structural preconditions

for a shared identity. Finally, I offer some perspectives from skeptics of the notion of new social movements on the Internet.

Cultural politics includes changing moods, attitudes, and sensibilities about aspects of social relationships that were previously taken for granted. Critical theory, well suited to respond to these changes, has addressed the international cultural ferment of World War II, the 1960s countercultures, and the new social movements of the 1980s, in each case by analyzing how "the new sensibility has become a political factor" and how to "incorporate the new dimension into its [own] concepts [and] project its implications for the possible construction of a free society" (Marcuse in Eyerman and Jamison 1998, 6).

The historical role of the music and cyberliberties project, writ large, is to prepare a strategy by which artists, musicians, and their fans can bypass the Celestial Jukebox, together with its copyright maximalism, criminalization of sharing, and its punitive enforcement mechanisms. The first part of the strategy involves opting out of Big Four products and services, boycotting copy protection, and rejecting abusive contract and license terms. The second part is to build an alternative mode of cultural production and distribution, from the bottom up, in communicative action. At the cusp of the PC age in the United States, video games, microcomputers, networking, community-access cable-television programming, satellite television, and advanced services for telephony began to diffuse across the country. Before the Internet became a consumption norm, libertarian visionaries of communication promoted alternative modes of media production and distribution, such as community-access television production, low-power broadcasting, electronic bulletin board systems (BBSs), and cassette-tape trading networks—all of which democratized access to music, information, and culture. All accomplished alternative forms of networking.

I review some literature in social studies that assesses broad-based resistance to the Celestial Jukebox, treating it either as a social movement or as presenting coherent stakeholder interests in institutions of civil society. Either literature can be interpreted to lend credence to the existence of a political agency that *could* unify activists, citizens, fans, musicians, and other creators in a counterhegemonic project. Music and cyberliberties activism could unify or fuse the horizons of otherwise splintered activists, such as those pursuing fair use, privacy, FOSS [free and open source software], and hacktivism. To some observers, the explosion of cyberlibertarian action plans indicates a new awareness of alternative modes of music distribution and new networking strategies, and is seen as a variety of political action for recovering social spaces that have been lost to the colonizing and rationalizing pressures in politics and the economy. Whether these potentials are realizable depends largely upon the characteristics of political social agency of cyberlibertarian activist groups and political opportunity structures. Using approaches that have been examined and utilized in contemporary critical theory, I shall evaluate the social agency of the alternative, radical, culture-jamming, and hacktivist cyberlibertarians. If collective action, solidarity, and ideological representations of a shared identity obtain, then taking a new social movement approach to cyberliberties makes sense. Nonetheless, there are also good reasons for remaining skeptical about characterizing media and cyberliberties activism as a type of new social movement. According to Harris M. Berger, "Radical skepticism has never been conducive to coordinated social action" (personal communication). This chapter will explore all of these positions more fully.

While they do not exhaust the range of research on cyberliberties as a social movement, public-sphere theory, resource mobilization (RM) theory, and new social movement (NSM) theory all adopt a modernist concept of politics as a rational, practical project in pursuit of individual autonomy and identity achieved through self-definition. The public-sphere approach emphasizes the pragmatics of positioning and maneuvering in campaigns for reforms, and analyzes their discourses; the NSM approach tends to idealize the social conditions for emancipation from suffering and injustice and thereby participates in a long tradition of utopianism. Both approaches reconceptualize politics, shifting its concerns from decision-making about wealth redistribution to conflicts over "quality of life and life-style concerns" in democratic self-defense against corporate and state attacks on autonomous and independent living (Pichardo 1997, 414). The theory of communicative action finds examples of praxis—free and rational politics—expressed in political solidarity and collective action and informed by anti-authoritarian ideals.

As political activities organized around the Internet have gained some traction, these two approaches—public-sphere and NSM theories—have expressed conflicted dynamics of cyberspace. Similarly, the dominant ideologies of cyberspace appear conflicted by a state-capitalist impetus to regulate and police cyberspace and by an "organic" resistance to regulation, policing, and hierarchical social relationships in cyberspace.[1] The regulation-based regime is oriented to accomplishing financial and other instrumental transactions online (Braman 2007), while the resistance regime is a participation-based universe of discourse oriented to "non-market" sociality (Benkler 2006). Each scheme is an ideology, because each scheme legitimizes social hierarchies and habits of thinking that are preconditioned by dominant configurations of power and money. Benkler argues that the resistance paradigm is the less harmful ideology, offering more communicatively rational potentials than the Celestial Jukebox does. By implication, it is less ideological and less based on coercion. Activism for free and open-source software, unregulated peer-to-peer file sharing, nonproprietary data and soft-ware standards, fair use, online privacy, and the freedom to tinker, for example—all have developed within the "networked public sphere." Benkler argues, however, that, structurally, the political agency collected behind these efforts is unlikely to exert hegemonic influence over the regulationist ideology. But the resistance ideology contains a teleology that aims for social justice, inclusion, and an expansion of recognized human rights; it can therefore serve as a normative standard for policymakers, activists, and informed consumer-participants in the technoculture.

Critical theory looks for empirically identifiable expressions of social conflict, and then discovers, to the best of its ability, whether they are cases of oppositional agency, and whether they are linked to political and economic changes. The visibility and viability of campaigns like Grey Tuesday, Downhill Battle, Recording Industry vs the People, FOSS, and so many others, together with the philosophical coherence among their many collective actions, call for a closer examination of traditional distinctions between interest groups and social movements. In the history of media reform, political economists ascribe political agency and pressures for change to social-movement politics. For example, Mosco argues that "numerous social movements have taken on national and local policy-making processes, including efforts to democratize decisions about licensing, spectrum allocation, industry structure, and media content" (1996, 241).

The mobilization of nonprofit, nongovernmental, and professional organizations around the impending Telecommunications Act of 1996 responded to the perceived antidemocratic effects of the deregulation of telecommunications in the United States. "Universal access to the information infrastructure, freedom to communicate, democratic policy-making, and privacy protection" are the democratic policy objectives of specific political constituencies that lobby, litigate, and educate, including the American Civil Liberties Union (ACLU), the American Library Association, the Association of America's Public Television Stations, the Center for Media Education, the Consumer Federation of America, Computer Professionals for Social Responsibility, and Public Citizen (Mosco 1996, 241). These organizations have enjoyed success in selecting policies and procedures to challenge. They "take advantage of political opportunities unique to a historical moment, strategically mobilize the resources available to them, and successfully frame issues in ways that appeal to the public" (Mueller 2004, 18).

Kriesi and others see participation in social movements by skilled professional workers as being stimulated by "encroachments on their work autonomy by colleagues who are primarily involved in the administration of the large private and public employers for whom the former work" (quoted in Pichardo 1997, 417). Skilled middle-class professionals who are at risk for micromanagement, Taylorization,[2] and downsizing "constitute a crucial structural potential for the new social movements, all of which attack in one way or another the unrestricted reign of technocracy" (Pichardo 1997, 417). As Marc Edelman (2001) puts it: "Although the 'old' labor movement upheld class as the primary social cleavage, category of analysis, organizational principle, and political issue, NSMs emerge out of the crisis of modernity and focus on struggles over symbolic, information, and cultural resources and rights to specificity and difference" (289).

The development of thinking about computers and human rights together did not become popular enough to warrant a social movement until there was a catchy slogan that could position it rhetorically. The cyberlibertarian slogan "Information wants to be free" was linked to the hacker ethic of sharing knowledge. It has a corollary: "Information wants to be expensive." The full argument was made in a speech by Stuart Brand to a conference on "hacker ethics" in 1984: "On the one hand information wants to be expensive, because it's so valuable. The right information in the right place just changes your life. On the other hand, information wants to be free, because the cost of getting it out is getting lower and lower all the time. So you have these two fighting against each other" (Brand 1984, in Clarke 2000).

Brand's argument about the market value of information reflected the realities of the corporate mass media in 1984. His syllogism expressed, on the one hand, a realism about the production of scarcity in late capitalism, and, on the other, an expectation for the economics of digital media to generate nonrival information goods at lower and lower marginal costs. As it became a popular slogan among computer hobbyists trading software and home tapers trading cassettes, "information wants to be free" was stripped of its grounding in an argument about information and media economics, and took on vague and elusive implications for culture and society. Brand's argument, thus misconstrued, became a libertarian slogan for popular participation in new information-sharing practices at about the same time that federal information policy and telecommunications policy were poised for thoroughgoing deregulatory reforms.

The Message of Music

As the system and the lifeworld "decouple," or differentiate, the operation of the Celestial Jukebox becomes independent of people's attitudes, beliefs, and expectations about being music fans. The identities of the participants in music and cyberliberties activism are symptomatically fractured between client-consumer and citizen roles, and the political responses to the Celestial Jukebox, so far, have been limited to boycotting and rebuking the system and to trying to tweak its most harmful features. As Sitton (1998) puts it, "Resistance to lifeworld colonization is difficult, because the lifeworld is only *partly* rationalized, denying the plausibility of traditional understandings but not having the cultural resources, mobilized by an intact public sphere, to block the extension of media-steering" (70). Not selling out to the Celestial Jukebox's terms is only half the battle. Is music and cyberliberties activism a social movement with a political agency capable of doing more than this, such as preparing an Alternative Jukebox for free culture?

The social agency of music scenes has been tied to the cultural reproduction of local "places of music" (Leyshon et al. 1998) that support the creation and distribution of music. Negus (1996) provides models of social agency that have been ascribed to music scenes, movements, and people who belong to them. In popular-music theory, social agency is associated with artists and their audiences, who are tied together through the messages in music and in the places of music (Negus 1996). Music in social-movement activism has been associated with the political messages in the music, and scholarship in this area has emphasized the political histories of music activism and the cultural traditions that have informed the transformative political events of radically democratic, civil-liberties–based movements (Eyerman and Jamison 1988; Garofalo 1992).

These accounts of political and social agency, however, leave out activism opposed to the production and distribution of music in the culture industries—activism driven by the message *of* music, rather than the messages *in* music. Music and cyberliberties activists have exploited linkages between media reform, radical media, and alternative music, but for them, the messages associated with specific genres and styles of music matter less than the channels and modes of communication they employ. Activism around the conditions of cultural reproduction takes advantage of the "political opportunity structures" (Brown 2002, 272) that are tilted in favor of activists using cyberspace strategically. The "downhill battle" of the indie-artist collective by the same name is being fought in cyberspace.

The goals, tactics, structures, and participants in music and cyberliberties activism, broadly construed, share features of new social movements, public-sphere activism, and media institutions in global civil society. Renouncing a materialistic and consumerist worldview is part of the post-punk identity, as is participation in music scenes and striving for autonomy from corporate music. Post-punk sensibilities reject the corporatization of culture, politics, and everyday life, as Klein (2000) portrays in *No Logo* and Barber (2007) portrays in *Consumed*. The broad-based opposition to the culture industries' domination of the production and distribution of music is also reflected by Coombe (2006) and Lessig (2004), who refer to a growing popular unease about the disappearance of the underpinnings for public-sphere institutions and "free culture."

As the "rising bad mood" about global capitalism (Marc Edelman 2001, 309) has fed concern with the corporate transnationals that supply most of the world's commercial music, the ideology of the Celestial Jukebox has been rendered suddenly visible. Coombe writes:

The recording industry that tends to control the greatest concentration of copyrights in musical works has also learned to deploy contract law, trademark law, common law, unfair competition suits, and even publicity rights to limit listening practices and creative use of music without authorization and payment. This legal situation leaves us with a musical culture structured primarily in favor of the financial interests of corporate intellectual property holders and shaped by the contractual conditions they establish. Any presumption that music serves public purposes and helps support social objectives seems to have vanished, just as any notion that the state should act to protect the public interest and to secure access to a range of public goods has become illegitimate. Even the long tradition of socializing the next generation into society's norms and values through music is rendered suspect when underfunded school systems and nonprofit social groups must pay royalties to pass down a nation's cultural heritage to its children (in Demers 2006, viii–ix).

When we recognize the diminution of the music lifeworld, we also recognize our vanishing expectations about a shared culture as well as the shrinking sources of support for free culture.[3] Coombe describes the sociological preconditions for conflict in the music and cyberliberties arena. She identifies a combination of strategies of domination that affect all members of society in innumerable ways, producing control over more and more intimate areas of life, in systems that prove to be irreversible unless countered by political intervention from unconventional sources. In this spirit, Lessig communicates the need to "liberate the music—again" for the sake of preserving a free culture: "the battle that got this whole [culture] war going was about music, so it wouldn't be fair to end this book [*Free Culture*] without addressing the issue that is, to most people, most pressing—music. There is no other policy issue that better teaches the lessons of this book than the battles around the sharing of music" (2004, 296).

An influential study of popular music addresses changes in the musical culture that accompanied the U.S. civil rights movements, but does not cover technology-oriented activism. Eyerman and Jamison (1988) search for "representative figures" (13) in the "mobilization of tradition" around democratic ideals: "By combining culture and politics, social movements serve to reconstitute both, providing a broader political and historical context for cultural expression, and offering, in turn, the resources of culture—traditions, music, artistic expression—to the action repertoires of political struggle" (7). Music mediates the traditional roles, values, and habitus that assist in reproducing society rather than transforming it radically (14–16). Eyerman and Jamison call collective action in these movements varieties of "cognitive praxis" organized around performative rituals. The songs of traditional struggle, protest, and national identity, especially when televised, "engendered" movement politics by providing a "reservoir of images" and symbols to inform and inspire political action (42). The work of Eyerman and Jamison demonstrates that, rather than demarcating separate "spheres" of communicative action, the social reproduction processes involving music in the lifeworld can be interdependent with those involving political development and identity formation.

In making the point that every movement has its own identifiable sound, Eyerman and Jamison argue that "there must . . . be some fit, some congruence, between the traditions carried in a particular song or piece of music, and the ideas and ideals of an emerging social movement" (1988, 46). Their point is that each movement's identity shares historical and cultural affinities with the music of the movement; by implication, however, their argument renders music a sort of marker of political activism rather than a mobilizing force or cause for solidarity in its own right. Yet music and cyberliberties activism, which is activism about music, does not have its own sound, because it stands in for all sounds (and intentional silences). Eyerman and Jamison have sidestepped the fact that there can be activism — ironically, in this case, about music itself — that does not have a distinct "sound" all its own.

Media and Social-movement Politics

Resource-mobilization and NSM approaches provide the benefits of a stereoscopic, resource-and-identity view of political action and, used together, can ascertain the identity, composition, and wherewithal of incipient social movements. And, just as important, both views are compatible with the understanding of communication as form of social action. A social movement is a "kind of campaign, parallel to an electoral campaign, [but] whereas an electoral campaign pays off chiefly in votes . . . a social movement pays off in the effective transmission of the message that its program's supporters are (1) worthy, (2) unified, (3) numerous, and (4) committed" (Tilly 2002, 88). Tilly argues that social movements operate largely symbolically to mobilize bias rather than strategically to seize state power: "In social movements the relationship between actions and the goals of the movement are diffuse and indirect . . . as compared with striking, voting, smashing the loom of a non-striking weaver, or running a miscreant out of town, [a social movement's] actions remain essentially symbolic, cumulative, and indirect. . . . Social movement mobilization gains its strength from an implicit threat to act in adjacent arenas: to withdraw support from public authorities, to provide sustenance to a regime's enemies, to move toward direct action or even rebellion" (88).

Yet media activists have demonstrated that effective rhetoric and use of symbols, especially in court battles, are also forms of strategic action. Lovink (2002) calls them "tactical." Moreover, social movements can be "invisible" to political scientists and to public authorities by remaining underground or in submerged groups, or by practicing a type of cultural politics that does not become institutionalized or fully "visible" to the political system. In the 1980s and 1990s, Jean Cohen and Andrew Arato, Alain Touraine, Alberto Melucci, Agnes Heller and Ferenc Feher, Nancy Fraser, Axel Honneth, Claus Offe, and Klaus Eder, among many others, uncovered some important and shared characteristics among seemingly unconnected causes and groups. From Western European cases, social-movement theory connected the experiential and political commonalities of disparate groups such as the anarchistic Dutch Weeds, antinuclear movements, and punk-rock scenes with examples from the United States, including EarthFirst! and Queer Nation. As Downing (2001) points out, the role of the media in NSMs goes unaccounted for.

NSM politics seems to be tailor-made for the networking logic of the Internet. For example, Kellner (2004) evaluates online activism by leftist activist subcultures, including hacktivism and culture jamming, as contemporary examples of Situationist praxis. In Kellner's analysis, cyberliberties activism would unite multiple sources of opposition around the goal of decrying the globalization of capitalism and the Bush administration's surveillance regime, and pursue its aims via hacktivism, blogging, open-source peer-to-peer (P2P) software development, the use of encryption for private communication, and the use of open-data formats for sharing information: "The internet activism of today is best perceived as informed by the spirit of the EZLN, the 'Battle of Seattle,' and the diverse amalgams of social movements and subcultures that have matured along with the new media over the last five years. This is the internet as a living, historical force and one of the keys to understanding and shaping the political and cultural life of the present age" (88–89).

Schweidler and Costanza-Chock (2008) describe movementlike resistance to global intellectual-property (IP) rights. At the level of "daily practice," fair-use exercises, file sharing, the use of copyleft and Creative Commons materials, remix culture, and piracy are goal-oriented activities that mobilize resources against IP rights. Resistant technologies include DeCSS, hacking, encryption bypassing and cracking, and P2P. Internationally, resisters use various rhetorical "frames" to characterize their opposition, including piracy, free culture, cultural sovereignty, the commons, and indigenous and traditional knowledge. At the policy level, the "Access to Knowledge" agreement signed by developing countries proposes a reform agenda at WIPO that loosens IP rights restrictions on poor countries. For these oppositional activities to register in the discourses of the public sphere to the extent that they alter public opinion and shape the political will of democratic governments is still an aspiration and a goal rather than an accomplished fact.

Rather than demonstrating the political agency of cyberliberties and media activism in the United States and worldwide, the public-sphere approach merely postulates it. The extent to which music fandom, daily technology practices, Situationist happenings, and software tools, together with alternative media, radical media, culture jamming, and hacktivism, all hang together as a coherent form of political agency with social subjectivity is the concern of the rest of this chapter.

NSMs and Resource Mobilization

There is a "systems" and a "lifeworld" distinction between the two methods most commonly used to study NSMs: one looks at the resource mobilization (RM) of movements, and the other looks at shared identities. To engage with the system, cyberliberties activists mobilize resources when the system offers opportunities for tinkering with social, legal, and technical code. The RM approach considers a "successful" showing of agency to be a specific policy outcome or a step taken in the direction of a policy change, rather than any of the "broader processes of cultural transformation" (Marc Edelman 2001, 290) occurring in the lifeworld. RM analyzes how disparate and often far-flung groups with roughly similar grievances have mobilized collectively for strategic political purposes and often for purely symbolic purposes. RM has also addressed the informal modes of organization of social movements and their existence as mere "preference structures" rather than as historical actors or social subjects (Buechler 1993, 223). Because policy changes will be needed to dismantle the Celestial Jukebox and to replace it with an Alternative Jukebox, the RM approach is useful for tracking debates about policy reforms in IP law, telecommunications policy, and information policy. As music fans abandon the new orthodoxy that comes with the Celestial Jukebox, they exit the formalized channels for colonizing the music lifeworld, advocating trading in the "copyright cops" (Vaidhyanathan 2001, 159) for a more humane IP regime and restoring balance to the system through copyright equality.

However wonkish and reformist the policy environment may seem for radicals of any stripe, it is still the case that the critical cyberlibertarian goals and ideologies complement those of precursor social movements that are broadly democratic. The NSM literature that grew out of comparative political studies of European and U.S. social movements beginning in the 1980s has much in common with cyberliberties. These commonalities include middle-class participation, a goal of creating more participatory forums for public speech, the making of greater opportunities for democratic participation, an awareness of ecological concerns in culture as well as in the environment, and the sparking of socially transformative communicative practices. Drawing from James Boyle, Lessig claims that the world needs an "environmentalism" for culture (Lessig 2004, 129): "It is an environment of creativity that we seek, and we should be aware of our actions' effects on the environment" (130).

NSM theory in many ways updates labor studies by looking for visible conflict and less visible forms of resistance to capitalist forms of domination: "In the US class conflict has always existed alongside cultural, ethnic, and racial struggle, never as a pure form for other movements to express" (Plotke, 1990, 89). NSMs express "cultural conflicts [that] have intensified because of new links between cultural and socioeconomic processes" and new "legal and distributive issues" (Plotke 1990, 90, 91). NSM theory addresses "broad, macro-sociological transformations that have created new contexts for collective-identity formation," viewing movements "less as organizations of common interest and more as new forms of collective identity engaged in discursive struggles that not only transform people's self-understandings but also contest the legitimacy of received cultural codes and points of view" (Carroll and Hackett 2006, 86–87). Taking NSM and RM perspectives into consideration together, it is possible to see music and cyberliberties activism as engaging both materially and symbolically with both system and lifeworld structures. Yet even with the benefit of the stereoscopic view of cyberliberties history, we are still seeing double. The incipient movement contains both reformist and radical political identities.

Two Cyberlibertarianisms

Emerging social movements need not be politically progressive to qualify as NSMs (Downing 2001). Speech, privacy, and information-access rights have become the centerpiece of civil libertarians' cyberspace activism, which draws on ACLU or EFF models. The private-property rights of owners of property and capital are the focus of economic libertarians. These two camps and their discourses have intermingled and intermixed in the history of cyberliberties. Cyberlibertarian political philosophy has evolved into twinned democratic-socialist and neoliberal ideologies to the extent that civil libertarians have found themselves positioned alongside economic neoliberals as sharers of the same "cyberlibertarian" values. "Progressives" who identify with civil liberties need not relinquish a claim to redistributive justice, and may in fact subordinate personal property rights to free speech, access, and privacy rights. However, while private-property rights and IP rights are typically the rallying cry for economic libertarians, at the end of the day, "progressive" cyberlibertarians show mostly ambivalence about the legitimate legal basis for capitalist IP rights.

The early proponents of cyberliberties as a rights-based worldview were the "digerati," or cultural elites who wielded money, power, and influence in the computer and software industries in the 1980s and 1990s. Although the digerati contributed to the commodification of cyberspace by commercializing it and marketing it (most notably in *Wired* magazine), they also sought to preserve some of its "public goods" characteristics as normative values of cyberlibertarianism. These values include the notion of an information and cultural "commons" and the notion of "peering" as a democratic communication practice.

Benkler, Vaidhyanathan, and Godwin exemplify the radical democratic and anti-authoritarian attitude in the literature of resistance. Vaidhyanathan's (2005) "manifesto" for "critical information studies" intends to root out abusive restrictions on personal autonomy in cyberspace. Benkler's critical theory likewise critiques regulationist norms in cyberspace, using individual autonomy as a yardstick. As the needs of the economy, politics, and family make demands on the Internet as an available communication resource, the urges to regulate the Internet as a coordinating platform for media distribution and consumption-driven daily life build and build. Godwin (2003) describes how a "fear of freedom" led to a "Net backlash" that formalized speech and behavior codes on the Internet. "Dismissive contempt for Net culture in all its frivolity, diversity, and perversity" accompanied the popularization of new "threats" from the Internet's open communication platform, including anonymous access to bomb-making instructions, hacker threats, and cyberporn (63–68). Cyberlibertarians have been on the defensive ever since the Net backlash.

The anti-authoritarianism of the cyberlibertarians presents a romanticized vision of Internet "pioneers" pushing social "frontiers," and of cyberspace, setting itself apart from the rest of civilization both rhetorically and juridically. Pioneering cybernauts wanted to be able to express maximal autonomy in a new world that was not despoiled by arbitrarily contrived rules and regulations imported from the real world. In the "Declaration of Independence of Cyberspace," Barlow (1996) captures the cowboy-libertarian attitude well: "Governments of the Industrial World, you weary giants of flesh and steel, I come from Cyberspace, the new home of Mind. On behalf of the future, I ask you of the past to leave us alone. You are not welcome among us. You have no sovereignty where we gather.... Your legal concepts of property, expression, identity, movement, and context do not apply to us. They are all based on matter, and there is no matter here."

With new communalist roots and strong links to music and political countercultures, early cyberlibertarians emphasized participatory, democratic ways to build communities (Turner 2006). Participation and access were key to the collaborations among MIT and Stanford mainframe hackers, ARPANET (Advanced Research Projects Agency Network) engineers, cyber- and cipher-punks, BBSers, MUDders and MOOers, and of course, WELL denizens.[4] The early cyberlibertarians shared both the beginnings of a lifeworld and expectations about the distinctiveness of cyberspace as a realm for self-exploration and pushing the boundaries of personal identity and social agency. Private property and state authority were dubious concepts that simply got in the way of the pursuit of personal autonomy.

The first and second "wired" generations provided a reservoir of norms, values, and expectations about social life online that persist today. Of course, not all of these norms were mutually consistent or even broadly shared. However, attitudes common to early "netizens" included hubris about technical competence as well as geeky enthusiasm for sharing their knowledge of hardware, software, and computer-networking skills. Turner (2006) ascribes to the burgeoning cyberculture of the 1990s a quest for the preservation of personal autonomy, antistatism, and a "libertarian orientation" toward regulation (248). This ideology was informed by a theory of human agency in which "human power was an individual possession, born of the proper use of technologies for the amplification of awareness through access to information" (261). In the gradual proliferation of new communication channels via cable, satellite, computer networking, and home recording equipment, the citizen-led media promoters commingled with computer experts and hobbyists. Turner argues that their shared values "[conjure] up visions of a disembodied, peer-to-peer utopia" (261), that are ultimately in conflict with other values, such as a "longing to return to an egalitarian world" (248) and "a return to a more natural, more intimate state of being" (261).

The life's work of Stuart Brand helped forge social networks that became the terrain of the earliest cyberlibertarians. His *II Cybernetic Frontiers* publication (1974) revealed an extant, pre-Internet hacker culture of computer hobbyists and networking geeks for a curious audience of technophiles.

Turner's biography of Brand and social history of the Whole Earth Network traces networks of active technology users associated both with the hippie counterculture and with New Left activists. Brand's *Whole Earth Catalog* project and his experiences in cofounding the WELL led him to communities that were actively constructing an original "electronic frontier" using networked computers. As mentioned previously, Brand also stimulated a discourse on hacking as a form of free-speech activism and addressed the concept of "hacker ethics" in a presentation to the first Hacker Conference, in 1984 (Clarke 2000). Together with John Perry Barlow, who had been a comparative religion major in college and then became a cattle rancher in Wyoming and a lyricist for the Grateful Dead, Brand became a founding member of the Electronic Frontier Foundation (Turner 2006, 172).

Turner portrays cyberliberties as a worldview that emerged from new communalist, back-to-the-land practices that "often embraced the collaborative social practices," but also relied on technological innovation and "the cybernetic rhetoric of mainstream military-industrial-academic research" from the cold war (Turner 2006, 33). Barlow's participation in the WELL "transformed the local norms" there, "including its Whole Earth–derived communitarian ethic, its allegiance to antihierarchical governance, and its cybernetic rhetoric" (162). The WELL cultivated expectations of democratic communication, participation, and access among its user group. In the WELL and other early virtual communities, "digital utopianism" in cyberlibertarian treatises blended strains of classic Enlightenment thinking with countercultural inspirations.

This utopianism did not rest easily once regulationist pressures began to impinge on the digerati. The saga of Steve Jackson Games (Godwin 2003), the "hacker crackdown" (Sterling 1992), and the suppression of encryption and encryption research by the U.S. executive branch were precedents that illustrated a new state interest in policing and regulating the social penumbrae of the digerati for the first time.[5] Barlow's cofounding of the EFF anticipated the expansionism of the regulationist state; in leaving his imprimatur of cyberlibertarian thinking on the organization, he created a defense mechanism for the technocultures of cyberspace.

A second attitude in cyberlibertarian literature, while sharing an anarchistic yearning for autonomy, has been put to use in "selling the market" as a project of neoliberal social and economic reforms (Aune 2001). The neoliberalism of the "neoclassical" Austrian school of economics and "rational choice" political theory have crept into cyberlibertarian discourse. Winner's "abbreviated" (1997, 15) sketch of cyberlibertarianism portrays it as a technologically determinist worldview that unnecessarily diminishes human

agency by mistaking human history as an outcome of technological developments. Winner argues that this *amor fati* (love of fate) can lead to an acceptance of false social choices that are dictated by technology rather than social needs. Moreover, the resulting ideology produced a "radical, right-wing" political agenda in the United States (1997, 15). Winner critiques "ecstatic enthusiasm for electronically mediated forms of living," which promoted "radical, right-wing libertarian ideas about the proper definition of freedom, social life, economics, and politics in the years to come" (1997, 14).

The evangelical style of rhetoric shared by the ascendant Republicans and the "third wave" vanguard has, at times, blurred the substantive differences between the digerati and the Republican revolutionaries. Aune (2001) links the popularization of the postindustrial thesis on networking to the suffusion of neoliberal discourses that accompanied the buildup to the Republican Revolution of 1994. Upbeat assessments of the liberating potential of the new information paradigm began to compete for prominence. Alvin Toffler's libertarian economic program for postindustrial society combined a popular "third wave" metaphor with the rhetoric of "post-industrial" society (derived from Daniel Bell) to promote a popular acceptance of a laissez-faire approach to the regulation of high-tech industries (Toffler 1980). Winner's critique highlights that cyberlibertarianism began as an elite worldview and that its elaboration into a progressive, democratic theory has taken decades.

The neoliberal reflex of the digerati was a self-serving class interest. In business, the reflex inspired efforts to curtail state powers in emergent markets for e-commerce and telecommunications services, to promote entrepreneurial commercial efforts in those areas, and to promote the products and services serving the new cyberculture. Implicit in the elite plan for management of cyberspace was to defer the eventual commercialization of online content, to use free content to stimulate the production of cultural objects online, and to experiment with business models for aggregating online audiences. The digerati were "netheads" who were in competition with the monopolistic Bell Telephone and AT&T, and they intended to bypass the taxation, regulation, subsidies, and other redistribution schemes of the incumbent technologists, the telephone "bellheads" (Frieden 2002). In the 1980s, they rode the financial boom in software-copyright and patent claims that began the process of privatizing cyberspace. The capitalist ideology of cyberlibertarianism, then, is derived from an interest in applying the rule of law to protect the new markets for computers, software, and online services.

The emergence of a capitalist camp among cyberlibertarians became explicit in the publication of the hodgepodge manifesto written by Esther

Dyson, George Gilder, George Keyworth, and Alvin Toffler: "Cyberspace and the American Dream: A Magna Carta for the Information Age" (Dyson et al. 1994). Turner argues that this manifesto, together with joint appearances made by Esther Dyson and Newt Gingrich, demonstrated that the new communalist movement as a whole had sold out to reactionary political forces. Indeed, politically and as a movement, the digerati's long migration from their communitarian roots in the 1960s to the loose affiliation of some of their members with Republican revolutionaries of the 1994 national elections in the United States alienated many cyberlibertarians along the way. Turner (2006) proposes that the new communalist identity and the cyberlibertarian political philosophy became so dissociated that "a social movement devoted to critiquing the technological bureaucracy of the cold war [came] to celebrate the socio-technical visions that animated that bureaucracy" (39). Winner (1997) critiques the technological determinism and "radical right-wing" political program for telecommunications and media deregulation that he identifies "cyberlibertarianism" with generally. Aune (2001) likewise distrusts the evangelical attitude of Toffler and other authors of postindustrial or "third-wave" literature, which has been harnessed by reformers to "sell the market" and advocate the full neoliberal package of deregulation, free trade, and fiscal and structural reforms.

Winner (1997) and Turner (2006) focus on "Cyberspace and the American Dream" as a cyberliberties manifesto. However, as competing positions on cyberliberties have evolved, there are more choices of position statements on information and communication rights in cyberspace. While some prominent cyberlibertarians, such as Esther Dyson, may have strayed into an experimental right-wing phase, most have shown themselves more capable of participating in progressive political action to defend lifeworld structures from colonization. A "Manifesto for Bad Subjects in Cyberspace," for example, promoted democratic-socialist perspectives on cyberliberties in 1993 (Bad Subjects Collective 1995). Nadine Strossen and Ann Beeson spoke frequently on the ACLU's progressive, cyberlibertarian program in the late 1990s; as Strossen points out, cyberliberties had to be asserted and defended in the wake of new, federal "cybercrimes" being created (Strossen 2000).

Cyberlibertarians agree to disagree about the ideological disposition of personal property in cyberspace. While some cyberlibertarians, such as Richard Stallman, oppose the concept of software being treated as private property imbued with legitimately commercializable rights, others, such as EFF staff attorneys, do not. "Hacktivist" cyberlibertarians see wisdom in purposefully withholding computer code from market-based exchanges and reserving it for the intellectual commons, where it can accrue potential benefits in ongoing innovation and in distributive social justice.

The Fan, the Smart Mob, and the Multitude

The RM and NSM approaches provide a stereoscopic view of the potential for social agency to engage in political praxis. RM looks for resources and strategies, while NSM looks for evidence of solidarity and shared identity in collective action, politics as symbolic action, and certain speech acts. Together, they insist that proof of political agency is in the pudding: the collective identities forged, strategies pursued, and goals attained in social action. Taken together, RM and NSM update the theory of communicative action by demonstrating the commingling of processes of social reproduction in identity formation, political articulation, and culture. They also reveal the conflicted nature of the ideologies motivating politically active cyberlibertarians.

As I have argued in chapter 2, other approaches have identified the mere activity of file sharing with a politically enhanced social agency, and still others have equated fandom with social agency. Whereas fandom studies and cultural studies tend to ascribe social agency to audiences that are "active" with respect to both their interpretations of cultural objects and their creative powers, these approaches risk attributing "movement" politics to every edgy conjuncture of song and fan, or illicit download. The social agency of the fan is more or less constrained by his or her relationship to the mode of access to, and consumption of, cultural objects. It may be that participatory fandom is a necessary, but not sufficient, condition for music and cyberliberties activism. Nevertheless, although they can depict oppositional politics in isolated instances, these approaches do not singly or together offer a robust view of social agency. Principally, this weakness is because they do not provide examples of either transformational social agency created in collective action or the potential for such.

The identification of structural constraints upon social agency does not necessarily lead to the detection of a coherent oppositional social agency, even if it seems as though it should. For example, Wark declares that "file sharing is a social movement in all but name" and presents an "alternative model" to capitalism (Wark 2006, 175, 176). In a similar vein, Hardt and Negri (2004) postulate the existence of "the multitude" as an organic or even mechanical reaction of the global disenfranchised to the power structures and violence of "empire." These approaches, informed by NSM theories and developed in conversation with them, infer the coherence of antisystemic agents and activities, and then reconstitute them, ex post facto, as historical subjects in a postlabor history of oppositional politics.

File sharing per se is not, and cannot be, the basis for an antisystemic social movement: it lacks institutionalization, does not demonstrate a movement politics, and lacks self-conception and social agency. Even if file sharing were a social movement, it would not automatically be considered oppositional, as there is some evidence to support a claim that the file sharing of music improves Big Four record sales (Burkart and McCourt 2006). So even if file sharing is a "new sensibility," to use Marcuse's words, it does not provide a basis for saying that it is therefore a "political factor" as a form of opposition. Instead, the case must be made for the linkage between the structural preconditions and the conscious expression of the sensibility. They must be both conceptualized and demonstrated to qualify as forms of praxis. Hadl (2004), for example, argues that "changing the media system as a whole, as well as the organizations within it" (78) is the end point of cyberliberties activism, while an intermediate step might be the development of a new media system that is "relatively autonomous of the state and market" (Curran, in Hadl 2004, 90). According to Hadl, "civil society media" provide the required "tools for decolonizing the lifeworld" (2004, 77).

The critical cultural-studies approach to fandom finds oppositional readings of texts that might otherwise seem to carry an orthodox ideological payload. The elucidation of such critical and reflexive responses to the culture industries can be inspiring. However, problems with this approach arise in the search for grounds for activism if text reading becomes erroneously treated as a social movement with its own historical subjectivity and agency. In the fields of media studies and performance studies, the ascription of social action to the private internalization of texts, and the imputation of a collective social identity as the result of a "radical" reading of a selection of texts, are frequently offered as contributions to social-movement theory. Notwithstanding, these claims are both fallacious, and even more so when joined together in the same analysis. Even if self-identification results from practices of fandom, evidence for the subsequent political expression of a shared and radicalized identity can be elusive.

Fandom, therefore, can be excluded from consideration as a form of political participation. Nonetheless, as I proposed earlier, fandom may be a prerequisite for music and cyberliberties activism. Fans express adoration, excitement, devotion, and loyalty for artists and solicit access to them (Théberge 2005, 497–499) while seeking to form "affective alliances" with them (Grossberg, quoted in Théberge 2005, 497). Fan clubs, including online fan clubs, can form "a network of repeatable relations" that are important to people's personal identities (Sterne, quoted in Théberge, 500). These social networks may anchor a symbolic basis for a collective identity. Of course, some fans in online portals may think that they are in symbolic interaction with other fans, when in fact they are interacting with a Turing test of machine simulations of other fans (McCourt and Burkart 2007). Critics of fandom have also suggested that fandom may inhibit cultural activism because the underlying behaviors exhibit "syncopated rhythms of manipulation and desire, profit-making and identity formation" (Théberge 2005, 500). These considerations suggest strongly that fandom cannot be relied upon as a category of political agency, from the perspective of communicative action, because it is already a colonized or co-opted social relationship that is detached (or detaching) from the lifeworld.

Another model that can be dispensed with as a prospective theory of agency for music and cyberlibertarian activism is the so-called smart mob (Rheingold 2002), which has been glimpsed in advanced network societies, and which *may* be poised to spread outward to the rest of the world. Rheingold's model of communicative agency resembles the "hive mind" model, which lacks central coordination, intent, and, often, even purpose. The smart mob can enable a culture-jamming campaign, but may just as easily become a twitch relayed among a few dozen nodes on an arbitrarily constructed and ad hoc network or a commercial viral marketing campaign. Rheingold claims that smart mobs facilitate collective action, which can lead to a consolidation of political agency into distinctive movement or party politics. The case of the Philippines—in which pro-democratic protestors formed smart mobs during the overthrow of Estrada—proves the concept of political mobilization through mobile messaging: "President Joseph Estrada of the Philippines became the first head of state in history to lose power to a smart mob. More than one million Manila residents, mobilized and coordinated by waves of text messages, assembled. . . . Estrada fell. The legend of 'Generation Txt' was born" (Rheingold 2002, 157–158). Other smart mobs, such as Critical Mass and Reclaim the Streets, likewise utilize text-message–based communication.

As tools for political resistance movements, smart mobs may facilitate political engagement and participation. Even so, smart mobs are only part of a repertoire of activist mobilization techniques, like culture jamming or hacktivism, and should not be properly understood as historical subjects themselves. A smart mob organized around a political goal, such as toppling a dictator, demonstrates more social solidarity and collective action mobilized behind a technology than, say, a smart mob responding to a department-store fire sale. Rheingold subtitles *Smart Mobs* "the next social revolution," which suggests in a technologically deterministic fashion that social transformations follow technological innovations as a matter of course. However, if revolutionary actors make their own history, then their technological repertoires are pressed into service and do not work autonomously.

Before turning to the model of agency provided by the public-sphere approach, I offer a final note on another dead-end path in the study of agency in oppositional politics. A rival discourse to Habermas and sociological approaches to social agency is the account of the "multitude" by Hardt and Negri (2004). Hardt and Negri address "network power" enabled by the "multitude," which they define variously as "the living alternative that grows within Empire" (xiii); as "an open and expansive network in which all differences can be expressed freely and equally, a network that provides the means of encounter so that we can work and live in common" (xiii–xiv); and as "the new global class" (xvii). In postmodern style, they dissolve "the people" into "innumerable internal differences that can never be reduced to a unity or a single identity—different cultures, races, ethnicities, genders, and sexual orientations; different forms of labor; different ways of living; different views of the world; and different desires" (xiv). The internal differentiation of the people into a multitude eclipses "the mass," which is the global population whose differences have been "submerged" in the operation of Empire (xiv).

The multitude is a more pluralist notion than "working class" insofar as it is "composed potentially of all the diverse figures of social production" and not merely waged workers (xiv). "Biopolitical" conflicts (xvi) emerge around a "new project of democracy" (xvii) that has been enabled despite, or because of, a "general global state of war" (5). Imperial war is a threat to democracy because it "creates law and jurisdiction from the inside," in "closed juridical systems" and "functional systems that, above all in complex societies, serve as surrogates for democratic expression—and thus function against democracy" (22). Hardt and Negri describe the uniqueness of NSMs as being automatically generated in "biopolitical" conflicts: "One distinctive feature of the network struggle of the multitude, like post-Fordist economic production, is that it takes place on the biopolitical terrain—in other words, it directly produces new subjectivities and new forms of life" (83). This approach to social-movement agency merely asserts its existence as a natural consequence of the transformation of politics into "biopolitics" in the age of the network society. The technological form dictates the terms of the political relationship. The limits to our political agency are encoded at the lowest level into our sociality.

The Deliberative Paradigm

Another approach to political agency informed by the theory of communicative action appears in work on the mediated public sphere. The public sphere is part of Habermas's empirical political theory of democracy, modeled after European experiences with state-owned media sectors and public-interest regulation. Communication researchers, and media social-movement researchers especially, find the public-sphere approach to cyberliberties appealing. If we insist on falsifiability for NSM studies, then we must also examine the claims made on behalf of the public sphere, the "networked public sphere" (Benkler 2006), and the "virtual public sphere" (Lovink 2002).

The existence of a public sphere is not a foregone conclusion. Schudson (1992) has criticized scholarship on U.S. political history that presumes, rather than demonstrates, evidence of a public sphere in the United States. That U.S. political communication discloses a history of rational and critical discussion is, in his perspective, too often "retrospective wishful thinking" (160). Because critical-communication scholars continue to employ public-sphere political theory and to develop it as an important aspect of the "deliberative paradigm" (Habermas 2006, 413), exploring media activism as a feature of public-sphere politics places a burden of proof on a public showing.

Within the theory of communicative action, the deliberative paradigm links politically democratic institutions to mass media through the formation of public opinion and political will. It offers as its main empirical point of reference a democratic process that is supposed to generate legitimacy through a procedure of opinion and will formation that fosters (1) publicity and transparency for the deliberative process, (2) inclusion and equal opportunity for participation, and (3) a justified presumption for reasonable outcomes (mainly in view of the impact of arguments on rational changes in preference) (Habermas 2006, 413).

The "established political public sphere" of mass-media gatekeepers is dominated by elites, experts, and professionals playing a variety of roles, including journalists, politicians, lobbyists, advocates, experts, moral entrepreneurs, and intellectuals (Habermas 2006, 416). The legitimation function of the political public sphere "prepare[s] the agendas for political institutions" (416) of European democracies.

Mass-media channels for news and debate, including print media and electronic media, have, in political systems with mixed public and private media ownership, provided the social spaces needed by deliberative democracies to put communicative reason to use for the perpetuation of the liberal model of government. But Habermas's model is based on the European experience with media ownership and regulation, which has emphasized public-interest regulation and a larger degree of public accountability for programming than has existed in the United States and nearby countries, including Canada and Mexico. The U.S. model, moreover, encroached broadly into Latin American media markets, and is starting to exert more pressures for change in Europe and elsewhere as support for public media dries up and as media-privatization measures find new opportunities for implementation.

New-media scholarship has resuscitated public-sphere theory. The opportunities for the bottom-up production and distribution of media are still robust. But, as the history of the Celestial Jukebox shows, the corporate gatekeepers of the mass media have partially converged with those of new-media enterprises, and are poised to foreclose those aspects of new media that have the greatest potential for access and participation by nonelites and grassroots organizations. Demands for a robust set of civil liberties that should accrue to citizens of the information society have emerged from various academic disciplines that identify with the democratic ideals of the public sphere (Benkler 2006; Hamelink 2004; Cunningham 2008; Vaidhyanathan 2005; Striphas and McLeod 2006). The public-sphere discourse on cyberliberties activism positions both the public sphere and "civil society" as zones of communicative action that are formally unmoored from state power centers and from the marketplace. Civil society itself is a construct designed to signify an intellectual commons at the heart of the public sphere.

"Global civil society" research connects civil liberties claims made by networked political actors around the world with antiglobalization activism. The notion of a global civil society reflects an awareness that globalization of the capitalist commodity form is accompanied by a globalization of resistance and opposition to the terms of the imposition of capitalism into new zones of life: "In 1993, Falk introduced the phrase globalization-from-below to refer to a global civil society linking 'transnational social forces animated by environmental concerns, human rights, hostility to patriarchy, and a vision of human community based on the unity of diverse cultures seeking an end to poverty, oppression, humiliation, and collective violence'" (Marc Edelman 2001, 304). I see nongovernmental organizations (NGOs) as important agents defending the music lifeworld.

NGOs as the Principal Networking Agents of Global Civil Society

Global civil society is best expressed in the global nongovernmental movement. As a group, NGOs are diverse and multifaceted. Their perspectives and operations may be local, national, regional, or global. Some are issue-oriented or task-oriented; others are driven by ideology. Some have a broad public-interest perspective; others have a more private, narrower focus. They range from small, poorly funded, grassroots entities to large, well-supported, professionally staffed bodies. Some operate individually; others have formed networks to share information and tasks and to enhance their impact (Schuler and Day, 2004, 1).

Schuler and Day identify public-sphere characteristics with "a fundamental aspect of democratic systems" (2004, 4) built on equitable, citizen-based, and deliberative public processes (5). Schuler and Day proclaim "the strong role—largely unacknowledged—that global civil society is playing in shaping the 'network society,'" and say that "practitioners of civil-society ICT [information and communication technology]...[and their] projects need to be considered as elements of a broader 'movement,' however unorchestrated that movement may be" (1–2).

The Internet's diffusion allowed transnational actors, particularly NGOs, to link with one another in the wake of the breakup of the Soviet Union and Eastern Bloc, amid the democratic and "velvet" revolutions there, and during the period of the indigenous rebellion of the Zapatistas in Mexico. The Internet facilitated the coordination of many activists besides NGOs in supporting globalization from below, and the cumulative experience of adapting the Internet for activism has led some cyberlibertarians to speak of the "virtual public sphere" (Dahlberg 2001).

The virtual public sphere has been used as a launching pad for campaigns to reform media and telecommunication policies, protest IP law, and, in general, oppose the use of the Internet and other technologies to transfer the legitimate distribution of media from the communication lifeworld to new system functions. The virtual public sphere introduces a recursive, or self-reflexive, dimension to media activism by utilizing the Internet as a communication medium, as a subject of political interest, and as an object for reforms. The diverse campaigns reviewed by Schweidler and Costanza-Chock (2009), for example, object to the removal of fair-use rights under the Digital Millennium Copyright Act (DMCA) and to broader changes globally ushered in with the World Trade Organization (WTO), WIPO, and other market-oriented reforms of the media, IP, financial, and information sectors. Schweidler and Costanza-Chock illustrate a coordinated and networked syncopation of public education and lobbying groups since the year 2000. The antiglobalization mobilizing of "Internet Zapatismo," the convergence of anti-WTO activists at the 1999 anti-WTO street demonstrations "Battle for Seattle," and the birth of Indymedia[6] proved the concept and demonstrated the utility of the Internet for transnational solidarity-building campaigns by anticorporate media (Downing 2001). The reverberations of this online activism illustrated the incipient relationship of networking the Internet for political campaigns to the potential for "mobilizing bias" (Brown 2002) and influencing the political system.

The theory of communicative action encourages us to look for the normative claims that underlie the expressions of these diverse and loosely connected rebellions, to uncover a common articulation of communicative rationality. We can find evidence of communicative rationality in the oppositional politics themselves. The rights talk of global civil society forces a public deliberation about expanding formal categories of freedom to protect a lost or threatened lifeworld, and about a robustness of citizens' rights that has yet to be realized in actual social practices. The deliberative model of cyberliberties activism argues that citizens of an information society have the right to organize in opposition to the social side effects of global capitalism in a global civil society. They have the right to a balanced IP regime: one that protects and expands fair use, access to knowledge and culture, and access to communications resources that, broadly conceived, can influence unjust and lopsided power relationships in society. Specifically, social benefits of the information society should include the right to require open networks for exercising free speech, for diverse programming (and for public access thereto), and the right of access to decision-making channels for public policy about media, telecommunications, information, culture, and knowledge (Burkart, 2008b, 277–278).

In *The Wealth of Networks* (2006), Benkler develops a democratic theory specifically adapted to the Internet, a clear critique of the commodification of the Internet, and a normative theory of cyberliberties. He critiques private-property relations expressed in commercial search engines and Web surveillance as systematically distorted communications, perpetrated by the profit motive. He also promotes nonmarket, sharing relationships online. For Benkler, an "ideal speech situation" is a peering relationship in an Internet commons, whereas for Habermas, it is power-free discourse aimed at reaching agreement. The two perspectives align nicely.

As far as political agency is concerned, Benkler hedges his bets. He is absorbed by the "conditions for emergence" of noncapitalist and "non-market relations" on the Internet. But he also identifies a "networked public sphere." It is free so far of control by steering media, but contains social relationships that deliberate "political and social action" will need to "protect" from colonization by market forces or state regulation (Benkler 2006, 23). Yet he offers "no reassurances" that such action "will in fact come to pass" (23).

Like the networked public sphere, the "virtual public sphere" (Lovink 2002, 262) remains outside of, but connected to, institutions of the public and private sectors. Lovink identifies cyberliberties activism as an updated variety of media activism and as operating on behalf of a virtual public sphere that is under construction:

What is of interest are the ideological structures written into the software and network architecture. It is not enough to just subvert or abuse this powerful structure. There is an equal challenge to develop new standards by writing free software and interfaces. The same can be said of the efforts to develop databases of free content, a still marginal activity that will soon gain importance once everyone will have to pay for content to download. The virtual public sphere cannot come into being in a purely global, commercial environment, neither in places where the state has absolute control over the nation's intranet and firewalls. It is in this "third place" the public part of cyberspace, in-between state and market, that media activism flourishes. (262–263)

By this account, online media activism is the purest form of contemporary democratic politics, and it can easily jump nation-state boundaries into transnational and global contexts.

Because "civil society" or a "public sphere" was once constrained by the political borders of nation-states, it is in this international context that the deliberative paradigm is stretched to its limits. In acknowledging contentious transnational activism over North-South disparities, identity politics, neoliberal reforms, and newly globalized corporate and multilateral power structures, the United Nations has begun to designate "global civil society" as a formally independent social sector alongside state and corporate stakeholders. The World Summit for the Information Society (WSIS) put "global civil society" to the test of self-presentation at its triennial events, with mixed results for media reform and cyberliberties activists: "The commercial agenda is supported by a strong constituency of the leading members of the WTO and powerful business lobbies (such as the Software Business Alliance and the Global Business Dialogue).... At present, the humanitarian agenda...is still in search of an active constituency in the world communications arena" (Hamelink 2004, 76).

Hadl (2004) argues that the WSIS created a consensus around the notion that "democracy requires a third media sector, consisting of media that are 'non-commercial and non-state'" (79). Susanna George describes media democracy and communication-rights movements as separate groups, but sees them both "mounting a broad-based resistance against the effects of globalizing economic liberalism" (quoted in Hadl 2004, 78). Nonetheless, the civil-society representatives of the Media Caucus at WSIS, including those from community media and civil-society media, were marginalized in the structure of the symposium (Hadl 2004, 88–89). The denouement of the WSIS suggests that the lasting aspect of the symposium has been the development of the CRIS (Communication Rights in the Information Society) campaign (CRIS n.d.), which has updated and reaffirmed some of the principles of the transnational opposition group the New World Information and Communication Order (CRIS 2005, 15–16). Hadl's case study supports my basic argument in this chapter, which is that the music lifeworld is decoupling from the economic and political institutions of the system, making it possible for it to support organizations geared for gaining independence from corporate media systems and for creating new alternatives.

Global civil society and the virtual public sphere may provide plausible constructs for cyberlibertarians who are political actors, and these concepts provide a valuable frame of reference for oppositional transnational political activity. But these concepts do not breathe any new life into existing social movements, nor do they animate new social movements. Besides remaining inventions of political theorists, global civil society and the networked public sphere may not be desirable choices, politically speaking. Fraser (1985) enumerated the exclusive, discriminatory, and nonparticipatory aspects of Habermas's public-sphere concept, especially for women, and Downing (2001) reminds us that not all alternative and radical media organizations are politically progressive.

Exactly who does and does not participate in the process of globalization from below, from networks to alliances to movements, likewise remains uncertain. Positions of power in NGOs and most oppositional groups are typically self-selected, or otherwise unelected. And globalization from below may retain some unappealing characteristics of globalization. For example, Hadl's category of "civil society media" has a built-in instrumentalist orientation, lacks the legitimacy derived from a popular mandate, and suggests hierarchical organizations that can mirror those of commercial or governmental media organizations.

Hadl concedes that because of these instrumentalist features, civil-society media are always at risk of institutionalizing undemocratic processes and generating antidemocratic discourses (2004, 89), but she conjectures that they are probably less risky than their commercial and state-run counterparts. Marc Edelman (2001) cautions against the technological determinism of the global-civil-society model of political agency and social change: "Such assertions suggest that changing international political norms and new technologies have fundamentally and universally altered the balance of power between state and society" (306). Yet as the Celestial Jukebox shows, the repeated and emboldened incursions of state and market forces into lifeworld structures would seem to challenge the claim that civil society has stuck it out, or maintained the upper hand, relative to the state or the market. It may be the case that the international political economy will tolerate an importuning global civil society as long as the neoliberal project of setting up supranational governance institutions and dismantling welfare-state institutions moves ahead, but will move to disconnect global civil society before it attains any real power.

More Room for Skepticism

There is plenty of room for skepticism about the adaptation of NSM discourse to media activism and cyberliberties activism in the United States. The post-punk sensibility itself is radically skeptical and unconducive to coordinated social action so asking about the appropriateness of NSM discourse for skeptical, even disenchanted, individualists is worthwhile at this point. Key values for cyberlibertarians, such as anonymity, are not conducive to solidarity. Some individuals and groups may think they are developing a counterhegemonic practice, but given their low levels of solidarity and collective action, the visibility and effectiveness of any counterhegemonic movement can be called into question.

One response to this objection is to qualify the NSM characteristics of music and cyberliberties activism while reemphasizing the political stakes of the game. The music and cyberliberties project, which is to create an alternative system to the Celestial Jukebox, strongly resembles prior social struggles and is not an entirely new variety of oppositional social agency. Plotke (1990) considers cultural politics to be continually infused by the politics of equality and social justice, and not a "new" social movement at all. Disruptive cultural politics may appear to be relatively recent (since the 1960s) but in the United States, class conflict has always been commingled with other conflicts:

> In seeking equity, autonomy, and cultural change, contemporary collective action is immersed in politics, both in the form of its action and its aims. Movements and interest groups are political—concerned with shaping social relations—at the level of the state and elsewhere. They politicize previously uncontested relations, or repoliticize previously settled relations. In doing so, they become involved with the national and local state, with legislatures and courts, and with all the routine forms of political decision-making. (100–101)

Plotke reminds us that new social movements are not sui generis, but "thoroughly political" in recognizable ways.

The concern remains that music and cyberliberties activists appear to be—organizationally and from the perspective of their "resource mobilization" among fans, activists, and creators—only loosely connected, providing few important examples of collective action. For example, the radical and hacktivist domains identified above tend to express "tactical," and not strategic, ends (Lovink 2002). Therefore, there are few if any overarching plans of action. Benkler (2006) envisions a "transformation" of the current regulationist model of cyberspace, but hedges his bets with his claim to "offer no reassurances" about the likelihood or inevitability of a meaningful transformation (23). For Benkler, who remains an idealist, the proof of social agency behind protective political action is still in the pudding.

Computer hacking may be a sign of social-movement politics or political potential, albeit a sign that remains "unfulfilled" (Taylor 2005, 634) and lacking "an explicit political target to which normative judgments can be applied" (634). Philosophical hackers, or hacktivists, refocus "upon the political nature of the end to which technological means should be put: a normative element has been put back into objectified computer code" (626). Taylor thinks that hacking, as a social movement, has "failed to develop the radical potential of its original celebration of human ingenuity over technological systems and has largely become an uncritical celebration of those systems for their own sake" (626). In particular, Taylor notes that the sloganeering around "information wants to be free" stands in for a "well-articulated political position" (630). However, Richard Stallman, from the Free Software Foundation, Ian Clark, Ricardo Dominguez of Electronic Disturbance Theater, and other open-source hacker-activists are in the process of articulating a political position from which to orient open-source development as a social movement for cyberliberties.

The utopianism of cyberlibertarianism is also a cause for concern to political realists, policy reformists, and many professionals. Although the social agency seems fragmented, the ideologies expressed in opposition to colonization share a strong family resemblance to a variety of technological utopianisms with a Western, and U.S.-oriented, influence. These ideologies are not always internally consistent and demonstrate many conflicted interests and identities. Utopianisms carry articles of faith: belief in individual or social transcendence, and liberation through new technologies. Technological utopianism mistakenly places technology, and not human agency, at the source of human history-making. Moreover, despite the litany of promises made for new ICTs by innovators, marketers, and modern-day physiocrats with a penchant for high-tech escapism, delivery on utopian promises always comes up lacking, and nothing fundamental changes in the way society is organized:

Each new generation of technology revived the discourse of salvation, the promise of universal concord, decentralized democracy, social justice and general prosperity. Each time, the amnesia regarding earlier technology would be confirmed. All these methods—from the optical telegraph to underwater cable, the telephone, the radio, the television and the Internet—intended to transcend the spatial and temporal dimensions of the social fabric brought back the myth of the recovery of the lost agora of Attic cities. Neither the often radically different historical conditions of their institutionalization, or the flagrant failure to fulfill their promises regarding their supposed benefits, could make this millenarian world of technological images falter. (Mattelart 2003, 23)

Today, the potentials of P2P networking substitute for varieties of social agency formerly reserved for the "lost agora of Attic cities."

These utopian visions still inform cyberlibertarian values, as indicated by the discrepancies between democratic theory and actually existing practices. The thoroughgoing commercialization of the Internet has defused most of its radical potential for subverting the most oppressive features of techno-capitalism. Particularly, the privacy violations of near-ubiquitous surveillance, restrictions on access to knowledge, and suppression of intertextuality and borrowing in the cultural reproduction of cyberspace have curbed the enthusiasm for the Internet originally expressed by the new communalist luminaries in the pages of *Wired* in the 1990s. However, cyber-utopianisms persist in discourses by and for technology innovators.

Winston (1998) points out the recurrence of utopian expressions of exuberance for innovative information and communication technologies in U.S. popular culture. Winston critiques the utopian and neo-utopian perspectives for their persistent idealism. Idealism is unwarranted from a historical perspective, which recognizes a pattern of recurring suppression and subversion of the "radical potential" of each new communication technology—which is ultimately brought into conformity with the more conservative needs of the market and the state. Cartels, legal prohibitions on disruptive technologies, and even outright censorship mark commercial media which routinely tout their offerings as "revolutionary." In the music business, experimental and underground musicians who pushed the limits of creativity in music collage by symbolically challenging copyright laws were boycotted by commercial music-pressing plants and music distributors in the 1990s (McLeod 2001, 125, 145). The conservative needs of the music industry tamed many incipient threats from the Internet, including demands for copyright equality by fans and consumers, and P2P file sharing.

There is an argument to be made that the Internet may be the last place to look now for oppositional social-movement agency. Dahlgren critiques the view that cyberspace is becoming a vital link for NSMs and NGO activists and contributing to the formation of "multiple mini-public spheres" (quoted in Pajnik 2005b, 79). Pajnik sees the Internet as a legitimation tool for neoliberals. It has the potential to empower, but in fact is used "to practice political action as a solitary activity," so much so that "deliberative forums may be useful for promoting a rather abstract form of political competence" (80). This criticism is reminiscent of Habermas's description of the disintegration of the public sphere into "acts of individuated reception, however uniform in mode" (Habermas, quoted in Pajnik 2005b, 80). Pajnik cultivates a "suspicion...that the Net is primarily a medium through which people construct and reconstruct their individuality, rather than a vehicle to promote civic association and communities" (80). People remain in "isolated groups, conversing among themselves" (80). Similarly, Dahlberg says,

"Although the Internet provides for the articulation and contestation of diverse views in multiple spaces, corporate portals and media sites are directing much online attention toward conservative news and consumer practices. This situation goes against the vision of the Internet operating as an alternative medium to the mass media, as a space where positions and critique excluded offline are foregrounded" (Dahlberg 2005, 172). The corporate Internet channels people's social aspirations into a "system of democratic development on the basis of a predefined logic where the option of a citizen to practice rationalization is limited" (Pajnik 2005b, 84).

Reframing progressive political reforms as counterhegemonic practices offers an alternative perspective for evaluating music and cyberliberties activism as a variety of political praxis. Hegemony is "the process of constituting the common-sense, taken-for-granted reality in society," achieved through consensus-building communication and consent (Mosco 1996, 242). Hegemony has been operating to normalize the social relations of production around the Celestial Jukebox and its punitive IP-law regime. Because hegemonic processes are a "contest for consent" that "is sufficiently unstable to admit oppositional and alternative hegemonies" (Mosco 1996, 244), an oppositional counterhegemony can unveil or disclose ideological distortions and misrepresentations of reality, and challenge values manipulated for the gain of elites. This chapter has addressed the political agents and actors who are widely thought to support an alternative project, and the challenging task of ascribing to them a coherent identity and strategy.

CHAPTER FIVE

Ethics and Aesthetics

✳

In this book I have tried to show that the social struggles of the new politics of music distribution disclose social agency in some kinds of communicative action, however fractured and partial the agency may be.[1] There is no singular movement, coalition, or vanguard leading the charge against the Celestial Jukebox. However, support for increased participation and access to places of music on the Internet is demonstrated among broad sections of society, and there are examples of collective symbolic action and political solidarity to point to.

Now that commercial, digital music distribution is becoming a consumption norm, or a dominant consumer practice, music studies needs answers to some basic questions about music that is provided as a service. What are some costs, and what are some benefits to music fans who are accustomed to collecting records and CDs? How will the changes in distribution affect the ways in which people buy and "consume" music? Record collectors who once participated in the social reproduction of the norms of popular-music scenes face making trade-offs to participate in digital music distribution.

There is no definitive formula for the commodification of digitally distributed music yet, although Apple appears to have nearly perfected one with the iTunes store. McCourt (2005) discusses how the experiences of obtaining and listening to music have changed in the transition to digital music distribution and music services. McCourt is attuned to the effects of format changes on the activities of music collectors, and to the evolution of formats over time: "Each subsequent format has less physical presence while allowing for more storage and greater possibilities for user programming" (2005, 249). But for music fans who collect music obtained through an Internet connection, digital music is not handled physically. The pleasure of music "consumption" cannot be obtained in its packaging or shelving.

Even so, there are new pleasures that come with the game of obtaining access and consolidating a database of music files.

Music fans who are record collectors participate in fan cultures through their purchases, musical appreciation and enjoyment, and their shared affinities. Record collectors are especially sensitive to the physical qualities of cultural objects like LPs and CDs, and take these factors into consideration when selecting objects for acquisition. Good quality vinyl and packaging creates allure and the perception of economic value worth spending money on. McCourt (2005) focuses on a record collector's desire for engaging in "emotive" consumption that lies behind the urge to collect tangibly packaged music, observing that "digital sound files lack potential emotive contexts altogether" (250). How is it that an ascendant format can make up for a "degraded" emotive context? How can it create the missing "aura"? McCourt's answer is that the collector's participation in the distribution of digital music files to peers, in music-sharing practices, creates a new sense of value related to a personal collection of digital music files. The value comes in communication and in sharing cultural objects as well as ideas and information about them. Spreading the fan-club base wider through personal distribution channels becomes more important than building personal archives of records and CDs. As Rodman and Vanderdonckt (2006) put it, the "free circulation of music through the culture" creates "a set of affectively charged social relationships" (248). This participatory and collectivist spirit is still left over from the heady days of Napster P2P, and the music industry depends on it implicitly (even if not explicitly) for the eventual dominance of digital distribution over CDs.

In this chapter, I perform a rudimentary cost-benefit analysis on the conversion of a record collector into a music-service user, and argue that the music industry's own attempts to create and instill economic value and aesthetic desire in digital distribution channels are probably doomed to fail. Specifically, I argue that the hoarding (or gorging) fetish associated with free music file sharing, and the associated music-sharing fetish, are complementary values to music fans who turn to the Internet as a place of music. I contend that the fetish of hoarding free music files that has developed since the Napster days may be successfully replaced by the fetish of sharing music with others. But while the sharing fetish is cultivated by commercial music marketing, it is not supported within the new technology regime; in fact, the regime seems to continually undermine sharing by introducing usability problems.[2] In its current stage of evolution, the business model for digital distribution is banking on whatever gratifications can come from a substituted fetish that cannot be gratified.

After addressing the question of the missing value underlying the contemporary media economics of digital music distribution, I conclude with an ethical argument about switching over from lifeworld-sustained music distribution to receiving music as a commercial service. I argue that a record collector who "switches" from physical formats to service consumption jeopardizes the music lifeworld, as do policymakers who impose filters and other restrictions on public networks. Finally, I speculate that a reconstituted online music lifeworld would look very much like a universe of post-punk music scenes maximized for access and participation.

Evolution of the Collector's Role in the Music Industry

Paul Théberge criticizes the notion that record collectors should enjoy privileged treatment in studies of fandom, calling the idea "elitist" (2005, 493). After all, he is aware that Benjamin's critique of the art collector still pertains to record collectors who consider records strictly for their investment value; collectors only barely conceal commodity fetishism in their accumulation and fetishization of cultural objects.[3] Commodity fetishism presents a distorted view of a commodity's value as being intrinsic in the object itself, and not constituted in the labors of its production.

Still, in the heyday of vinyl-record collecting, record collectors were pillars of normative support for, not to mention patrons of, the record industry. They bought and traded the newest releases, composed detailed histories of the records themselves as well as of the producers, musicians, and other artists involved in the record project. Many record collectors edited and contributed to music magazines and fanzines (Burns 2004), which produced secondary and tertiary discourses about records and sustained fan cultures organized around music subcultures, affinity groups, and specialty genres.

Record collectors safeguarded the histories of recorded music by holding the recordings themselves, and created new cultural objects and commentaries from them or about them. Record collectors also helped put new music into circulation. Some record collectors opened record stores, which in themselves were places of music that provided outlets for other record collectors to exercise their right of first sale, in selling and purchasing used records. Record stores also facilitated the emergence of new music scenes by releasing new records, many of which came from local artists. Moreover, record stores often traded with local radio stations, including community and student radio stations. In many small- and medium-sized cities in the United States, where big-box retailers like Wal-Mart have come to dominate local markets for practically every consumable, one can gauge the importance of record stores on local music scenes by the disappearance of both (Zucco 2007). "Going to a store and buying a CD is no longer a rite of passage for many teenagers"; only half of U.S. teens bought any discs at all in 2007 (Quinn 2008). When record stores began going out of business in droves—first, the "mom and pop" shops, then the national chain stores—local music scenes lost a great deal of their groundedness in local places for listening to and sharing music. Record collectors and their spaces and places and habitus contributed to the material and cultural reproduction of music cultures; as these spaces disappear, so does some of the music lifeworld.

Record stores are going the route of the old dance halls, some of which still persist only thanks to the work of preservationists (Vertuno 2008). DJs, dance clubs, blogs, and other online spaces seem to be filling in some of the areas of fan culture that have been eroded in the migration to digital distribution (Théberge 2005). Théberge's sense for the daily communication rhythms of music fans with other fans on the Internet supports McCourt's claim that collectors ascribe more value to participating in the circulation and flows of digital music than they have before. New, online places of music distribution and consumption, like music blogs and social-networking sites, are growing up around the distribution changes.

Pricing frictions between the Big Four labels and Apple iTunes, and experimentation with DRM-free downloads, have kept digital distribution in a prolonged phase of prototyping. Continuing year-over-year declines in CD sales are raising the profile of digital distribution as a sales channel, but many labels are still reluctant to commit fully by releasing complete CDs and entire catalogs to online services. This hesitation has emerged because of a lack of coordination between the major labels and Apple (primarily) over standards setting and revenue sharing.

The pause permits music fans and music collectors more time to deliberate about the implications of making the turn to an archive of all-digital files. Pressures to convert to the new formats come from different sources, but ultimately, it is a consumption choice to switch a personal collection to all-digital file formats. Once the decision has been made to accumulate music downloads, however, participating in music flows as a collector becomes quite a different prospect from participating in music scenes as a collector. In important ways, it becomes impossible to "collect" digital music files; thus symbolic substitutes for collections stand in for the collections themselves. This process happens through software interfaces for enabling and restricting access to music and other cultural objects encoded digitally.

In the online music universe, when digital music isn't flowing from an Internet service, it resides in the form of a queue or playlist generated by media-player software.[4] McCourt addresses the queues as representations of a person's record collection. The lists are artifacts of prior queries in a search engine. It is in the context of the music's searchability—which is made possible by file indexing and searching software—that Goldberg (2005) says, "In the environment engendered by these search tools, music is less about an artist's self-expression than a customer's desire for self-reflection" (Goldberg 2005). The "value" of a centrally searchable, all-digital music collection comes from self-reflection, independently or with the aid of an "intelligent" software agent.[5] The desire to search would become presumably more intense if a music fan's entire database of digital music were accessible through a single software installation on a central computer, or networked computers, and if an exhaustive list of music holdings could be generated from an online catalogue. The original P2P Napster offered something like this experience to its users.[6] From this line of approach, then, online music searching is a form of soul-searching that relieves the collector's fetishes for packaging, acquisition, and handling of records. In a certain way, a successful search for a personally meaningful song, accomplished on demand within a comprehensive database, fulfills (at least temporarily) some of our expectations of the "digital sublime" (Mosco 2004). Yet doing so in a commercial domain places the music collector into a "digital enclosure" (Andrejevic 2002) that remains enclosed even if the space has access to certain shared lists and the collections of others.

Life of a Music Fan inside the Digital Enclosure

Collecting music from within a "digital enclosure" or online music service provider's portal is a different kind of activity from collecting music in physical formats. The formats themselves introduce user limitations, and their technological enclosures can tighten them. Music fans cannot become record collectors, so in an attempt to compensate for missing value, they share and hoard music files whenever possible. Thus, while sharing and hoarding music files and playlists may reduce the perceived collectable value of music to the fan, these same activities also increase a collector's sense of ownership or entitlement to share them or to incorporate them into new creative works. In a capitalist economy and society, "the necessity to create value for something that has no physical presence accelerates the need for and process of circulation" (McCourt 2005, 251). Therefore, file sharing—even more than hoarding—would appear to contribute to the psychological appeal of digital-music files to music collectors. And sharing is also a means to hoarding in many online communities.

Working at the social-systems level, Sterne (2006) takes a less intimate view of digital music collecting. Sterne finds sharing and hoarding practices to be encoded into the very design of the MP3 format, which he considers to be a "cultural artifact" with a set of inscriptions left from its historical place and time in late capitalism. Inscribed by the social codes of consumer culture, and then encoded into a CODEC [coder-decoder software], the MP3 is "a form designed for massive exchange, casual listening and massive accumulation" (Sterne 2006, 838). The MP3, therefore, is more likely to be favored over other formats by distracted consumers seeking to accumulate digital libraries. A clash between the youthful digital music culture and the music industry appeared in the criminalization of sharing and hoarding activities that circumvented copy protections. The unprotected MP3 addressed the needs of the 1990s digerati, but ruffled the music industry, which rebuffed it and tried various means to banish and outlaw the format. The Big Four have favored alternative formats encumbered with digital rights management (DRM).

There has been experimentation with MP3 releases since the early days of the Celestial Jukebox. The service eMusic, with financial participation by the major labels, has distributed DRM-free MP3s for several years. Likewise, EMI promoted supposedly DRM-free music on the Apple iTunes store, although these tracks retained AAC encoding. Universal Music Group has announced plans to release MP3 versions of selected tracks through its own Web site. And Amazon.com now offers MP3 downloads from all four major labels to users in the United States.

It is important to remember the technology steps that led music fans and the music industry to these conditions. With a standard CD collection and a standard CD player, the music fan's experience of playing music is mediated only by the CD and the CD player. There are no extra steps requiring authentication or any other transactions requiring a user interface. The turntable was also a "dumb" interface. The introduction of a computer changes the equation fundamentally. Digital music files put music fans utterly at the mercy of wonkish computer and software vendors. If the client software fails to initialize properly, it will be impossible for the computer or the portable device to find the music file names necessary to generate the queue or playlist. Software GUIs (graphical user interfaces) restrict user controls over music files in ways that cannot be compared to the more direct and hands-on access to music through a CD player, cassette player, or record player. The playing and sharing of music stored in a collection of MP3 or AAC or WMA files are subject to compliance with sharing and hoarding policies dictated by the new formats and by their software players. The content industries have tried to take away the record and copy buttons from consumer appliances for generations of media formats. Sony Betamax, TiVO, peer-to-peer, and MP3 players are all technology survivors of the content industry's attacks (although Betamax lost out to the VHS tape format in the marketplace).

The digital enclosure is tightened in communications online. Digital distribution through most online services is handled by legal transactions based on contract law. Music players also require users to agree to the terms of shrinkwrap or clickwrap contracts. Juridically, the Uniform Computer Information Transactions Act (UCITA) enabled "contractual enclosures" through clickwrap licensing (Benkler 2006, 444). The providing of music services is unregulated, so public-interest regulations related to communications do not apply. Thus, distributing music online as a service, rather than as a product for sale, improves intellectual property (IP) rights owners' control over newly licensed copies. This strategy also prevents music fans from becoming music collectors, even if they are paying customers of a music service. The relationship struck between a record label and a music service "user"—for example, in a EULA or terms of service agreement—accrues distinct advantages to the IP rights owners, as compared to the traditional relationship between a record label and a record buyer. As mentioned previously, Rhapsody's EULA strips fans of most rights as a condition of sale. The future right of first sale in general is a dubious prospect, based on the legal history of "digital phonorecords" (Hyde 2001). But the devil is in the details. The EULA, terms of service agreements, and other policies of iTunes run 10,500 words (26 pages), Rhapsody's run 7,700 words (19 pages), eMusic's is 6,500 words (16 pages), and Yahoo Music's come in at a whopping 14,554 words (36 pages), as of early 2008. These documents are subject to change without notice.

Because entire collections are made to "disappear" when subscriptions run out, or when authentication schemes break because of hardware or software problems, the music collector is always subjected to arbitrary conditions imposed by technology.[7] The rollouts of the iTunes music store and most of its competitors, therefore, have introduced deliberate bottlenecks to the new flows of music that emanated from the "Rip/Mix/Burn" distribution method and also from the P2P file-sharing culture. The shareability of the digital file formats, or the very source of new value that McCourt identifies with digital archives, is typically illegal outside most digital music enclosures.

"Users" who are "authenticated" are subjected to continual online surveillance, and must relinquish any rights to anything of value that they generate in the enclosure. Perhaps even more seriously, and more disturbingly, surveillance can become internalized emotionally, so that users willingly perform the "work of being watched" and contribute to the value of their own user profiles as cyber-commodities (Andrejevic 2003; Mosco 1996). The wage relationship created from music fans' participating in online digital "enclosures" introduces a new and internalized power dynamic tied to music fandom and to the activity of listening to music where one did not previously exist before digital distribution. In joining a digital enclosure like a music-service provider, a music fan not only gives up a personal right to property (a musical product), but also concedes to innumerable legal terms and conditions that do not expire. Consumers have attributes, preferences, spending power, and histories, and a narrow set of legal rights that are (at best) lightly enforced by state agencies and courts. Consumers, as clients of firms, take only what they can get, in individuated transactions, and follow rules enforced by contract law that overwhelmingly favor the interests of the firms.

The Internet's development in colleges and universities historically shielded university networks from unwanted attention by the culture industries and slowed the juridification and clientelization of Internet users at colleges and universities. But, as addressed in chapter 1, university networks have been under increasing pressure since the Napster Watershed, and now bear the brunt of the "new enclosure movement" (Benkler, 2006): "The institutions of higher education, which have found themselves under attack for not policing their students' use of peer-to-peer networks, have been entirely ineffective at presenting their cultural and economic value and the importance of open Internet access to higher education, as compared to the hypothetical losses of Hollywood and the recording industry" (411).

Networks once accepted as zones of experimentation now attract special scrutiny. The RIAA sponsors legislation that would commit federal funds for surveillance of university networks for P2P activity (N. Anderson 2007b); thus, federal lawmakers have targeted university networks with rules for policing, deterring, and providing "alternatives" to P2P file sharing (McCullagh 2007), under the threat of having all $100 billion a year in federal financial aid withdrawn. Many university network administrators, rather than investigating noninfringing uses of P2P networking protocols and defending students' rights to enjoy them, have opted instead for a heavy-handed approach of blocking or "dialing down," or reducing, bandwidth available for P2P transfers on university-managed networks. Various distributions of Linux depend upon P2P networks for reaching the free software community, because it is a cost-free approach to providing content on the Internet; thus, "dialing down" P2P on university campuses can also "dial down" access to free software, Skype, and other noninfringing uses of P2P.

While many universities oppose these intrusions, others have preemptively begun running filtering software on their networks, including Red Lambda technology at the University of Florida, and AudibleMagic at the University of Utah's and Wittenberg University's (Ohio) networks (McCullagh 2007). The AudibleMagic system automatically enforces online policies that resemble a system of high school hall monitors and passes. Audible-Magic's marketing materials divulge a regulationist intent for the networks of free thinkers, experimenters, and intelligentsia: "CopySense Network Appliance with new capabilities specifically tailored to campus networks. The CopySense Appliance can now help educate users toward appropriate network use with notices or messages that respond to attempts to violate network policy. It can also place pre-programmed temporary restrictions on a repeat violator's network access" (AudibleMagic n.d.). Even more draconian policies have crippled some campus networks: "Ohio University has taken the unusual step of banning peer-to-peer software on its campus... in response to the [RIAA's]... accusing students... of being the most prolific in swapping music files online in violation of copyright law" ("Ohio U. Bans P2P" 2007). University faculty are experiencing administrative pressures from network administrators to avoid researching with anonymizing software like Tor (Cesarini 2007).

More troubling still, the country of France has become among the first highly developed democracies to propose a countrywide filtering of the Internet for copyright regulation: "Internet users in France who download music and films without paying for them could find their access shut down by a government body, under a groundbreaking industry agreement backed by... the president" (Hall 2007). The notion of imposing an Internet ban on anyone evokes scorn and disbelief among cyberlibertarian techies ("There's some tough competition when it comes to 'most stupid politicians in the world.' Do French right wingers have some special advantage, like negative IQs?"),[8] as did earlier regulationist fantasies such as ubiquitous DRM. Yet the very existence of these discourses helps establish the boundaries and the frames of reference that will condition people's expectations and taken-for-granteds about online culture, and will help determine the extent to which cyberliberties activists must fight to "reappropriate society from the state" (Carroll and Hackett 2006, 418).

Copyright-term extension on the U.S. model is poised to take over in Canada and the European Union. Together with pan-European copyright licensing (Buck 2005) and software patents, the broadening and deepening of online enclosures is a current danger zone. In other parts of the E.U. bureaucracy, however, such as the Telecoms Commission, structural reforms such as telecom breakups have been promoted (Buck and Parker 2007), and the European Competition Commission has stepped up anti-trust pressures against Microsoft (including the imposition of heavy fines) since its 2004 findings of anticompetitive behavior (Ricciuti 2008). The ground underneath cyberliberties is constantly shifting.

Stepping outside the Enclosures

So where can collectors and fans assert their autonomy and communicative competence online without interference? The internal coherence of the concept of the popular-music scene is evasive, and has been theorized variously as refuge, locale, genre, and subculture (Hesmondhalgh 2005). I have mostly avoided the use of "scene" preferring the concept of "places of music" or "places for music" to denote aspects of a shared music lifeworld online and offline. Music fans have begun to migrate to MP3 blogs and other online affinity groups that fall outside of commercial music portals and other enclosures, some of which intersect with local music scenes, and some of which do not (Heuman 2008; Harvey 2008). If the online music world develops in such a way that music scenes are reproduced or extended in online contexts, then "spectators [can] become fans, fans [can] become musicians, [and] musicians [can] always already [be] fans" (Shank 1994, 131). In any of these contexts, the theory of communicative action enables us to think about a scene as potentially facilitating participation and access among its participants and reinforcing lifeworld processes.

There is a purposive, ethical, and normative dimension to the online art and music scenes organized in this way. Coombe and Herman (2001) offer something like an ethical duty of the culture industries to generate "new forms of responsibility and social accountability" (943), advocating a more negotiable set of norms for art and music scenes than those currently permitted under a punitive orthodoxy. For participant-fans, they valorize interventionist and interruptive art and music that broaden the discussion of the copyfights raging within the culture industries. In the spirit of John Perry Barlow and contemporary culture jammers, they portray "culture as a verb, not a noun" (2001, 922) and push for scenes in which "interactive ethics" might challenge "systems of univocal proprietary control" and their "impositions of privilege" (943). This interventionist conception of art scenes resembles the "semiotic democracy" imagined by Vaidhyanathan (2004, 303–304), and asserts the primacy of culture over technology (Vaidhyanathan 2001, 160); nonetheless, it rests on both a deliberative model of rationality and an expectation that deliberation will assist political actors in identifing and balancing the interests of all its stakeholders.

In new social movement politics, carving out a stakeholder identity begins with demands for recognition of, and respect for, a distinct cultural identity (Fraser and Honneth 2003). These demands are cultural and political at once, and are often expressed through messages handled in alternative media systems. The observable cultural politics of music and cyberliberties activists are disputes that are expressed in different modes or styles by artists, fans, artists, hackers, jurists, educators, and librarians, and by people with mixed roles. In reasserting a hacker ethic for cybercultures, Coombe and Herman (2001) see in art and music scenes social institutions for affective communication and self-discovery, as well as social laboratories for working through the new politics of the culture industries. Online music scenes may become the beginnings of a "cooperative search of deliberating citizens for solutions to political problems" through a "competition for better reasons . . . built into communicative action" (Habermas 2006, 413), semiautonomous zones for incubating debates and new ideas about cultural and information policies.

The incommensurability of the two "worlds" of collecting music emerged along with a broader change of worldviews about culture and information as intellectual property, and with a subsequent "change of state" that institutionalized these worldviews recently (Braman 2007). The impacts have yet to "sink in" completely in the music world. The rapid loss of user control over technology, in itself, strains against the music collector's ego, and the controlled life of the music fan within the digital enclosure seems incommensurable with the music fan who once went to record stores and bought, sold, traded, and collected CDs, LPs, and cassettes; who made and shared mix tapes; who retained rights of first sale; and who did not execute a losing legal transaction upon obtaining every recording or listening to every song in a collection. In the end, the major labels' approach to digital distribution tries to suspend commodity fetishism, which is at the heart of the collector's desire to collect. The restricted shareability of music outside discrete online enclosures reduces the chance that music fans, especially former collectors, will identify a value in digital music files worth paying for. Given their obsession with control over making choices about playing music, why would music collectors choose to become subscribers to a music service that extinguishes so many aspects of users' control over music collections? There is a good chance that most music fans will add digital distribution to a media mix that still retains access to physical-media archives. But at what price to the autonomy of the fans?

And will local music scenes pay a price for the absence of record stores or face-to-face encounters at shows and festivals? Besides the aesthetics of music collecting and participation in music scenes, there is an also an ethic of cyberliberties, shared in record collecting and fandom, that can inform the choices of becoming a music user or abandoning a recorded-music collection.

Gillespie (2007a) summarizes the predicament in which record collectors find themselves, in which they are partly excluded from the music cultures with which they identify:

Questions of ownership of music in the financial sense are tangled with, and thus have to deal with, a sense of ownership of music in other senses, i.e. cultural ownership. This is deeply part of what record collectors and fans are about, and is also very much what shared playlists is about—this is "my" music. So both fan orientations, hoarding and sharing, depend on this sense of ownership; but in the first case, it neatly aligned with financial ownership, whereas in the context of subscription services and licensed music, the sense of ownership inside of sharing is imagined to run counter to financial ownership. . . . It's a fundamental point to the investigation of copyright questions, but it too often goes unstated.

In the transition to all-digital music distribution, the collector's fetish, which is also a commodity fetish, is being tested with a substitute control fantasy. This fantasy is associated with searching, finding, and playing any song, any time—yet another media "pushbutton fantasy" (Mosco 1982). The pushbutton fantasy carries the music industry to its ultimate mode of production as a service by substituting precise and deep search-query returns for the desire to own and maintain a personal collection of material artifacts: "The disappearance of hard goods, in the form of physical recordings, heightens the transition from a world of cultural goods to a world of cultural services. The result is that 'value' is not an inherent character of the product, but the manner in which it reaches the consumer" (McCourt 2005, 251).

In the cultural enclosures created by IP law, contract law, and computer software, music collectors face losing property, control and usability, legal rights of first sale, consumer-product protections, and other customary rights and privileges associated with being a legal subject and a consumer. It remains largely unclear who and what are in charge of the manner in which music reaches the music fan who has signed up for cultural services. Fortunately, recourse to the physical world for access to music is, of course, very much still an option, though one undergoing transformation and, perhaps, disintegration.

Restoring practices of physical archiving may even become like an ethic to those who collect music diligently. The collector and the cyberlibertarian share the values of individual autonomy over technology and of shared access to culture. Access to art and culture is "a major and integral part of the transaction that engenders political behavior" (Murray Edelman 1995, 42). Art and culture form a "reservoir of images which inform political impulses and inspire politically motivated actions" (42). When music, art, and culture inspire politically motivated actions about the future conditions for making and enjoying media, reflexive and discursive expressions of social agency can emerge.

CHAPTER SIX

Conclusion

✳

In this book I have presented the flip side of the story of the rise of the Celestial Jukebox: that there is, at the very least, a "loyal opposition" to it. What I have asked is whether or not there is in it a spark of an incipient social movement. I began with an analysis of the whipsawing effects of the passing of the Napster Watershed on the music lifeworld, and on music fans' basic expectations about culture sharing on the Internet that are left over from this painful event. I have looked for evidence for strategy in the mobilization of symbols and resources in support of cyberlibertarian values, including continued access to, and participation in, shared music cultures. I have found elements of oppositional movements that are worldwide and savvy about new technologies, alternative business models, social solidarity, and music fans' obsession with communicating about and sharing music. But I have *not* found strong evidence for an offensive and strategically oriented movement, or for a convergence between linked modes of activism.

The developments in musical production and regulation I have covered are relevant to media, communication, and cultural studies, political economy of culture, and social and political theory. In posing the music and cyberliberties research question as a question about both agency and structure, I have tested the ability of second-generation critical theory to (1) offer explanatory and interpretive perspectives on music and cyberliberties activism, and (2) lend practical wisdom in the service of cyberlibertarian reforms. I have also provided reasons why other approaches in music studies — including political economy, media economics, and fan studies — are insufficient or otherwise inappropriate for addressing the social agency supporting music fandom and music activism.

In addressing the processes of identity formation, changing cultural politics, and social integration, second-generation critical theory offers some purchase on how and why cyberliberties activism such as hacktivism, culture jamming, radical media, and many other efforts to bypass or jam the record industry's influences are now occurring, and why any of it should matter at all to music fans, artists, and researchers. As music fans become entangled in the technocratic web of contract law, IP law, online payments, perpetual surveillance, and other abusive technology practices, simply to enjoy their music, they lose an important measure of freedom and autonomy that has been taken from the music lifeworld. Using the TCA's (theory of communicative action) basic explication of lifeworld colonization, I have tried to identify concrete social harms to cultural freedom that fans suffer worldwide in the expansionist, regulationist system that has been imposed on the Internet.[1] I have argued that music and cyberliberties activism expresses a basic revulsion toward technocratic controls over music culture. This sensibility suffuses and informs people's identities, cultural attitudes, and oppositional social action.

But without a doubt, the TCA also has some limitations and other weaknesses. I have argued that these are not built-in, and try to show where these are correctable and amenable to further debates and revisions. First, I have pointed to the interdependencies in lifeworld processes of identity formation, cultural politics, and socialization that exist in the music lifeworld. I have also highlighted examples of shared system-and-lifeworld domains, and provided evidence of uncoupling of the music lifeworld from the technocratic system. Second, I have pointed to work by Downing, Lovink, Benkler, Schuler and Day, and others that seems well suited to update Habermas's anachronistic public sphere model. Radical media, alternative media, tactical media, peering, and other networking activities arise from the music lifeworld; they are also often reflexively centered on lifeworld communication about individual rights and liberties, shared culture, and oppositional collective action. The real work of making the arguments for cyberliberties, again and again, is normatively based in the music lifeworld, where it also hopes to find worldwide appeal and political support.

Third, the broadly intercultural and international dimensions of struggle against the Celestial Jukebox, and creation of alternative services,[2] provide an opportunity for updating the TCA's restricted focus on public-sphere politics, as mediated by national media systems. As such concepts as "networked" or "virtual public sphere" demonstrate, the "original" public-sphere concept that was developed in the 1980s around mass-media models was soon to be upstaged by the Internet and personal networking. By 1996, it was recognized by the U.S. Supreme Court that the Internet provided "a never-ending worldwide conversation" and the "most participatory form of mass speech yet developed" (*ACLU v. Reno*). Finally, cyberlibertarian norms

exist globally among Internet users, requiring a broadening of scope for the public-sphere concept.

Technology studies and popular cultural studies go stale; new legal precedents, innovations in business models and genres, new hardware and software and networking systems, disruptive world-historical events, and other unpredictable and "external" factors can all challenge their validity and their relevance. For music and media scholarship on science and technology to provide lasting lessons and remain relevant, it should focus more on social problems that are related to changing forms of music production, distribution, and regulation, while admitting every opportunity for radical disruptions of everyday technology practices.

The Future of Music Coalition Manifesto
June 1, 2000

＊

We build this organization as an attempt both to address pressing music-technology issues and to serve as a voice for musicians in Washington, D.C., where critical decisions are being made regarding musicians' intellectual property rights without a word from the artists themselves.＊

- No longer will corporate media and big money be able to frame the discussion of music solely in terms of their industries, as we draw together the strongest voices in the technology and independent music communities to address questions of music in the marketplace with a clear-eyed focus on the interests of the artists.
- No longer will business interests or lobby groups for business interests drown out the voices of the musicians on whose art they have built an industry.
- No longer will idealistic techies and idealistic musicians find themselves locked into opposing sides of an issue that profoundly affects both of our communities.

We begin this organization with the intention of addressing three pressing areas of concern.

1. Piracy / Technological Innovation

The Future of Music Organization is founded on the belief that creation is valuable and should be compensated. Here we are speaking of both musical creation and technological creation. By drawing together advocates for musicians' rights and innovators in Internet technology, we will work to move

＊*Source:* http://www.futureofmusic.org/manifesto/.
As this book was going to press, the Future of Music Coalition was in the process of drafting a new manifesto. According to Casey Rae-Hunter, the organization's communications director, the new document will "frame our core convictions (musicians' middle class, equitable compensation structures for artists, access to tools of media, etc.) in a more contemporarily relevant context."

the discussion away from the narrow privacy vs. piracy discussions that dominate the general media, toward practical solutions leveraging the strengths of digital download technology on behalf of the artists. Our work will encourage the development of innovative Internet music business models to guard the value of musicians' labor and ensure that artists will continue to be paid for their compositions and performances despite drastic changes in methods of distribution.

2. The RIAA's Conflict of Interest

The Recording Industry Association of America is a special interest group that claims from time to time to lobby on behalf of musicians, but it is funded by, and represents the interests of, the major record companies—the same corporations traditionally known to be the primary exploiters of the musicians that the RIAA claims to represent. The RIAA simply cannot be trusted to serve two distinct masters—the record companies and the artists. An important example is the "work for hire" issue: the RIAA pushed legislation that gives major labels the right to own musicians' master tapes in perpetuity, changing an existing law that allowed some artists to regain the rights to their masters after 35 years. By advocating for this language, even while claiming to have the artists' interests at heart, the RIAA made it clear that it is compromised, and cannot be left to its own devices in the policy-making arena.

In a more frightening development, the RIAA is attempting to step beyond its traditional lobbying role in order to enter the music-licensing business by collecting and distributing royalties from webcasts. While there is clearly a need for an organization to manage these royalties (webcasting royalties could result in more money than currently collected by BMI and ASCAP combined), the Future of Music has no confidence in the RIAA's ability to represent the voice of musicians or to collect and distribute artists' royalties from the major labels who fund the RIAA.

The Future of Music therefore advocates for an impartial and accountable organization to guard the value of artists' webcasting royalties. By standing in opposition to the RIAA we hope to give voice to the concerns of musicians who are simply not represented by an organization whose core mission is promotion and protection of the record industry agenda.

3. SDMI

The Secure Digital Music Initiative (SDMI), spearheaded by the RIAA, was an attempt to pull together a limited group of powerful consumer electronics manufacturers; PC manufacturers, and record labels to develop a copyright-enabled alternative to the MP3 format. It is viewed by many as a misguided and desperate scramble by those in the existing music business monopoly to maintain their stranglehold on the channels of distribution through the application of a standardized encryption or watermarking program.

As with most technologies that are conceived and developed in a no-feedback vacuum, without the desires of potential consumers in mind (not to mention an understanding of the limits of encryption technology), it was destined to fail. As much has been said by Executive Director Leonard Chiariglione, whose comments at the May 2000 SDMI meetings revealed a combination of infighting between competing business interests and fatal flaws in the group's structure, which requires all decisions to be made by consensus. While SDMI members bicker and veto proposals based on the personal financial interests of their multinational corporations, consumers are presented with narrow, confusing options that alienate them and thus do more to promote piracy, which becomes the only viable mode of digital transfer for the great majority of the world's existing music.

The Future of Music believes SDMI is a perfect example of what happens when industry attempts to legislate technological advances without the crucial input of musicians and programmers.

Notes

✳

Introduction

1. The Celestial Jukebox is the actual or envisioned technology and policy regime that accommodates the media business model of the "pay-per society" (Mosco 1989).

2. The rate of change in the differentiation of the music market into digital music has been rapid: "Nielsen SoundScan reports that while album sales were down 4.9 percent in 2006 over the previous year, digital track sales increased by 65 percent with 582 million songs sold. Digital album sales more than doubled, reaching almost 33 million sold in 2006" (Plunkett Research 2007b, 7). However, total revenues from CD sales declined 6 percent from 2004 to 2005 (Plunkett Research 2007a, 22), and "digital music has not yet achieved the 'holy grail' of compensating for the decline in CD sales" (IFPI 2007, 4).

3. The lifeworld "remains at the backs of participants in communication" and "is present to them only in the prereflective form of taken-for-granted background assumptions and naively mastered skills" (Habermas 1984, 335). The concept of the lifeworld is derived from Husserl's phenomenology, which was adapted for social science by Alfred Schutz. "By the everyday life-world is to be understood that province of reality which the wide-awake and normal adult simply takes for granted in the attitude of common sense" (Schutz and Luckman 1973, 3).

4. Authority is "the right to command" and "the right to be obeyed," and is distinguished from power, which is "the ability to compel compliance, either through the use or the threat of force" (Wolff 1970, 4). I consider autonomy a concept of personal freedom that, after Benkler, can be measured as a combination of the capacity to do for and by one's self, to work and communicate "in loose commonality with others" independently of a market, and to participate in formal, noncommercial organizations (Benkler 2007, 8).

5. The music industry has ceded about 70 percent of all revenues from distribution to Apple, which was a nonindustry player until 2003, when the iTunes store was introduced.

6. "Culture" refers to the "stock of knowledge from which participants in communication supply themselves with interpretations as they come to an understanding about something in the world"; "society" denotes "the legitimate orders through which participants regulate their memberships in social groups and thereby secure solidarity"; and "personality" refers to the "competences that make a subject capable of speaking and acting, that put him in a position to take part in processes of reaching understanding and thereby to assert his own identity" (Habermas 1987, 138). These three zones are landmarks of the lifeworld.

7. The Frankfurt School's concept of reification of commodities drew on Marx and Weber in presenting the instrumental, rational processes of production in an unfree but rational capitalist industry. Lukács developed the concept further.

1. Saving a Place for Music

1. The industry has insisted on increasingly strict rules for the new generation of "home tapers" who now "rip" their CDs. Marc Fisher notes in the *Washington Post* (December 30, 2007, M5) that, more recently still, "In legal documents in its federal case against Jeffrey Howell, a Scottsdale, Ariz., man who kept a collection of about 2,000 music recordings on his personal computer, the industry maintains that it is illegal for someone who has *legally* purchased a CD to transfer that music into his computer."

2. The Windows Vista OS shuts off data bus functions on the computer motherboard if the software detects a violation of a DRM sharing policy from a peripheral device.

3. Examples of noninfringing uses of P2P include the distribution of public-domain, cost-free, copylefted, and Creative Commons–licensed IP, including music, text, and video.

4. Some indie hybrids get services such as distribution from the majors. This turn of events has followed the buyouts of major distributors of catalogue items from independent labels, such as Caroline (bought by Virgin, and then EMI) and Mordam (bought by Lumberjack and Warner). Working much closer to the big leagues, Matthew Garrahan writes in the *Financial Times* (April 10, 2007) of hybrid music producers, marketers, and distributors such as The Firm, a talent management group that represents Snoop Dogg, Ice Cube, and Kelly Clarkson, among others (April 10, 2007). Jeff Kwatinetz, founder of The Firm, says, "The industry is set up wrong and the business model is all wrong. . . . If I told you there were four companies making all the food in the world and that I owned one of them you would think I was a rich guy. Music isn't as essential as food but it's something that is everywhere and is consumed by everyone. Yet the four companies that control the industry don't make a billion dollars between them."

5. The main digital distributors for indie labels are IODA (International Online Distribution Alliance), DRA (The Digital Rights Agency), IRIS (the biggest distributor of electronic music online), and eMusic (in addition to having its own sales

portal, eMusic also sub-distributes its content to third-party online stores). They all claim to work with metadata catalogues and marketing. The application services tend to be handled by the front-end stores taking the music—i.e., iTunes—as well as a company called Loudeye, in Seattle, which streams many of these distributors' content to them (Schalit, 2007, personal communication).

6. The fair use doctrine of copyright law exempts some copyrighted materials from potential IP-rights claims in special circumstances.

7. In software and technology, "patent thickets" are set up purposefully to discourage innovations in an area dominated by one firm or by a cartel.

2. Creating the Music Lifeworld Online

1. Notwithstanding the record industry's own claim at court that ripping one's own CDs to a music player or backup disk may not be lawful (see note 2 to chapter 1), the practice continues.

2. A purely functionalist systems-theoretical approach cannot account for communicative rationality or access lifeworld processes, and therefore has a limited impact on technology and policy debates affecting culture. See Luhmann (1982). The ability of social systems theory to become critical is widely debated (McCarthy 1985, Baxter 1987, Calhoun 1995.)

3. Public radio stations that had also Webcast their programming were among the early movers against the royalty increases, and pressed for a legislative appeal in the Internet Radio Equality Act (HR 2060) (WTMD 2007).

4. The digital broadcast flag has repeatedly been pushed in the United States by the copyright lobby. Its defeat at court in 2005 was a legal victory won by Public Knowledge.

5. "Small worlds" file sharing is intentionally restricted sharing among a trusted circle.

6. Although fan studies, critical-cultural studies, and text-centered interpretive approaches to music also explore colonization, they do not offer normative social theories that are grounded in communication or communicative rationality. Nor do they ground human agency in communication.

7. In 2007, FCC chairman Martin succeeded in accomplishing his goal of lifting most remaining ownership caps among newspapers and broadcasters in the same markets.

8. Similarly, Google's page-caching function provides workarounds to legally required Internet filtering in U.S. libraries and schools.

9. To illustrate the first example, eJamming Audio has developed an Internet-based software platform for creating a live performance among geographically dispersed players. Other companies are also developing online music collaboration applications.

10. "Contributory infringement...requires (1) knowledge of the infringing activity and (2) a material contribution—actual assistance or inducement—to the alleged piracy" (Stanford Center for Internet and Society n.d.)

11. The Pho listserv and the Slashdot.org forums became important online venues for reporting and discussing the technical risks of both the rootkit and the deceptive rootkit "fix" that was not really a fix.

12. An assistant professor at Bowling Green State University has documented challenges of academic freedom for Tor researchers by campus "network security technicians" (Cesarini 2007).

13. Sony's proprietary Blu-Ray standard has since overtaken HD-DVD for consumer electronics, and Blu-Ray's encryption was hacked before the format even began its take-off stage.

14. Of course, corporate network security technologies have learned from and adapted to DDoS (distributed denial-of-service) attacks. See, for example, Juniper Networks (2008).

15. Searle (1969) and Mead (1967) contribute components of speech act theory that are incorporated into the theory of communicative action. Edelman (1971) anticipated some of Habermas's political insignts.

16. The Marxist imperialist thesis was enumerated by Lenin and Hilferding, and variants have been adopted in political economy in the notion of "cultural imperialism" (H. Schiller 1991).

17. Unencrypted AAC files still retain the FairPlay DRM "envelope" that contains copy-protected AAC files. "Songs sold without DRM still have a user's full name and account e-mail embedded in them, which means that dropping that new DRM-free song on your favorite P2P network could come back to bite you" (Fisher 2007).

18. "Small worlds" P2P file-sharing groups and CD-ripping circles remain private, and are not open to the entire world via the Internet, as are services like Morpheus and Kazaa.

19. The discrepancy arises between the estimates of the American Association of Independent Music (AAIM) and Nielsen SoundScan. AAIM estimates market share of indie music higher than Nielsen ("What is fair market share?" 2006).

3. Culture Clashes on the Internet

1. Another, the right of first sale, is precluded by the licensing terms of music-service providers.

2. Hatch is himself a recording artist. Examples of his works can be found at http://www.hatchmusic.com/.

3. As the last chapter explained, the sociological approach of the theory of communicative action considers processes of functional integration (occurring in institutions of the state and market) alongside processes of social integration (in culture and society).

4. Contract reform for iTunes Store sales is needed, because the iTunes store is a reseller for labels, because artists remain in their royalty agreements with labels,

and because these agreements still typically deduct from artists' payments charges for nonexistent CD packaging, breakage, and "new technologies" (FOMC n.d.).

5. Downhill Battle does not, however, critique DRM. In fact, it had endorsed a now-defunct "pay P2P" scheme called Weedshare.

6. Spiralfrog began offering users "free" downloads of catalog items from Vivendi-Universal in 2006 in return for watching advertisements on its Web site. The downloads offered are MP3s and WMAs wrapped in PlaysForSure DRM ("Free SpiralFrog" 2006). PlaysForSure DRM was cracked by Viodentia in 2006 ("Microsoft's Windows" 2006).

7. In 2007, the Free Software Foundation created "a fund to help provide computer expert witnesses to combat RIAA's ongoing lawsuits, and to defend against the RIAA's attempt to redefine copyright law" (Free Software Foundation 2007).

8. Subsequently, a temporary but renewable DMCA exemption for copying DVD clips for film studies classes was sought and won by university professors (see chapter 4).

9. Habermas introduced the notion of a legitimacy crisis of Western European political systems in 1975. While the music industry is not a political system, it has participated in processes of material and symbolic reproduction shared by political systems, and frequently makes appeals to clients that are noneconomic and normative.

10. There is a resistance movement in Canada against a DMCA-like law, led by Michael Geist, Canada Research Chair of Internet and Media Law, University of Ottawa, Canada.

11. Parts of the following section are taken from Burkart (2009) in *Making Our Media*.

4. Projects and Prospects

1. Ideology is an "instrumental distortion of image and information" that is "imposed by class power" and "based on...coercion" (Mosco 1996, 242–243).

2. Taylorization is the practice of managerial control over work that separates conception and execution of labor, both manual and intellectual. See Henry Braverman, *Labor and Monopoly Capital*. New York: Monthly Review Press, 1974.

3. Michael O'Donnell (2008) characterizes the cyberlibertarians' oppositional discourses as "shrill."

4. MUDs and MOOs were among the earliest interactive social spaces constructed for the Internet, and were text-only for a long time. MUDs were "multiuser dungeons," and MOOs were "MUD object oriented" virtual spaces.

5. The landmark 1993 case of Steve Jackson Games v. Secret Service (EFF n.d. e) "was the first step toward establishing that online speech IS speech, and entitled to Constitutional protection."

6. The Indymedia is a nonprofit collective of DIY journalists and "one of the more dynamic innovations in global social justice media use" (Downing 2008, 47).

5. Ethics and Aesthetics

1. This chapter is adapted from Burkart 2008b.

2. Recent attempts to build a "hybrid" pay-P2P service have failed, including the Weedshare program.

3. Walter Benjamin, who identified cultural disenchantment in the substitution of mechanically produced, modern reproductions for original works of art, also linked "original" pieces of art to an authentic "aura."

4. From a Webcaster's perspective, music flows are representable as lists. Licensed Webcasters are required to submit both playlists and listener logs in the United States to government-sanctioned auditors.

5. Apple's iTunes store unveiled its Genius music recommendation feature in 2008, late for a music service provider. Its recommendations, naturally, reflected the lapses of the iTunes catalog. Stiteler (2008) reported that Genius returns an error with Beatles songs (which had long been unavailable for digital distribution).

6. Users of unpaid peer-to-peer services are more likely to "gorge" on free music downloads than users of paid music services: "Peer-to-peer networks yielded five billion downloads in 2006, whereas 509 million songs were downloaded from iTunes-style services" (Mindlin 2007).

7. In 2008, Walmart notified its music store cutomers that, "Beginning October 9, we will no longer be able to assist with digital rights management issues for protected WMA files purchased from Walmart.com," because it was disabling its authentication servers (Doctorow 2008).

8. Blogger "MPE" on Slashdot.org/yro (http://yro.slashdot.org/article.pl?sid=07/11/23/1355220).

6. Conclusion

1. The new sensibility, and the new politics, of cyberliberties derive in part from the absurdity of the emergent conflicts. For example, University of Washington researchers have demonstrated that "it is possible for a malicious user (or buggy software) to implicate (frame) seemingly any network endpoint in the sharing of copyrighted materials," namely, by showing how inanimate (but networked) objects have received DMCA "takedown notices" (Piatek, Kohno, and Krishnamurthy, 2008). In the case of U.W. researchers, their laser printer received a DMCA takedown notice.

2. A new generation of commercial digital distribution services has grown up alongside and in competition with iTunes, including Amazon, Beatport, Bell Mobility Full Track, Bleep, Boomkat, eMusic, Fina, GroupieTunes, Lala, Last.fm Radio, Limewire Subscription, Limewire a La Carte, Livewire Mobile / Groove Mobile, Mbop Digital, Mix and Burn, Mod Systems, mTraks, Napster, Navio / gBox, Other Music, Puretracks, Rhapsody, Rogers Wireless, Ruckus Network, SecuryCast Download, Slacker, Spiral Frog, Sprint, T-Online, and Verizon (Schalit 2008).

References

✳

A2K [Access to Knowledge]. n.d. A2K Treaty. Http://www.access2knowledge.org/cs/taxonomy_menu/5?PHPSESSID=bf6842d4c5d699c5523f44.

ACLU [American Civil Liberties Union]. 2004. Combating the surveillance industrial complex. Http://aclu.org/safefree/resources/18512res20040809.html.

———. 2005. ACLU letter to Attorney General Gonzales requesting the appointment of Outside Special Counsel for the investigation and prosecution of violations, or conspiracy to violate, criminal laws against warrantless wiretapping of American persons. Http://www.aclu.org/safefree/general/23184leg20051221.html.

———. n.d. Cyber-Liberties. Http://www.aclu.org/cyberliberties/index.html.

Alderman, John. 2001. *Sonic boom: Napster, P2P, and the battle for the future of music.* Cambridge, Mass.: Perseus Press.

Alliance for Public Technology et al. 2003. Brief of amicus curiae in support of appellant Verizon Internet Services and urging reversal. September 16. Http://www.epic.org/privacy/copyright/verizon/Appeal_1_amicus.pdf.

Andersen, Heine. 1990. Morality in three social theories: Parsons, analytical Marxism and Habermas. *Acta sociologica* 33 (4): 321–339.

Anderson, Nate. 2006. Hacking digital rights management. *ArsTechnica*, July 18. Http://arstechnica.com/articles/culture/drmhacks.ars.

———. 2007a. New bill lets colleges use federal funds to fight P2P. *ArsTechnica*, April 2. Http://arstechnica.com/news.ars/post/20070402-new-bill-lets-colleges-use-federal-funds-to-fight-p2p.html.

———. 2007b. Universities help overturn P2P amendment, with help from you. *Ars Technica*, July 25. Http://arstechnica.com/news.ars/post/20070725-universities-help-overturn-p2p-amendment.html.

Andrejevic, Mark. 2002. The work of being watched: Interactive media and the exploitation of self-disclosure. *Critical Studies in Media Communication* 19 (2): 230–248.

———. 2003. Tracing space: Monitored mobility in the era of mass customization. *Space and Culture* 6 (2):132–150.

Apple iTunes Store. 2008. Terms of Service. Http://www.apple.com/legal/itunes/us/service.html.

Aronowitz, Stanley. 1993. *Roll over Beethoven: The return of cultural strife*. Hanover, N.H.: University Press of New England / Wesleyan University Press.

AT&T. 2007. *Daytona*. Http://www.research.att.com/~daytona/.

AudibleMagic. n.d. Peace of Mind with P2P. Http://www.audiblemagic.com/pdf/peace_of_mind.pdf.

Aufderheide, Patricia. 1999. *Communications policy and the public interest: The Telecommunications Act of 1996*. New York: Guilford Press.

Aune, James Arnt. 2001. *Selling the free market: The rhetoric of economic correctness*. New York: Guilford Press.

Bad Subjects Collective. 1995. Manifesto for bad subjects in cyberspace. Http://badeserver.org/issues/1995/18/manifesto.html.

Bangeman, Eric. 2005. "Analog hole" legislation introduced. *ArsTechnica*, December 18. Http://arstechnica.com/news.ars/post/20051218-5797.html.

———. 2007. "Day of silence" coming to Internet radio. *ArsTechnica*, June 21. Http://arstechnica.com/news.ars/post/20070621-day-of-silence-coming-to-internet-radio-on-june-26.html.

Bannon, Lisa. 1996. The birds may sing, but campers can't unless they pay up. *Wall Street Journal*, August 21, Eastern edition, A1.

Barber, Benjamin R. 2007. *Consumed: How markets corrupt children, infantilize adults, and swallow citizens whole*. New York: W.W. Norton.

Barlow, John Perry. 1996. A declaration of the independence of cyberspace. Http://homes.eff.org/~barlow/Declaration-Final.html.

Baudrillard, Jean. 1998. *The consumer society: Myths and structures*. Thousand Oaks, Calif.: Sage.

Baxter, Hugh. 1987. System and life-world in Habermas's *Theory of Communicative Action*. *Theory and Society* 16:39–86.

Benjamin, Walter. 1968. *Illuminations*. Translated by Harry Zohn. New York: Harcourt, Brace & World.

Benkler, Yochai. 2006. *The wealth of networks: How social production transforms markets and freedom*. New Haven, Conn.: Yale University Press.

———. 2007. *The wealth of networks: how social production transforms markets and freedom*. New Haven, Conn.: Yale University Press.

Berger, Harris M. 2007. Personal communication. September 1.

Berger, J. 1991. The linguistification of the sacred and the delinguistification of the economy. In *Communicative action: Essays on Jürgen Habermas's The Theory of Communicative Action*, edited by Axel Honneth and Hans Joas, 163–180. Translated by Jeremy Gaines and Doris L. Jones. Cambridge, Mass.: MIT Press.

Berland, Jody. 1998. Locating listening: Technological space, popular music, and Canadian mediations. In *The place of music,* edited by Andrew Leyshon, David Matless, and George Revill, 129–150. New York: Guilford Press.

Born, Joe. 2006. Letter to the Honorable Chairman James Sensenbrenner Jr. and the Honorable Representative John Conyers, U.S. House of Representatives. Http://open.neurostechnology.com/files/dtcsa.html.

Boucher, Rick. n.d. Congressman Rick Boucher urges reaffirmation of fair use rights. Boycott-RIAA.com. Http://www.boycott-riaa.com/editorials/boucher.

Braman, Sandra. 2004. The emergent global information policy regime. In *The emergent global information policy regime*, edited by Sandra Braman, 12–38. New York: Palgrave Macmillan.

———. 2007. *Change of state: Information, policy, and power*. Cambridge, Mass.: MIT Press.

Braman, Sandra, and Stephanie Roberts. 2003. Advantage ISP: Terms of service as media law. *New Media and Society* 5(3): 422–448.

Brand, Stuart. 1974. *II cybernetic frontiers*. New York: Random House.

Brown, Robin. 2002. The contagiousness of conflict: E. E. Schattschneider as a theorist of the information society. *Information, Communication and Society* 5 (2): 258–275.

Buck, Tobias. 2005. Moves to aid online music providers. *Financial Times*, July 8, 27.

Buck, Tobias, and Andrew Parker. 2007. EU Commissioner favours telecoms break-up. *Financial Times*, March 29, 8.

Buechler, Steven M. 1993. Beyond resource mobilization? Emerging trends in social movement theory. *Sociological Quarterly* 34 (2):217–235.

Burkart, Patrick. 2005. Loose integration in the popular music industry. *Popular Music and Society* 28 (4):489–500.

———. 2008a. The Internet and American life. In *Battleground: The media*, edited by Robin Andersen and Jonathan Gray. Westport, Conn.: Praeger.

———. 2008b. Trends in digital music archiving. *The Information Society* 24 (4): 246–250.

———. 2009. Introduction to Kidd, Rodriguez, and Stein 2009, 153–160.

Burkart, Patrick, and Tom McCourt. 2004. Infrastructure for the Celestial Jukebox. *Popular Music* 23:349–362.

———. 2006. *Digital music wars: Ownership and control of the Celestial Jukebox*. Lanham, Md.: Rowman and Littlefield.

Burns, Gary. 2004. Fan culture, the Internet, and the British influence in popular music studies. *Journal of American Culture* 27 (2):199–209.

Buskirk, Eliot Van. 2007. MediaDefender leaked on BitTorrent. *Listening Post*, September 20. Http://blog.wired.com/music/2007/09/source-code-of-.html.

Calhoun, Craig. 1995. *Critical social theory: Culture, history, and the challenge of difference*. Cambridge, Mass.: Blackwell.

Carlson, Scott. 2006. Scholars win exemptions to digital-copyright act. *Chronicle of Higher Education* 53.16 (December 8):A31.

Carroll, William K., and Robert A. Hackett. 2006. Democratic media activism through the lens of social movement theory. *Media Culture and Society* 28 (1):83–104.

Castells, Manuel. 1996. *The rise of the network society*. Cambridge, Mass.: Blackwell.

CDD [Center for Digital Democracy]. n.d. X marks the spot. Http://www.demo craticmedia.org/news/washingtonwatch/BrandXfiles.html.

Cesarini, Paul. 2007. Caught in the network. *Chronicle of Higher Education*, 53.23 (February 9):B5.

CFP [Computers, Freedom, and Privacy]. 2006. About CFP. Http://www.cfp2006 .org/about.html.

Clarke, Ian. n.d. Background information on Ian Clarke. Http://locut.us/publicity/.

Clarke, Roger. 2000. Information wants to be free. Http://www.anu.edu.au/people/ Roger.Clarke/II/IWtbF.html.

Cohen, Jean L., and Andrew Arato. 1992. *Civil society and political theory*. Cambridge, Mass.: MIT Press.

Consumer Council of Norway. 2006. Complaint against iTunes Music Store. Http:// forbrukerportalen.no/filearchive/Complaint%20against%20iTunes%20Music%20 Store.pdf.

Coombe, Rosemary. 2006. Making music in the soundscapes of the law. In Demers 2006, vii–ix.

Coombe, Rosemary, and Andrew Herman. 2001. Culture wars on the net: Intellectual property and corporate propriety in digital environments. *South Atlantic Quarterly* 100 (4):919–947.

Cooper, M. 2003. Media ownership and democracy in the digital information age: Promoting diversity with First Amendment principles and market structure analysis. Washington, D.C.: Stanford University, Center for Internet and Society. Http://cyberlaw.stanford.edu/blogs/cooper/archives/mediabooke.pdf.

Coppock, Akua, Piper Nieters, Gunther Oakey, and Samantha Thompson. n.d. Comments on the promulgation of a broadcast flag rule: Before the Federal Communications Commission in the matter of Digital Broadcast Copy Protection, MB Docket 02-230. Http://www.ll.georgetown.edu/aallwash/BFComment.pdf.

Copps, M. 2005. The FCC past and present. Paper presented at National Media Reform Conference, St. Louis, Missori, May.

Couldry, Nick. 2003. *Media rituals: A critical approach*. New York: Routledge.

CPSR [Computer Professionals for Social Responsibility]. 2002. Digital rights management: Whose rights are being managed? White paper. April 22. Http:// trout.cpsr.org/program/ip/icac_drm_brief.html.

CRIS [Communication Rights in the Information Society]. 2005. *Assessing communication rights: A handbook*. Http://www.crisinfo.org/pdf/ggpen.pdf.

——. n.d. Http://www.crisinfo.org/.

Cunningham, Carolyn. 2009. The right to communicate: Democracy and the digital divide. In Kidd, Rodriguez, and Stein 2009, 207–222.

Curiel, Jonathan. 2004. The Yes Men. *San Francisco Chronicle*. October 1. Http://www .sfgate.com/cgi-bin/article.cgi?file=/chronicle/reviews/movies/YESMEN.DTL& type=movies.

Dahlberg, Lincoln. 2001. Democracy via cyberspace. *New Media and Society* 3 (2): 157–177.

———. 2005. The corporate colonization of online attention and the marginalization of critical communication? *Journal of Communication Inquiry* 29 (2):160–180.

D'Ambrosio, Antonio. 2004. Let fury have the hour: The punk rock politics of Joe Strummer. In *Let fury have the hour: The punk rock politics of Joe Strummer*, edited by Antonio D'Ambrosio 3–18. New York: Nation Books.

D.C. Circuit Court of Appeals. 2003. No. 03-7015, *Recording Industry Association of America, Inc., Appelee, v. Verizon Internet Services, Appellant.* Appeal from the United States District Court for the District of Columbia. Http://www.epic.org/privacy/copyright/verizon/dc-cir-op.pdf.

Deetz, Stanley A. 1992. *Democracy in an age of corporate colonization: Developments in communication and the politics of everyday life*. Albany: State University of New York Press.

Demers, Joanna. 2006. *Steal this music: How intellectual property law affects musical creativity*. Athens: University of Georgia Press.

"Digital music soars while revenues fall." 2008. Emarketer, January 30. Http://images.emarketer.com/Article.aspx?id=1005875.

Doctorow, Cory. 2003. *Down and out in the magic kingdom*. New York: Tor.

———. 2008. Wal*Mart shutting down DRM server, nuking your music—only people who pay for music risk losing it to DRM shenanigans. Boingboing, September 26. Http://boingboing.net/2008/09/26/walmart-shutting-dow.html.

———. 2005. Why some "piracy" can increase overall revenues. *Boing Boing*, August 24. Http://www.boingboing.net/2005/08/24/why-some-piracy-can-.html.

Downey, John, and Natalie, Fenton. 2003. New media, counter publicity, and the public sphere. *New Media and Society* 5 (2):185–202.

Downhillbattle.org. n.d. iTunes music store: Facelift for a corrupt industry. Http://www.downhillbattle.org/itunes/.

Downing, John. 2001. *Radical media: Rebellious communication and social movements*. With Tamara Villarreal Ford, Genève Gil, and Laura Stein. Thousand Oaks, Calif.: Sage.

———. 2008. Social movement theories and alternative media: An evaluation and critique. *Communication, Culture, and Critique* 1:40–50.

Drew, Rob. 2005. Mixed blessings: The commercial mix and the future of music aggregation. *Popular Music and Society* 28 (4):533–551. Http://www.informaworld.com/smpp/title~content=t713689465~db=all~tab=issueslist~branches=28-v28.

Dyson, Esther. 1995. Friend and foe. *Wired* 3 (August). Http://www. wired.com/wired/archive/3.08/newt.html.

Dyson, Esther, et al. 1994. Cyberspace and the American Dream: A Magna Carta for the Information Age. Http://www.alamut.com/subj/ideologies/manifestos/magna Carta.html.

Edelman, Marc. 2001. Social movements: Changing paradigms and forms of politics. *Annual Review of Anthropology* 20:285–317.

Edelman, Murray. 1971. *Politics as symbolic action: Mass arousal and quiescence*. Chicago: Markham.

———. 1995. *From art to politics: How artistic creations shape political conceptions.* Chicago: University of Chicago Press.

Edgecliffe-Johnson, Andrew. 2005. A new musical arrangement for the Internet age. *Financial Times,* November 15, 14.

EFF [Electronic Frontier Foundation]. n.d.a. Digital Millennium Copyright Act (DMCA). Http://www.eff.org/IP/DMCA/.

———. n.d.b. Digital rights management and copy protection schemes. Http://www.eff.org/IP/DRM/.

———. n.d.c. FTAA & Bilateral FTA Resources. Http://www.eff.org/IP/FTAA/.

———. n.d.d. RIAA v. The people: Two years later. Http://www.eff.org/IP/P2P/RIAAatTWO_FINAL.pdf.

———. n.d.e. Steve Jackson Games v. Secret Service case archive. Http://w2.eff.org/legal/cases/SJG/.

———. n.d.f. Wanted: Acacia Technologies. Http://www.eff.org/patent/wanted/patent.php?p=acacia.

———. n.d.g. Wanted: Seer Systems. Http://www.eff.org/patent/wanted/patent.php?p=seer.

Eggerton, John. 2006. CBS radio settles with NY over payola. *Broadcasting and Cable,* October 19. Http://www.broadcastingcable.com/article/CA6383282.html?display=Breaking+News.

Elson, Shane. 2007. A Habermasian perspective on the alternative radio program. *Social Alternatives* 26 (1):32–38.

Engadget. 2006. The Engadget interview: Viodentia, creator of FairUse4WM. September 25. Http://www.engadget.com/2006/09/25/the-engadget-interview-viodentia-creator-of-fairuse4wm.

English, Simon. 2006. U.S. launches price-fixing probe into online music market. Independent, March 4. Http://findarticles.com/p/articles/mi_qn4158/is_2006 0304/ai_n16191331.

EPIC [Electronic Privacy Information Clearinghouse]. 2006. Complaint for injunctive relief. Http://www.epic.org/privacy/nsa/aclu_complaint.pdf.

Eyerman, Ron, and Andrew Jamison. 1998. *Music and social movements: Mobilizing traditions in the twnetieth century.* Cambridge: Cambridge University Press.

Fairtlough, Gerard H. 1991. Habermas' concept of "lifeworld." *Systems Practice* 4(6): 547–563.

FCC [Federal Communications Commission]. 2003. Digital broadcast content protection: Report and order and further notice of proposed rule, 18 F.C.C.R. 23.550 (adopted 2003).

Felten, Edward, and Andrew Appel. 2000. Technological access control interferes with noninfringing scholarship. *Communications of the Association for Computer Machinery* 43:9.

FFII [Foundation for a Free Information Infrastructure]. 2006. FFII statement given at EU patent policy hearing, July 12. Http://wiki.ffii.de/PatHearing060712En.

Finquelievich, Susana. 2000. ICT and local governance: A view from the South. In *Community informatics: Enabling communities with information and communica-*

tions technologies, edited by Michael Gurstein, 232–250. Hershey, Pa.: Idea Group International.

Fisher, Ken. 2007. Apple hides account info in DRM-free music, too. *ArsTechnica*, May 30. Http://arstechnica.com/news.ars/post/20070530-apple-hides-account-info-in-drm-free-music-too.html.

FOMC [Future of Music Coalition]. 2000. The Future of Music manifesto. Http://www.futureofmusic.org/manifesto.

———. 2007. FMC and ACS invite you to a technology and IP policy day. Http://www.futureofmusic.org/events/dcpolicyday07/index.cfm.

———. n.d. iTunes and digital downloads: An analysis. Http://www.futureofmusic.org/itunes.cfm.

Foucault, Michel. 1983. The subject and power. In *Beyond Structuralism and Hermeneutics*, edited by Hubert L. Dreyfus and Paul Rabinow, 208–228. Chicago: University of Chicago Press.

Fraser, Nancy. 1985. What's so critical about critical theory? The case of Habermas and gender. *New German Critique* 35 (Spring–Summer):97–131.

———. 1989. *Unruly practices: Power, discourse, and gender in contemporary social theory.* Minneapolis: University of Minnesota Press.

———. 1992. Rethinking the public sphere: A contribution to the critique of actually existing democracy in *Habermas and the public sphere*, edited by Craig Calhoun, 109–142. Cambridge, Mass.: MIT Press.

Fraser, Nancy, and Axel Honneth. 2003. *Redistribution or recognition? A political-philosophical exchange.* New York: Verso.

Free Press. n.d. Stamp out the rate hikes. Http://freepress.net/postal/=history.

Free Software Foundation. 1989. GNU general public license. In Stallman 2002, 195–202.

———. 2007. RIAA Lawsuits—Expert Witness Fund. https://www.fsf.org/associate/riaa.

Free SpiralFrog Music Store to Use PlaysForSure. 2006. *Wired* Blogs, August 26. Http://blog.wired.com/music/2006/08/free_spiralfrog.html.

Frieden, Rob. 2002. Revenge of the Bellheads: How the Netheads lost control of the Internet. *Telecommunications Policy* 26 (7–8):425–444.

Gamet, Jeff. 2007. Norway declares iTunes DRM technology illegal. *Mac Observer*, January 25. Http://www.macnewsworld.com/story/ZRuDFbsV7LKwh5/Norway-Declares-iTunes-DRM-Technology-Illegal.xhtml.

Garcia, D. Linda. 2004. Networks and the evolution of property rights in the global, knowledge-based economy. In Braman 2004, 130–153. New York: Palgrave Macmillan.

Garofalo, Reebee. 1987. How autonomous is relative: Popular music, the social formation and cultural struggle. *Popular Music* 6 (1):77–92.

———, ed. 1992. *Rockin' the boat: Mass music and mass movements.* Boston: South End Press.

Gates, Kelly. 2006. Will work for copyrights: The cultural policy of anti-piracy campaigns. *Social Semiotics* 16 (1):57–73.

Giddens, Anthony. 1984. *The constitution of society: Outline of a theory of structuration*. Berkeley and Los Angeles: University of California Press.

Gillespie, Tarleton. 2007a. Personal communication, December 7.

———. 2007b. *Wired shut: Copyright and the shape of digital culture*. Cambridge, Mass.: MIT Press.

Godwin, Mike. 2003. *Cyber rights: Defending free speech in the digital age*. Cambridge, Mass.: MIT Press.

———. 2008. After the revolution. Lecture given at the Glasscock Center for Digital Humanities, Texas A&M University, January 28.

Goldberg, Michelle. 2005. Mood radio. *San Francisco Bay Guardian*. Http://www.sfbg.com/noise/05/mood.html.

Graham, Paul. 1996. Habermas's rectifying revolution. *International Politics* 33 (March):3–25.

Granneman, Scott. n.d. The big DRM mistake. Http://www.securityfocus.com/print/columnists/390.

Greene, Paul D. 2005. Introduction: Wired sound and sonic cultures. In *Wired for sound: Engineering and technologies in sonic cultures*, edited by Paul D. Greene and Thomas Porcello, 1–22. Hanover, N.H.: University of New England Press / Wesleyan University Press.

Gumiela, Josh. 2007. Netlabels. Paper presented at Global Fusion 2007, St. Louis, Missouri.

Habermas, Jürgen. 1970. Systematically distorted communications. In *Recent sociology*, edited P. Dreitzel, 2: – . London: Collier-Macmillan.

———. 1979. *Communication and the evolution of society*. Boston: Beacon Press.

———. 1984. *The theory of communicative action*. Vol. 1, *Reason and the rationalization of society*. Translated by T. McCarthy. Boston: Beacon Press.

———. 1987. *The theory of communicative action*. Vol. 2, *Lifeworld and system: A critique of functionalist reason*. Translated by T. McCarthy. Boston: Beacon Press.

———. 1990. What does socialism mean today? The rectifying revolution and the need for new thinking on the left. *New Left Review* 183 (September–October): 3–21.

———. 1992. Further reflections on the public sphere. In *Habermas and the public sphere*, edited by Craig Calhoun, 421–461. Cambridge, Mass.: MIT Press.

———. 2006. Political communication in media society: Does democracy still enjoy an epistemic dimension? The impact of normative theory on empirical research. *Communication Theory* 16:411–426.

Hadl, Gabriele. 2004. Civil society media theory: Tools for decolonizing the lifeworld. *Ritsumeikan Social Sciences Review* 40 (3):77–96. Http://www.ritsumei.ac.jp/acd/cg/ss/sansharonshu/403pdf/hadl.pdf.

Hall, Ben. 2007. France proposes to cut off persistent Internet pirates. *Financial Times*, October 23, 2.

Hamelink, Cees. 1994. *The politics of world communication: A human rights perspective*. Thousand Oaks, Calif.: Sage.

———. 2004. Did WSIS achieve anything at all? *International Communication Gazette* 66 (3–4):281–290.

Hammond, Allen S., IV. 2005. Universal service: Problems, solutions, and responsive policies. *Federal Communications Law Journal* 57 (2):187–200.

Hardt, Michael, and Antonio Negri. 2000. *Empire*. Cambridge, Mass.: Harvard University Press.

———. 2004. *Multitude: War and democracy in the age of empire*. New York: Penguin.

Harold, Christine. 2004. Pranking rhetoric: "Culture jamming" as media activism. *Critical Studies in Media Communication* 20 (3):189–211.

Harvey, Eric. 2008. Keep on Freeing in the Rock World: MP3 Blogs, Music Fandom, and Participatory Promotion. Paper presented at Exploring New Media Worlds conference, Texas A&M University, March.

Hesmondhalgh, David. 1998. Post-Punk's attempt to democratize the music industry: The success and failure of Rough Trade. *Popular Music* 16 (3):255–274.

———. 2005. Subcultures, scenes or tribes? None of the above. *Journal of Youth Studies* 8 (1):21–40.

Heuman, Joshua. 2008. Hardcore takedown: Alternative MP3 blogs and the everyday life of copyright on the Web. Paper presented at Exploring New Media Worlds conference, Texas A&M University, March 1.

Hintz, Arne, and Gabriele Hadl. 2009. Framing our media for transnational policy: The World Summit of the Information Society and beyond. In Kidd, Rodriguez, and Stein 2009, 103–122.

Holdorf, Adam. 2002. Another battle of Seattle. *Real Change News*, September 5. Http://www.realchangenews.org/2002/2002_09_05/features/another_battle_of_seattle.html.

Honneth, Axel. 1991. *The critique of power: Reflective stages in a critical social theory*. Translated by Kenneth Baynes. Cambridge, Mass: MIT Press.

———. 2002. Grounding recognition: A rejoinder to critical questions. *Inquiry* 45 (4):499–520.

Hyde, Bob. 2001 (May 31). The first sale doctrine and digital phonorecords. *Duke Law and Technology Review* 0018. Http://www.law.duke.edu/journals/dltr/articles/2001dltr0018.html.

IFPI [International Federation of the Phonographic Industry]. 2007. *Digital Music Report 2007*, January 17. Http://www.ifpi.org/content/library/digital-music-report-2007.pdf.

Jay, Martin. 1984. *Marxism and totality: The adventures of a concept from Lukács to Habermas*. Berkeley and Los Angeles: University of California Press.

Jeschke, Rebecca. 2007 (February 5). EFF Battles Gambit to Freeze Telecom Surveillance Cases. Http://www.eff.org/deeplinks/2007/02/eff-battles-gambit-freeze-telecom-surveillance-cases

Jobs, Steve. 2007. Thoughts on music. Http://www.apple.com/hotnews/thoughtsonmusic.

Jones, Steve. 2002. Music that moves: Popular music, distribution and network technologies. *Cultural Studies* 16 (2):213–232.

Jordan, Tim. 2002. *Activism! Direct action, hacktivism, and the future of society*. London: Reaktion Books.

Jordan, Tim, and Paul A. Taylor. 2004. *Hacktivism and cyberwars: Rebels with a cause?* New York: Routledge.

Juniper Networks. 2008. Network security. Http://www.juniper.net/solutions/service_provider/network_security/.

Kaplan, Debra. 2005. Broadcast flags and the war against digital television piracy: A solution or dilemma for the digital era? *Federal Communications Law Journal* 57 (2):325–344.

Katyal, Sonia. 2004. Privacy vs. Piracy. *Yale Journal of Law and Technology* 7:1–126.

Keane, John. 1975. On tools and language: Habermas on work and interaction. *New German Critique* 6:82–100.

Kellner, Douglas. 1989. *Critical theory, Marxism, and modernity*. Baltimore: Johns Hopkins University Press.

———. 1998. Boundaries and borderlines: Reflections on Jean Baudrillard and critical theory. Http://www.uta.edu/huma/illuminations/kell2.htm.

———. 2004. New media and Internet activism: From the "Battle of Seattle" to blogging. *New Media and Society* 6 (1):87–95.

———. 2005. *Media spectacle and the crisis of democracy: Terrorism, war, and election battles*. Boulder, Colo.: Paradigm.

Kettler, David, and Volker Meja. 1996. Legal formalism and disillusioned realism in Max Weber. *Polity* 28 (3):307–331.

Kidd, Dorothy, Clemencia Rodriguez, and Laura Stein, eds. 2009. *Citizens' movements and the democratization of the public sphere*. Vol. 2 of *Making our media: Global initiatives toward a democratic public sphere*. Creskill, N.J.: Hampton Press.

Klein, Naomi. 2000. *No space, no choice, no jobs, no logo: Taking aim at the brand bullies*. New York: Picador.

Knight, Will. 1999. Hackers: BO2K "child's play" remark draws fire. ZDNet UK, July 16. Http://news.zdnet.co.uk/internet/0,1000000097,2072701,00.htm.

Knowles, Joe. 2003. The pirates of Hollywood. *In These Times*, January 13. Http://www.inthesetimes.com/article/540/the_pirates_of_hollywood/.

Koivisto, Juha, and Esa Väliverronen. 1996. Resurgence of the critical theories of public sphere. *Journal of Communication Inquiry* 20 (2):18–36.

Kraft, James P. 1995. Artists as workers: Musicians and trade unions in America, 1880–1917. *Musical Quarterly* 79 (3):512–543.

Lee, Kwang-Suk. 2009. The electronic fabric of resistance: A constructive network of online users and activists challenging a rigid copyright regime. In Kidd, Rodriguez, and Stein 2009, 189–206.

Lemos, Robert. 2004. RIAA to face MyDoom's music? *Cnet News*, February 20. Http://news.com.com/RIAA+to+face+MyDooms+music/2100-7355_3-5162833.html.

Lessig, Lawrence. 1999. *Code, and other laws of cyberspace*. New York: Basic Books.

———. 2001. The future of ideas: The fate of the commons in a connected world. New York: Random House.

———. 2004. *Free culture: How big media uses technology and the law to lock down culture and control creativity*. New York: Penguin.

Levine, Robert. 1999. Senza Sordino. June. Http://www.icsom.org/pdf/senza373.pdf.

Leyshon, Andrew. 2003. Scary monsters? Free software, peer-to-peer networks and the spectre of the gift. *Environment and Planning D: Society and Space* 21:533–558.

Leyshon, Andrew, David Matless, and George Revill, eds. 1998. *The place of music*. New York: Guilford Press.

Leyshon, Andrew, Peter Webb, Shaun French, Nigel Thrift, and Louise Crewe. 2005. On the reproduction of the musical economy after the Internet. *Media, Culture and Society* 27 (2):177–209.

Lopes, Paul D. 1992. Innovation and diversity in the popular music industry, 1969 to 1990. *American Sociological Review* 57:56–71.

Lovering, John. 1998. The global music industry: Contradictions in the commodification of the sublime. In Leyshon, Matless, and Revill 1998 , 31–52.

Lovink, Geert. 2002. An insider's guide to tactical media. In *Dark fiber: Tracking critical Internet culture*. Cambridge, Mass.: MIT Press.

Lucchi, Nicola. 2007. Countering the unfair play of DRM technologies. New York University Public Law and Legal Theory Working Paper No. 50. Http://lsr.nellco .org/nyu/plltwp/papers/50.

Luhmann, Niklas. 1982. *The differentiation of society*. Translated by Stephen Holmes and Charles Larmore. New York: Columbia University Press.

Maloney, Paul. 2002. Copyright Office to hold public roundtable on recordkeeping. RAIN [Radio and Internet Newsletter], April 15. Http://www.kurthanson.com/ archive/news/041502/index.shtml#story2.

Mariano, Gwendolyn. 2001. Judge waves MP3Board suit into court. *CNet News*, March 19. Http://news.com.com/Judge+waves+MP3Board+suit+into+court/ 2100-1023_3-254356.html.

Mark, Roy. 2003. RIAA settles 63 more infringement suits. DC Internet.com. September 29. Http://dc.internet.com/news/article.php/3085051.

Marson, Ingrid. 2006. Sony rootkit victims in every state, researcher says. *CNet News*, January 17. Http://news.com.com/Sony+rootkit+victims+in+every+state,+resea rcher+says/2100-1029_3-6027857.html.

Mattelart, Armand. 2003. *The information society: An introduction*. Thousand Oaks, Calif.: Sage.

May, Christopher. 2006a. The denial of history: Reification, intellectual property rights and the lessons of the past. *Capital and Class* 88 (Spring):33–56.

———. 2006b. The World Intellectual Property Organization. *New Political Economy* 11 (3):435–445.

McCarthy, T. 1985. Complexity and democracy, or the seducements of systems theory. *New German Critique* 35 (Spring–Summer):27 – 53.

McChesney, Robert W. 2004. *The problem of the media: U.S. communication politics in the twenty-first century*. New York: Monthly Review Press.

McCourt, Tom. 2005. Collecting music in the digital realm. *Popular Music and Society* 28 (2):249–252.

McCourt, Tom, and Patrick Burkart. 2007. Customer relationship management: Automating fandom in music communities. In *Fandom: Identities and communities in a mediated world,* edited by Jonathan Gray, Cornel Sandvoss, and C. Lee Harrington, 261–270. New York: New York University Press.

McCullagh, Declan. 2004. "Pirate act" raises civil rights concerns. *CNet News,* May 26. Http://news.com.com/2100-1027-5220480.html.

———. 2005. Copyright lobbyists strike again. *CNet News,* August 1. Http://news.com.com/Copyright+lobbyists+strike+again/2010-1071_3-5811025.html.

———. 2007. Democrats: Colleges must police copyright, or else. News.com, November 9.

McLeod, Kembrew. 2005. *Freedom of expression: Overzealous copyright bozos and other enemies of creativity.* New York: Doubleday.

———. 2001. *Owning culture: Authorship, ownership, and intellectual property law.* New York: Peter Lang.

McMillan, Robert. 2006. Sony rootkit settlement with states reaches $5.75 m. *Infoworld,* December 21. Http://www.infoworld.com/article/06/12/21/HNrootkitgrows_1.html.

Mead, George Herbert. 1969. *Mind, self, and society: From the standpoint of a social behaviorist.* Chicago: University of Chicago Press.

Meyer, David. 2006. Anti-DRM day set for next month. ZDNet UK, May 9. Http://www.zdnetasia.com/news/business/0,39044229,39418947,00.htm.

Microsoft's Windows Media DRM Cracked. 2006. *Wired* Blog, August 28. Http://blog.wired.com/music/2006/08/microsofts_wind.html?entry_id=1546765.

Mindlin, Alex. 2007. Peer-to-peer downloaders gorge on songs. *New York Times,* April 2, C3.

Mnookin, Seth. 2007. Universal's CEO once called iPod users thieves. Now he's giving songs away. *Wired,* November 27. Http://www.wired.com/entertainment/music/magazine/15-12/mf_morris.

Moore, Ryan. 2004. Postmodernism and punk subculture: Cultures of authenticity and deconstruction. *Communication Review* 7:305–327.

Mosco, Vincent. 1982. *Pushbutton fantasies: Critical perspectives on videotext and information technology.* Mahwah, N.J.: Greenwood.

———. 1989. *The pay-per society: Computers and communication in the information age.* Norwood, N.J.: Ablex.

———. 1996. *Political economy of communication: Rethinking and renewal.* Thousand Oaks, Calif.: Sage.

———. 2004. *The digital sublime: Myth, power, and cyberspace.* Cambridge, Mass.: MIT Press.

MP3 player buyers guide. n.d. CNet. Http://reviews.cnet.com/4520-7964_7-5134106-2.html.

Mueller, Milton. 2004. Reinventing media activism: Public interest advocacy in the making of U.S. communication- information policy, 1960–2002. Syracuse University. Http://dcc.syr.edu/ford/rma/reinventing.pdf.

———. n.d. Publications and papers by Milton Mueller [personal Web page]. Http:// istweb.syr.edu/~mueller/onlinepubs.htm.

Mules, Warwick. 2001. That obstinate yet elastic natural barrier. *M/C: A Journal of Media and Culture* 4 (5). Http://journal.media-culture.org.au/0111/Mules .php.

Murray, Andrew D. 2005. The role of the cyberlawyer. *Nthposition.* Http://www .nthposition.com/theroleof.php.

Napoli, Philip M. 2001. *Foundations of communications policy: Principles and process in the regulation of electronic media.* Cresskill, N.J.: Hampton Press.

Negus, Keith. 1996. *Popular music in theory: An introduction.* Middletown, Conn.: Wesleyan University Press.

Newitz, Annalee. 2001. Not your girlfriend: The next generation of women hackers are doing it for themselves. *SFGate*, October 11. Http://www.sfgate.com/cgi-bin/ article.cgi?file=/gate/archive/2001/10/11/womhackers.DTL.

———. 2005. Dangerous terms: A user's guide to EULAs. Http://www.eff.org/wp/ dangerous-terms-users-guide-eulas.

O'Brien, Lucy. 1999. The woman punk made me. In *Punk rock: So what? The cultural legacy of punk*, edited by Roger Sabin, 186–198. New York: Routledge.

O'Donnell, Michael. 2008. Remix: Making art and commerce thrive in the hybrid economy [book review]. *San Francisco Cronicle*, October 12, M-1.

Offe, Claus. 1987. Challenging the boundaries of institutional politics: Social movements since the 1960s. In *Changing boundaries of the political*, edited by Charles Maier, 63–106. New York: Cambridge University Press.

Offe, Claus, and Helmut Wiesenthal. 1980. Two logics of collective action: Theoretical notes on social class and organizational form. *Political Power and Social Theory* (1):67–115.

Ohio U. bans P2P. 2007. *The Chronicle of Higher Education*, April 27. Http://chronicle .com/wiredcampus/article/2027/ohio-u-bans-p2p.

Orbitcast. 2006. CEA speaks out against RIAA lawsuit against XM. May 17. Http:// www.orbitcast.com/archives/cea-speaks-out-against-riaa-lawsuit-against-xm.html.

Pajnik, Mojca. 2005a. Citizenship and mediated society. *Citizenship Studies* 9 (4): 349–367.

———. 2005b. "New media" limitations to citizenship. Proceedings of "TIC I Participación Pública," Fourth International Conference on Communication and Reality, Barcelona, 77–86.

Piatek, Michael, Tadayoshi Kohno, and Arvind Krishnamurthy. 2008. Challenges and Directions for Monitoring P2P File Sharing Networks -or- Why My Printer Received a DMCA Takedown Notice. Http://dmca.cs.washington.edu/dmca_ hotsec08.pdf.

Pichardo, Nelson A. 1997. New social movements: A critical review. *Annual Review of Sociology* 23:411–430.

Plotke, David. 1990. What's so new about new social movements? *Socialist Review* 20:81-102.

Plunkett Research. 2007a. Entertainment and media industry statistics. January 19.

———. 2007b. Entertainment and media industry trends. January 19.

Popular music under siege. n.d. Arts Censorship Project. Http://www.eff.org/Censorship/music_censorship_aclu.article.

Post, David G. 2000. Cyberspace and privacy: A new legal paradigm? *Stanford Law Review* 52:1439–1459.

Quinn, Michelle. 2008. More teenagers ignoring CDs, report says. *Los Angeles Times*, February 26. Http://www.latimes.com/business/la-fi-music27feb27,0,4432240.story.

Racine "Rave Raid." 2003. ACLU, January 17. Http://www.aclu.org/drugpolicy/raves/10730res20030117.html.

Rappeport, Alan. 2006. Web warriors play cat-and-mouse with censors to free the Internet. *Financial Times*, March 4–5, 6.

ReasonableAgreement.org. n.d. The Small Print Project. Http://smallprint.netzoo.net/reag/.

Recording Industry vs The People. 2007. RIAA accused of extortion and conspiracy in Tampa, Florida, case, *UMG v. Del Cid*. June 4. Http://recordingindustryvspeople.blogspot.com/2007/06/riaa-accused-of-extortion-and.html.

RE/Search. 1986. *RE/Search #11: Pranks!* Edited by V. Vale. San Francisco, Calif.: RE/Search Publications.

Rhapsody. 2006a. Rhapsody End User License Agreement. Http://rhapreg.real.com/rhapsody/freeform?freeformname=RhapC%20EULA.

———. 2006b. Rhapsody Service Terms and Conditions. June 8. Http://rhapreg.real.com/rhapsody/freeform?freeformname=RhapC%20Terms.

Rheingold, Howard. 2002. *Smart mobs: The next social revolution*. Cambridge, Mass.: Perseus.

RIAARadar.com. 2008. Http://www.riaaradar.com/ (accessed December 9).

RIAA's student extortion letter. 2007. P2Pnet.net. Http://p2pnet.net/story/11515.

Ricciuti, Mike. 2008. EU Slaps Microsoft with $1.35 billion fine. *CNet News*, February 27. Http://www.news.com/8301-10784_3-9880256-7.html.

Robins, Kevin, and Frank Webster. 1999. *Times of the technoculture: From the information society to the virtual life*. New York: Routledge.

Rodman, Gilbert B., and Cheyanne Vanderdonckt. 2006. Music for nothing; or, I want my mp3: The regulation and recirculation of affect. *Cultural Studies* 20 (2–3):245–261.

Rojas, Viviana, Debasmita Roychowdhury, Ozlem Okur, Joe Straubhaar, and Yinan Estrada-Ortiz. 2001. Beyond access: Cultural capital and the roots of the digital divide. Http://www.utexas.edu/research/tipi/research/Beyond_Access.pdf.

Ross, Brian, Richard Esposito, and Vic Walter. 2006. Pay to play: Music industry's dirty little secret. ABC News, February 8. Http://abcnews.go.com/WNT/story?id=1591155.

Rothenbuhler, Eric W. 1998. *Ritual communication: From everyday conversation to mediated ceremony.* Thousand Oaks, Calif.: Sage.

———. 2007. Personal communication.

Rubin, Alvin B. 1987. Does law matter? A judge's response to the critical legal studies movement. *Journal of Legal Education* 37 (3):307–314.

Samuelson, Pamela. 1996. The Copyright grab. *Wired* 4 (January). Http://www.wired.com/wired/archive/4.01/white.paper_pr.html.

———. 2003. DRM (and, or, vs.) the law. *Communications of the ACM* 46 (4):41–45.

Sassen, Saskia. 2000. *Cities in a world economy.* Thousand Oaks, Calif.: Pine Forge Press.

Sawhney, H. 2003. Universal service expansion: Two perspectives. *Information Society* 19:327–332.

Schalit, Joel. 2007. Personal communication.

———. 2008. Personal communication.

Schement, Jorge Reina, and Terry Curtis. 1995. *Tendencies and tensions of the information age: The production and distribution of information in the United States.* New Brunswick, N.J.: Transaction.

Schiller, Dan. 1999. *Digital capitalism: Networking the global market system.* Cambridge, Mass.: MIT Press.

Schiller, Herbert I. 1991. Not yet the post-imperialist era. *Critical studies in mass communication* 8:13–28.

Schneier, Bruce. 2007. DRM in Windows Vista. Schneier on security, February 12. Http://www.schneier.com/blog/archives/2007/02/drm_in_windows_1.html.

Schudson, Michael. 1989. How culture works: Perspectives from media studies on the efficacy of symbols. *Theory and Society* 18:153–180.

———. 1992. Was there ever a public sphere? If so, when? Reflections on the American case. In *Habermas and the public sphere*, edited by C. Calhoun, 141–163. Cambridge, Mass.: MIT Press.

Schuler, Douglas, and Peter Day. 2004. Shaping the network society: Opportunities and challenges. In *Shaping the network society: The new role of civil society in cyberspace*, edited by Douglas Schuler and Peter Day, 1–16. Cambridge, Mass: MIT Press.

Schutz, Alfred, and Thomas Luckmann. 1973. *The structure of the life world.* Evanston, Ill.: Northwestern University Press.

Schwartz, John. 2003. ACLU challenges music industry in court. *New York Times*, September 29. Http://query.nytimes.com/gst/fullpage.html?res=9A01E1DD113DF93AA1575AC0A9659C8B63.

Schweidler, Christine, and Sasha Costanza-Chock. 2009. Common cause: Global resistance to intellectual property. In Kidd, Rodriguez, and Stein 2009, 161–188.

Scott, James C. 1985. *Weapons of the weak: Everyday forms of peasant resistance.* New Haven: Yale University Press.

Searle, John R. 1969. *Speech acts: An essay in the philosophy of language.* Cambridge: Cambridge University Press.

Seltzer, Wendy. 2005. The broadcast flag: It's not just TV. *Federal Communications Law Journal* 57 (2):209–214.

SFLC [Software Freedom Law Center]. 2006. Software freedom law center files brief with Supreme Court arguing against software patents. December 15. Http:// www.earthtimes.org/articles/show/news_press_release,35629.shtml.

Shank, Barry. 1994. *Dissonant identities: The rock 'n' roll scene in Austin, Texas*. Hanover, N.H.: University Press of New England.

Singstad, Jo. 2007. The Consumer Council of Norway is on track to win case against iTunes. Norwegian Consumer Council. Http://forbrukerportalen.no/Artikler/ 2006/1149587055.44.

Sitton, John F. 1998. Disembodied capitalism: Habermas's conception of the economy. *Sociological Forum* 13 (1):61–83.

Sohn, Gigi B. 2005. Statement of Gigi B. Sohn, president, Public Knowledge, before the House Judiciary Committee Subcommittee on Courts, the Internet and Intellectual Property: Oversight hearing on "Content Protection in the Digital Age: The Broadcast Flag, High-Definition Radio, and the Analog Hole," November 3. Http://www.publicknowledge.org/news/testimony/20051103-gbsohn-testimony.

Solomon, John, and Barton Gellman. 2007. Frequent errors in FBI's secret records requests. *Washington Post*, March 9, A1.

Spaul, M. W. J. 1995. Critical systems thinking and "new social movements": A perspective from the *Theory of Communicative Action*. *Systems Practice* 9(4):317– 332.

Stahl, Matthew. 2003. To hell with heteronomy: Liberalism, rule-making, and the pursuit of community in an urban rock scene. *Journal of Popular Music Studies* 15 (2):140–165.

Stallman, Richard. 2002. *Free software, free society: Selected essays of Richard M. Stallman*. Edited by Joshua Gay. Boston: Free Software Foundation.

Stanford Center on Internet and Society. n.d. Question: What is contributory infringement? Http://www.chillingeffects.org/dmca512/question.cgi?QuestionID =268.

Sterling, Bruce. 1994. *The hacker crackdown: Law and disorder on the electronic frontier*. Http://www.mirrors.wiretapped.net/security/info/books/bruce-sterling--the-hacker-crackdown.txt.

Sterne, Jonathan. 2006. MP3 as cultural artifact. *New Media and Society* 8 (5):825– 842.

Stiteler, Bill. 2008. iTunes 8 and Genius first impressions. Appletell, September 9. Http://www.appletell.com/apple/comment/itunes-8/.

Strangelove, Michael. 2005. *The empire of mind: Digital piracy and the anti-capitalist movement*. Toronto: University of Toronto Press.

Streeter, Thomas. 1999. That deep Romantic chasm: Libertarianism, neoliberalism, and the computer culture. In *Communication, citizenship, and social policy: Rethinking the limits of the welfare state*, edited by Andrew Calabrese and Jean-Claude Burgelman, 49–65. Lanham, Md.: Rowman and Littlefield.

Striphas, Ted, and Kembrew McLeod. 2006. Strategic improprieties: Cultural studies, the everyday, and the politics of intellectual properties. *Cultural Studies* 20 (2–3):119–144.

Strossen, Nadine. 2000. Cybercrimes v. cyberliberties. *International Review of Law, Computers and Technology* 14 (1):11–24.

——. 2004. Reflections on the essential role of legal scholarship in advancing causes of citizen groups. *New York Law School Law Review* 49. Http://www.nyls.edu/pdfs/Strossen_ReflectionsOn.pdf.

Taylor, Paul A. 2005. From hackers to hacktivists: Speed bumps on the global superhighway? *New Media and Society* 7 (5):625–646.

Théberge, Paul. 2005. Everyday fandom: Fan clubs, blogging, and the quotidian rhythms of the Internet. *Canadian Journal of Communication* 30:485–502.

Tilly, Charles. 2002. *Stories, identities, and political change*. Lanham, Md.: Rowman and Littlefield.

Toffler, Alvin. 1980. *The third wave*. New York: Morrow.

TOR [The Onion Router]. 2007a. Tor: Anonymity online. September 1. Http://tor.eff.org/.

——. 2007b. Tor: Overview. October 24. Http://www.torproject.org/overview.html.en.

Touraine, Alain. 1998. *Return of the actor: Social theory in postindustrial society*. Minneapolis: University of Minnesota Press.

Tristani, G. 2005. FCC past and present. Paper presented at the National Media Reform Conference, St. Louis, Missouri, May.

Turner, Fred. 2006. *From counterculture to cyberculture: Stewart Brand, the Whole Earth Network, and the rise of digital utopianism*. Chicago: University of Chicago Press.

U.S. Department of Justice. 2006. Notice of motion and motion to dismiss or, in the alternative, for summary judgment by the United States of America. Http://www.eff.org/legal/cases/att/GovMotiontoDismiss.pdf.

Vaidhyanathan, Siva. 2000. MP3: It's only rock and roll and the kids are alright. *Nation* 271 (4):31–34.

——. 2001. *Copyrights and copywrongs: The rise of intellectual property and how it threatens creativity*. New York: New York University Press.

——. 2005. *The anarchist in the library: How the clash between freedom and control is hacking the real world and crashing the system*. New York: Basic Books.

——. 2006. Critical information studies: A bibliographic manifesto. *Cultural Studies* 20 (2–3):292–315. Available at Http://ssrn.com/abstract=788984.

Vertuno, Jim. 2008. Old dance halls in danger. *Bryan-College Station (Texas) Eagle*, February 9. Http://www.theeagle.com/PrinterFriendly/Old-dance-halls-in-danger.

von Lohmann, Fred. 2005a. DMCA triennial rulemaking: Failing consumers completely. EFF Report, November 30. Http://www.eff.org/deeplinks/archives/004212.php.

——. 2005b. Now the legalese rootkit: Sony-BMG's EULA. EFF Report, November 9. Http://www.eff.org/deeplinks/archives/004145.php.

——. 2006. Personal communication.

———. n.d. IAAL: peer-to-peer file sharing and copyright law after Napster. White paper. Http://www.law.upenn.edu/polk/ip/2003sp/downloads/readings.feb7.pdf.

Wall, David S. 2000. Cybercrimes, cyberspeech, and cyberliberties. *International Review of Law, Computers and Technology* 14 (1):5–9.

Wark, McKenzie. 2006. Information wants to be free (but it is everywhere in chains). *Cultural Studies* 20 (2–3):16–183.

What is fair market share? 2006. Billboard.com, March 16, 10.

Winner, Langdon. 1997. Cyberlibertarian myths and the prospects for community. *Computers and Society* (September):14–19.

Winston, Brian. 1998. *Media, technology, and society: A history: From the telegraph to the Internet*. New York: Routledge.

Wirtén, Eva Hemmungs. 2006. Out of sight and out of mind: On the cultural hegemony of intellectual property (critique). *Cultural Studies* 20 (2–3):282–291.

Wolff, Robert Paul. 1970. *In defense of anarchism*. New York: HarperCollins.

WTMD (FM). 2007. Public radio webcasting fees. Radio for Music People [blog], May 10. Http://wtmd.blogspot.com/2007/05/public-radio-webcasting-fees.html.

Zucco, Tom. 2007. Vinyl carves out groove. *St. Petersburg (Florida) Times*, April 17, 10.

Index

A&M Records v. Napster, 85
AAC. *See* advanced audio coding
"Access to Knowledge" agreement,
102–3
ACLU (American Civil Liberties Union),
23–25, 97, 109
ACLU v. Reno (1997), 24, 138
active audience approach, 35–36, 86, 110
activism. *See* Alternative Jukebox; cyberliberties activism; hacktivism; new
social movement (NSM) theory;
social movement theory
activist scholarship, 15
Adobe Systems, 55
advanced audio coding (AAC): behavioral
controls of, 17–18; EMI releases with,
60, 144n1; Johansen hack of, 54; as proprietary format, 40; unencrypted AAC
file releases, 60, 146n17
Advanced Research Projects Agency Network (ARPANET), 106
AIMster, 51–52
Alpert, Herb, 50
Alternative Jukebox: autonomous markets
as intermediate steps to, 111; as cyberliberties strategy, 95; Napster as component
of, 86; necessity of policy reforms for,
103–4; noninfringing use of, 60; overview of changes entailed by, 13; social
movement theory and, 22, 98–99, 110.
See also Celestial Jukebox business
model; social movement theory
alternative media, 43–45, 46–48, 63, 138
alternative music scenes: autonomous markets and, 111; democratizing influences
of, 22, 28; fan awareness in, 78, 110–11.

See also music scenes; post-punk move-
ment
alternative-radical dialectic, 44, 47
Amazon.com, 60, 129, 144n1
American Civil Liberties Union (ACLU),
23–25, 97, 109
American Library Association, 97
American Society of Composers, Authors,
and Producers (ASCAP), 31, 141
anarchism, 51–52
Andrejevic, Mark, 59, 80
anonymity, 30, 47, 50, 52–54, 72–73, 120.
See also surveillance
antinuclear movement, 102
AOL, 80
Apple: FairPlay media format, 40, 146n17;
as information service, 62; opposition to
DRM, 40–41; RIAA enabling of, 16–17.
See also iPod; iTunes
Argentina, 82, 90
ARPANET (Advanced Research Projects
Agency Network), 106
artists: artist-advocacy support networks, 23;
collective action among, 81–82; as cyberliberties concern, 74; fair use rights and,
30; fandom studies and, 35–36; FOMC
advocacy for, 140–42; music industry
wage relationships, 16; performance royalties, 31; recording industry relationships with, 18, 79; RIAA appeals on behalf of, 18; rights to master recordings,
141; royalties from digital sales, 79,
147n4; views of sharing, 72.
See also fans
ASCAP (American Society of Composers,
Authors, and Producers), 31, 141

167

Center for Internet and Society, 28
Center for Media Education, 97
Chiariglione, Leonard, 143
Child Online Protection Act, 24
Chile, 69
chillingeffects.org, 30
China, 69
cipher-punks, 106
civil liberties: ACLU cyberliberties program and, 23–24; civil liberties violations experiences, 38; collective vs. individual rights and, 25–27; economic/property liberties compared with, 104–10; first principles issues in, 27–28; personal autonomy, 3, 143n4; scholarship on cyberliberties, 89. *See also* free speech rights; privacy rights; right to communicate
civil rights movement, 100–101
civil society media, 111, 115, 119
Clarke, Ian, 52, 120
Clarke, Rebecca, 30
class: crisis of modernity and, 98; "digerati" elites as cyberliberties proponents, 105, 108–9; digital divide, 62–63; fandom studies and, 35–36; Habermas neglect of, 11; Internet social stratification and, 26–27; middle-class activism, 97–98; relationship with cultural, ethnic, and racial conflict, 104, 120; social agency and, 113
clientelization: defined, 14, 39–40; industry fostering of, 4–5; legal status of clients, 73–74; online fan spaces and, 79–81; terms of service agreement, 62, 74–75. *See also* subscription services
Clinton, Bill, 67–68
Cloak, 47
Cohen, Bram, 51
collecting: copy-protected files and, 17; desiccation of music scenes and, 57; digital vs. physical collecting, 124–25, 130–31, 134–35; ethics of record collectors, 40; financial ownership vs. cultural ownership and, 135; hoarding fetish, 124, 135; as music lifeworld component, 127; physical collecting as cyberliberties activism, 135–36; public archivist role and, 63; record collectors, 14, 40; value in digital collecting, 127–28. *See also* records; sharing
collective action: absence of coherent cyberliberties movement, 137; collaborative music, 145–46n9; collaborative programming networks, 55–56; collective action among artists, 81; collective mobilization of disparate groups, 103–4; collective vs. individual activism and, 50, 52, 63, 82, 122–23; collective vs. individual rights and, 25–27; consumer boycotts and write-in campaigns, 78–79; cyberliberties initiatives as, 56; do-it-yourself (DIY) artist collectives, 5, 88; fan clubs as social networks, 111–12; fan collectivity and, 110–11; Internet as mobilization tool, 102, 116–17; multitudes, 56, 110–13; postpunk sensibility and, 120; tactical vs. strategic ends, 120. *See also* Alternative Jukebox; cyberliberties activism; hacktivism; social movement theory
collective bargaining, 81
colonization: alternative media initiatives and, 43–44; clientelization of fans and, 39–40, 73–74; communicative rationality as resistance to, 42; "contours of consciousness" effects, 88–89; disruptive technologies and, 37; of fandom, 111–12; global civil society as refuge from, 36; Habermas on, 7; internal colonization of the lifeworld, 58–59; international resistance to, 90–92; of the musical lifeworld by copyright law, 15, 59; postmodern imperialism, 57; power/money influence on, 38; spatialization and, 61; steering media role in, 67; theory of reification and, 6–7, 58
Comcast, 62
commodification: commercialization strategy for online content, 108; commodity fetishism, 126, 148n3; cybernetic commodities, 58–59, 61–62; of digital music, 88–89, 124; emotive context of music consumption, 124; information as commodity, 98; of online user information, 59, 62; social movement resistance to, 2
communication communities, 29
communication rights, 25, 27–28, 36, 118
Communication Rights in the Information Society (CRIS), 27, 118
Communications Decency Act, 24
communicative rationality, 6–8, 42, 56–58, 117
Company of Us (USCO), 84
Computer Professionals for Social Responsibility (CPSR), 24, 97
concurrent versions system (CVS) code management, 55

conservatism, 107–9

Consumer Federation of America, 97

content scrambling system (CSS) media format, 54

Coombe, Rosemary, 8, 87, 99–100, 133–34

CopyLeft initiative: as alternative media initiative, 44, 81–82; availability of music and, 60; fair use assertions and, 87; as global initiative, 92; visibility of system-lifeworld dialectic in, 42

copy protection. *See* digital rights management

copyright activism, 44–45, 122. *See also* CopyLeft initiative; Creative Commons alternative-copyright project

"copyright grab," 5

copyright law. *See* intellectual property law

copyright maximalists, 38

Copyright Term Extension Act of 1998, 71

Cordless Recordings, 44

Costanza-Chock, Sasha, 91–92, 102, 116

cost-benefit analysis, 124

counterculture, 83–84, 95, 106–7

Creative Commons alternative-copyright project, 28, 44, 81–82, 87, 92

"crippleware." *See* digital rights management

CRIS (Communication Rights in the Information Society), 27, 118

critical information studies, 27–28

critical legal studies, 11–12

Critical Mass, 112

critical media studies, 7, 29–30

critical social systems theory, 38, 57–58, 65, 95, 97, 145n2

CRM (customer relationship management) software, 80

CSS (content scrambling system) media format, 54

Cult of the Dead Cow, 54

cultural environmentalism, 104

cultural politics, 36, 95, 120

cultural studies: on "active audiences," 86; approach to fan collectivity, 111; as cyberliberties activism approach, 137; research on hackers, 51; research on social movements, 35–36, 94

culture industry, 15, 19–21, 24, 83–84

culture jamming, 48–50, 78, 112

customer-relationship-management (CRM) software, 80

cyberliberties: defined, 7–8; "change of state" and, 3, 88–89, 134; civil liberties scholarship on, 89; conflicting versions of, 14; cyberlibertarian ethics, 14; as normative good, 105, 137–38

cyberliberties activism: absence of coherent cyberliberties movement, 137; ACLU cyberliberties program, 23–24; alternative vs. radical activism, 43–45; capitalist cyberlibertarianism, 107–10; collective vs. individual activism and, 50, 52, 63, 122–23; cyberlibertarian lifeworld, 82; "daily practices" in, 102–3; disruptive technologies and, 37; DMCA as target of, 18; DMCA coverage of, 32; early-Internet experiences and, 82, 84; file-sharing rebellion, 16, 25; free-culture rights and, 27; "information wants to be free" slogan, 98, 121; overview of strategies for, 2–3, 95, 137–38; political philosophy of, 104–10; political vs. marketplace freedoms and, 25; property rights theory and, 26, 82, 89–90; resistance ideology as normative paradigm, 97; social agency of fans and, 110; social movement theory and, 13, 22, 56–58, 95–96; as symbolic action, 57–58; TCA adaptation and, 11; uncoupling (system from lifeworld) and, 98–99; virtual public sphere as site for, 117–18, 138. *See also* hacktivism; social movement theory

cybernetic commodities, 61–62

cyber-punks, 106

cyberterrorism, 54–55

dance halls, 127

Danger Mouse, 15–16, 49

Darknet, 16, 20, 42

Day, Peter, 116, 138

DeCSS hack, 54, 92

Deetz, Stanley A., 66

Deleuze, Gilles, 80

deliberative paradigm, 14, 114, 117, 134

Demers, Joanna, 15, 18, 87

democratization: alternative media and, 44; democratic theory of music scenes, 3, 21–23; post-punk contributions to, 22; theory of communicative action and, 8–9; theory of radical democracy, 27–28; third media sector and, 118–19

digital enclosure: overview, 128–33; avoiding digital enclosure, 133–36; civil disobedience in, 91; fan-worker consciousness and, 80–81; as surveillance site, 59, 62; ubiquitous-DRM and, 41

digitally correct hacking, 52–53

fair use doctrine: civil liberties scholarship on, 89; erosion of rights in, 14, 58, 67–68; exemption from some IP claims, 145n7; fair use civil disobedience, 87, 103; instructional use of media and, 32, 69, 100, 147n8; international campaign for, 45, 91–92, 102, 116; international norms for, 90–92; IP intimidation cases, 30–31; juridification and, 29–31; Napster affiliation with, 85–86; netizen rights and, 62; research on, 74; sampling by artists, 87. *See also* intellectual property law

Falk, Richard, 115

Fanning, Shawn, 51–52

fans: civil liberties violations experiences, 38; clientelization of fans, 4–5, 14, 39–40, 73–74; college/university fans, 18–19, 24, 70–71, 86; commodification of online user information, 59, 62, 131; contract law as component of fan experience, 58–59; criminalization of fans, 19–21, 24; digital vs. record consumer experience, 124, 127–28; fandom studies, 35–36, 86, 110, 137; fan fiction, 30; fanzines, 37, 81, 88, 126; as "netizens," 36, 62; online fan spaces, 79–81; privatization of fan space, 39–40; production role of, 35–36; rejection of monitored portals, 82; RIAA mass litigation initiative, 70–71, 147n7; rituals of fandom, 3, 21, 30, 57, 81, 101; sharing as fan-base production, 124; social agency in fan clubs, 111–12; ubiquitous-DRM effects on, 41–42; uncoupling (system from lifeworld) and, 98–99; as users vs. consumers, 1, 4–5, 14, 20, 61–63, 73. *See also* artists

fanzines, 37, 81, 88, 126

Fasttrack, 51–52

FCC (Federal Communications Commission), 43, 46, 145n7

Felten, Edward, 32, 55

file sharing. *See* sharing

filtering software (for ISPs), 132, 145n8

Firm, The, 144–45n5

FloodNet, 54–55

FOMC (Future of Music Coalition), 43, 74, 140–42

FOSS (free and open source software). *See* open-source software

Foucault, Michel, 80

Fowler, Mark, 43

France, 69, 132

Frankfurt School of critical theory, 6, 144n7. *See also* critical social systems theory

Fraser, Nancy, 10–11, 102, 119

free and open source software (FOSS). *See* open-source software

free culture: alternative media and, 44; Lessig free-culture rights argument, 27; music industry challenges to, 12–13; sharing as component of, 32–33; strategies for challenging media business, 2, 13

"Freedom of Expression" trademark, 49

Freenet, 51–52

Free Press, 45

Free Software Foundation, 28, 44, 120, 147n7

free speech rights: ACLU cyberliberties program and, 23–24; civil liberties scholarship on, 89; communitarianist conflicts with, 82; criminalization of performance, 31; culture jamming and, 49; as cyberliberties concern, 7; hacker assertion of, 55; online speech protection, 147n5; property rights conflicts with, 27; right to communicate and, 25, 28; right to tinker and, 32. *See also* censorship

free trade agreements (FTAs), 69

Future of Music Coalition (FOMC), 43, 74, 140–42

gaming, 40, 51–52

Garcia, D. Linda, 89

Garofalo, Reebee, 83

Gates, Bill, 51

Gates, Kelly, 18, 21

Gates, Robert, 30–31

Geist, Michael, 147n10

gender: fandom studies and, 35–36; female hackers, 51; Internet social stratification and, 26–27

genetics as legal property, 45

Genius music recommendation feature, 148n5

Geocities, 78

George, Susanna, 118

Germany, 69

gift economy, 1, 86, 110. *See also* sharing

Gilder, George, 109

Gillespie, Tarleton, 135

Gingrich, Newt, 84–85, 109

Girl Scouts of America, 31

Global Business Dialogue, 118

global cities, 62–63
global civil society studies: overview, 14; globalization-from-below, 115; global public sphere and, 118–19; right to communicate and, 27, 36; WSIS alternative media initiatives and, 44–45, 47
globalization of capitalism, 57, 100, 102, 113, 116–17
Gnutella, 51–52
"God Bless America," 31
Godwin, Mike, 65, 67, 105
Goingware, 60
Google, 37, 47, 145n8
Graham, Paul, 12
Gramsci, Antonio, 43
graphical user interfaces (GUIs), 17
Grateful Dead, 84, 107
Grey Tuesday, 15–16, 97
Grokster, 16, 21
Grossberg, Paul, 111

Habermas, Jürgen: colonization thesis, 7, 42, 74; on the communication media of money and power, 30; on the deliberative paradigm, 114; functionalist systems theory of, 9–10; intellectual sources and concepts, 67, 144n6; on juridification, 29; on legitimation crises, 147n9; "lifeworld" concept of, 3, 6, 9, 143n3; on the norm-free society, 81; on power-free discourse, 117; on the public sphere, 7, 9, 113–14, 119, 122, 138; on "second nature" sociality, 41; theory of communicative action, 5–6. See also theory of communicative action
hacker culture: collaborative programming networks, 55–56; hacker crackdown, 20–21, 107; hacker ethics, 52–53, 107, 109–10; illegal code as art, 55; political philosophy of, 106, 120; visibility of system-lifeworld dialectic in, 42. See also hacktivism
Hackett, Robert A., 44, 56, 132–33
hacktivism: defined, 8, 13, 51; anonymizing (anticensorship) services, 54; anti-EULA initiatives, 77–78; bogus DMCA takedown notices, 148n1; computer viruses, 78; distributed denial-of-service attacks, 146n14; DRM hacking, 16, 54–55, 92, 146n13, 147n6; international initiatives for, 91–92; Napster role in, 51–52; political potential in, 121; position on private

property, 109–10; social movement theory and, 56–58. See also cyberliberties activism; hacker culture; social movement theory
Hadl, Gabriele, 42, 111, 118–19
Hall, Ben, 132
Hamelink, Cees, 8, 118
Hansen, Chris, 24
"Happy Birthday to You," 31
Hardt, Michael, 56–57, 110, 112–13
Hatch, Orrin, 71, 146n2
HD-DVD format, 146n13
hegemony, 123
Heller, Agnes, 102
Herman, Andrew, 133–34
Hesmondhalgh, David, 21–23, 28, 44
hip-hop music, 24
hoarding fetish, 124, 134. See also collecting
Holzman, Jac, 44
Honneth, Axel, 60, 102
Horkheimer, Max, 6
Howell, Jeffrey, 144n2
Husserl, Edmund, 143n3

imperialism, 57. See also colonization
independent record labels: alternative media initiatives and, 43–44; fan awareness in, 78; industry buyouts of, 144n5; music lifeworld and, 22–23; NCMR support of, 46; total market share of, 23, 61, 146n19; visibility of system-lifeworld dialectic in, 42; web publishing as facilitator for, 37
Indiana University Press, 30
Induce Act (Inducing Infringement of Copyrights Act), 21
Inducing Infringement of Copyrights Act, 21
IndyMedia news portal, 43, 116, 148n6
"information wants to be free" slogan, 98, 121
intellectual property law (IP law): absence of normative grounding, 38, 40, 72–73, 81; ACLU cyberliberties program and, 23–24; civil liberties scholarship on, 89; contributory/vicarious infringement, 85, 146n10; copyright activism, 44–45, 122; "copyright grab," 5; copyright term extension, 29–30, 71, 132; corporation as impetus for, 67; culture jamming and, 49; cyberliberties vs. property rights critique of, 26; derivative use, 49, 75, 77, 122;

ism, 104; cyberliberties research of, 8; on digital totalitarianism, 25–26; on the eclipse of the public sphere, 99–100; on the erosion of media use rights, 71; on free culture, 44; on Internet design, 27–28, 66; SFLC affiliation of, 24

Leyshon, Andrew, 4

lifeworld: as civil liberties focus, 36; Habermas concept of, 9; overview of, 143n3; as political resistance, 83, 87–88, 99; system vs. social integration and, 9. *See also* music lifeworld; system; uncoupling

Linux, 131

Loka Institute, 25

Loudeye, 145n6

Lovink, Geert, 50, 52, 102, 117–18, 138

LPs. *See* records

Lucchi, Nicola, 70, 73, 75, 77

Lukács, Georg, 58

Lumberjack Corp., 144n5

lyric server technology, 27

Magnatunes, 60

major music labels. *See* Big Four media conglomerates

Marcuse, Herbert, 95, 111

Marxism, 6–7, 8, 36, 58, 146n16

mashups, 75, 77

master recordings, 141

Mattelart, Armand, 121

McCarthy, Thomas, 8–10, 38–39

McCourt, Tom, 2, 79, 111–12, 124, 127–28, 131, 135

McCullagh, Declan, 21

McLeod, Kembrew, 15, 31, 38, 49, 87

Mead, George Herbert, 146n15

media economics, 13, 29, 34–35, 65, 98, 126, 137

media flows, 35, 127, 148n4

media players (online). *See* online music services

media players (portable): behavioral controls in, 17–18; hacker initiatives and, 52; locked-to-player copy protection, 17; user agreements for, 130–31. *See also* iPod

mediatization of the lifeworld, 58

Melucci, Alberto, 102

Merry Pranksters, 84

message boards, 80–81, 95, 106

Mexico, 89–90, 114, 116

microbroadcasting (FM radio), 43–44

Microsoft: Back Office server software, 54; cooperation with state-sponsored censors, 47; European anti-trust initiatives against, 133; as information service, 62; virus attacks against, 78; Windows Vista DRM schemes, 71–72, 144n3; Windows XP EULA restrictions, 76; WMA file format, 18, 40, 54, 148n7

Mill, John Stuart, 82–83

mind bombs, 50

Mitnick, Kevin, 51

monetization of interactions, 58

MOOs (MUD oriented objects), 106, 147n4

Mordam record label, 144n5

Morocco, 69

Morpheus, 146n18

Mosco, Vincent: on cybernetic commodification, 58–59; on hegemony, 123; on new social movements, 56; on online music services, 135; on the pay-per society, 143n1; on political agency in movements, 97; on public interest media reform, 43; on social networking sites, 80

Motion Picture Association of America (MPAA), 18, 71

MP3 audio format: Amazon.com distribution of, 60, 129; behavioral controls of, 18; as cyberliberties concern, 27; hacker initiatives and, 52; industry opposition to, 129, 141–42; sharing enabled by, 128–29

MUDs (multi-user dungeons), 106, 147n4

multitudes, 56, 110–13

multi-user dungeons (MUDs), 106, 147n4

music lifeworld: defined, 3–4; campfire songs and, 31; critical activities of, 30; displacement by online spaces, 79–81; industry view of, 19–20; institutions associated with, 22–23; juridification relationship with, 29–31, 39, 57–58; lifeworld as political resistance, 83, 87–88; Napster as component of, 85–86; political agency and, 100–101; record stores as lifeworld component, 22–23, 79–80, 88, 126–27, 135; resistance to colonization of, 56, 88–89, 99; "second nature" activities in, 41, 60; sharing as component of, 81; theory of communicative action approach to, 34–35. *See also* lifeworld; music scenes; places of music

MusicNet, 16, 62, 80

music players. *See* iPod; media players

music profiling, 24

music sales portals. *See* online music services

music scenes: communal and sharing practices, 4; democratic theory of music
scenes, 21–23; democratizing influences
of, 3; desiccation of sharing/collecting rituals, 57; displacement by online spaces,
79–81; effect of colonization on, 88; face-
to-face encounters in, 135; as "places of
music," 133; reinforcement by online
spaces, 133–34. *See also* alternative music
scenes; music lifeworld; places of music
music studies, 3
MyDoom.F, 78
MySpace, 37, 80

Napster: overview, 85–86; as disruptive
technology, 37; as evocative of cultural
assumptions on sharing, 72; Fanning
role in, 51; file-sharing rebellion role, 16,
51–52; Napster Watershed legal defeat,
14, 21, 66, 85–88; search features, 128;
social relationships in sharing, 124
National Conference for Media Reform
(NCMR), 45–46
Negativland, 49
Negri, Antonio, 56–57, 110, 112–13
Negus, Keith, 99
neoliberalism, 84–85, 104–5, 107–9, 122
Netherlands, 82, 102
Netlabels, 5, 43–44, 60, 81
networked public sphere, 14, 96–97, 103, 114,
117–19, 138
new communalism movement, 3, 14, 24,
83–85, 122
new-media studies, 14, 115
new social movement (NSM) theory: biopolitical conflict and, 113; cyberliberties
and music activism and, 56; cyberspace
role in, 122; deliberative paradigm, 14,
114, 117, 134; fan collectivity as component in, 110–11; methodology of, 110;
modernity as key concept in, 96, 98; natural affinity for Internet, 102; post-punk
sensibility and, 120; recognition of broad
cultural conflicts, 103–4; system-
lifeworld perspective in, 35
New World Information and Communication Order, 118
New Yorkers for Fair Use, 74
NGOs (nongovernmental organizations),
115–16
No Electronic Theft Act, 71
nongovernmental organizations (NGOs),
115–16, 122

Norway, 70, 75–76
NSM theory. *See* new social movement
theory

Offe, Claus, 27, 102
Ohio University, 132
onion routers, 54
online music services: Big Four revenue
sharing arrangements, 127; catalog features in, 127–28; commodification of
user information, 59, 62, 131; effect on
music consumers, 124; fan rejection of
monitored portals, 82; hacker role in development of, 52; music download statistics, 148n6; post-iTunes generation of
services, 148n2; pushbutton control fantasy, 135; user agreements for, 130–31. *See
also* iTunes; Rhapsody music service;
subscription services; Winamp
OpenNet Initiative, 47
open-source software: concurrent versions
system (CVS) code management, 55;
decolonizing influence of, 5; FOSS
open-source campaign, 95, 97; hacker
political agency and, 121; as IP counterproject, 92; SFLC support for, 24;
WTO–TRIPS agreement and, 45

Paper Tiger TV, 43–44
parental warning labels, 24
patent law. *See* intellectual property law
patent thickets, 145n8
pay-per society, 143n1
Peacefire, 47
peer-to-peer (P2P) technology: BitTorrent
design and, 47–48; as cyberliberties concern, 27, 65; as disruptive technology, 20,
37; Downhill Battle licensing system for,
79; file-sharing rebellion role, 16; hacker
developments in, 51–52; hybrid pay-P2P
design, 148n2; ideal speech situation
and, 117; juridical defense of, 86–87; lifeworld as origin of, 138; music download
statistics, 148n6; Napster/Grokster rul-
ings effect on, 21, 51–52; new communalism convergence with, 85; noninfringing
use of, 144n4; political philosophy associated with, 105–6; smear campaign
against, 21
phenomenology, 143n3
Philippines, 112
Phlow.de, 60
Pho Listserv, 40, 74, 146n11

Pichardo, Nelson A., 33, 96, 98
piracy. *See* sharing
Pirate Act, 71
Pirate Bay, 40
pirate radio, 44, 48–49
places of music: defined, 2; culture sharing
and, 32–33; music as counterhegemonic
action and, 83–84, 133–34; "music scene"
term and, 133; social movement activism
and, 99. *See also* music lifeworld; music
scenes
playlist software, 127–28
PlaysForSure DRM, 54, 147n6
Plotke, David, 87–88, 104, 120
Plunderphonics, 49
political economics: colonization as concept
in, 61; cultural imperialism and, 146n16;
cyberliberties activism and, 16, 20, 137;
global civil society and, 119; IP law and,
28–29, 69; social movement theory and,
97; TCA adaptation and, 11–13, 34–35
post-punk movement: antimaterialistic
worldview in, 99–100; democratizing influences of, 22–23, 28; disinclination to
collective action in, 120; industry legitimation crisis and, 88, 147n9; punk-rock
as social movement, 102. *See also* alternative music scenes
Postrel, Virginia, 85
Pressplay, 80
privacy rights: ACLU cyberliberties program
and, 23–24; as cyberliberties concern, 7;
FOMC position on, 140–41; pay-to-
labor Internet design and, 59, 62; property rights conflicts with, 27; traffic analysis systems and, 53–54; web anonymity,
30, 47, 50, 52–54, 72–73, 120
production/consumption blurring, 19, 33,
99
programmed society, 42
PRO-IP Act of 2008, 71
Prometheus community radio project,
43–44
property rights. *See* intellectual property law
Proxify, 47
psychoanalysis, 10
P2P technology. *See* peer-to-peer technology
Public Citizen, 97
public domain, 7–8, 89
Public Knowledge, 28, 145n4
public sphere: critical studies on, 114; cyberliberties as normative in, 105, 137–38; democratization as influence in, 9; discrim-

inatory aspects of, 119; disintegration of,
122; functionalist concept of, 9–11; networked public sphere, 14, 96–97, 103,
114, 117–19, 138; public-sphere theory, 96;
sphere of publics and, 11; transcendence
of political borders by, 118; uncontrollable public sphere, 56–57; virtual public
sphere, 114, 116–18, 138; as zone of communicative freedom, 115. *See also* Habermas, Jürgen

Queer Nation, 102
queuing software, 127–28

radical-alternative dialectic, 44, 47
radical democracy, 27
radical media, 138; alternative media compared with, 44, 47–48, 63; cyberliberties
activism and, 11, 22, 63, 99, 138; hacktivism and, 52, 77; social movement theory
and, 50; social/political agency of, 43–45,
56–57, 103, 119; system-lifeworld visibility
and, 42; as tool for decolonization, 36
radio: alternative radio, 43, 46; CopyLeft
radio guides, 60; digital broadcast access
agreements, 145n4; as lifeworld component, 126; microbroadcasting (FM
radio), 43–44; pirate radio, 44, 48–49;
Web radio broadcast royalties, 39, 145n3
"rational choice" political theory, 107–8
rationalization of society, 5–6, 29, 99
rave raids, 24
RealNetworks, 40, 75
reasonableagreement.org, 77–78
Rebecca Clarke Reader fair-use case, 30
reception-based media theories, 13
Reclaim the Streets, 112
recording industry: artist and repertoire
(A&R) departments, 5; consolidation of,
18; internet disruptions to distribution
channels, 20; status of labor in, 79. *See
also* Big Four media conglomerates
Recording Industry Association of America
(RIAA): Apple/iTunes as digital music
competitor for, 16–17; FOMC position
on, 141–42; legislative strategy of, 71,
131–32; moral appeals to consumers, 18;
post-Napster mass litigation initiative,
70–71, 147n7; power to subpoena ISPs,
68; RIAA Radar monitoring of, 60;
RIAA v. Verizon, 68; virus attacks against,
78
Recording Industry vs. the People, 97

records: behavioral controls of record players, 17; as Celestial Jukebox opt-out strategy, 60; consumer experiences with, 124; displacement by digital media, 143n2; ideology of sharing and, 72; record collectors, 14, 40; record stores as lifeworld component, 22–23, 79–80, 88, 126–27, 135; turntable as "dumb" interface, 129. *See also* collecting

Red Lambda filtering software, 132

regulationism: clash with cyberlibertarians, 2; hackers as impetus for, 21; ISP filtering software, 132, 145n8; "Net backlash" and, 105; P2P as response to, 85; regulationist ideology, 65; TCA critique of, 38

reification, 6–7, 58, 90

Reno v. ACLU (1997), 24, 138

research (cyberliberties research): collaborative research, 74; overview of, 8; suppression of DRM research, 30–31, 55, 107

RE/Search Magazine, 49

resource mobilization (RM) approach, 103–4, 110

Rhapsody music service (RealNetworks), 40, 75, 130

Rheingold, Howard, 83, 112

RIAA. *See* Recording Industry Association of America

right of first sale, 62, 92, 130, 134, 146n1

right to communicate, 25, 27–28, 36

right-wing libertarianism, 107–9

"Ring around the Rosie," 31

Rip-Mix-Burn marketing, 17, 19, 130–31

ripping: home tape mixing as precursor, 37; industry crackdown on, 144n2, 145n1; music-that-moves issue and, 36–37; production/consumption blurring and, 19; Rip-Mix-Burn marketing, 17, 19, 130–31; rootkit copy-protection and, 53

ritual, 3, 21, 30, 57, 81, 101

RM (resource mobilization) approach, 103–4, 110

rootkit technology, 17–18, 53, 76–77, 146n11

Rothenbuhler, Eric, 5

royalties: artist performance royalties, 31; major label policies for, 79; Webcasting licensing fees and, 39, 148n4

Russia, 69, 116

Russo, Wayne, 52

Samuelson, Pamela, 38, 41

Scalia, Antonin, 25

Schudson, Michael, 114

Schuler, Douglas, 116, 138

Schutz, Alfred, 143n3

Schweidler, Christine, 91–92, 102, 116

SDMI (Secure Digital Music Initiative), 141–42

search tools, 127–28

Searle, John R., 146n15

second nature sociality, 41

second self, 59

Secure Digital Music Initiative (SDMI), 141–42

semiotic democracy, 22, 28, 30, 86–87, 133

SFLC (Software Freedom Law Center), 24

Shank, Barry, 133

sharing: artists' views of, 72; criminalization of fans, 19–21, 24; culture sharing as cyberlibertarian concern, 32–33; Downhill Battle licensing system for, 79; fair use provision for, 30; file-sharing rebellion, 16, 25; FOMC position on, 140–41; as fundamental to copyright law tradition, 70; gift economy, 1, 86, 110; industry media player design initiatives, 129–30; information as commodity and, 98; international norms for, 90–92; MP3 design and, 128–29; as music lifeworld norm, 60, 72–73, 81, 86, 97, 137; piracy rhetoric, 26; post-Napster sharing sites, 51–52; small worlds file sharing, 41, 145n5, 146n18; social agency and, 110–11; social relationships in, 124. *See also* collecting

Singapore, 69

Sklyarov, Dmitry, 55

Skype, 131

Slashdot.org, 146n11

smart mobs, 83, 112

social control, 3, 13–14, 25–26

social movement theory: overview, 101–2; activist scholarship, 15; alternative vs. radical media, 43–45; collective vs. individual activism and, 50, 52, 122–23; collective vs. individual rights and, 25–27; communicative rationality as provisional initiative, 42; cultural studies perspective on, 35–36, 94; cyberliberties initiative and, 13, 22; "daily practices" in, 102–3; file sharing as a social movement, 86–87; mediation between system and lifeworld, 11–12; middle-class activist motivation, 97–98; music as social/political activism, 83–84, 99–100, 133–34; organic resistance strategies, 96–97; political agency in hacking, 120; resistance ideology as nor-

mative paradigm, 97; resistance to commodification, 2, 90–92; right to communicate and, 36; self-awareness role in,
110–11; technological freedom and, 14;
virtual public sphere as activist environment, 117–18, 138. *See also* Alternative
Jukebox; cyberliberties activism; new
social movement (NSM) theory
social networking sites, 37, 80. *See also* Facebook; MySpace
Software Business Alliance, 118
Software Freedom Law Center (SFLC), 24
Sonny Bono Copyright Term Extension Act,
30, 71
Sony Betamax media format, 129–30
Sony-BMG Corp.: anti-DRM lawsuits filed
against, 77; ownership structure of, 61;
payola scandal of, 21; rootkit technology
of, 17–18, 53, 76–77, 146n11; slow adaptation to cybertechnology, 4
Sony Walkman/Discman players, 37
South Korea, 82, 90–91
Soviet Union, 116
spatialization, 61–63
speech acts, 55, 146n15
sphere of publics, 11
Spiralfrog, 147n6
spyware, 77
Stallman, Richard, 24, 51, 109, 120
steering media, 30, 67
Steve Jackson Games, 107, 147n5
Steve Jackson Games v. Secret Service (1993),
147n5
Strangelove, Michael, 25–26, 56–57
Strossen, Nadine, 109
SubGenius Foundation, 49
subscription services: collectors as subscribers, 134–35; passive consumer reaction to,
58; physical formats compared with,
124–25, 130–31, 134–35; recording property rights and, 20. *See also* clientelization; online music services
surveillance (digital surveillance): acquiescence to, 81; colonization thesis and, 7,
53–54; CRM software and, 80; as cyberliberties concern, 2; by iTunes, 59; privacy rights and, 122; private property
rights and, 117; RIAA-sponsored legislation facilitating, 131; user authentication
and, 130–31. *See also* anonymity; digital
rights management
system: Habermas on, 3, 6, 9, 143n3; system
integration, 7, 9, 38–39, 67; system vs.

social integration and, 9; visibility of
system-lifeworld dialectic, 42. *See also*
lifeworld; theory of communicative
action; uncoupling

tactical media, 50, 138
Taylorization, 97–98, 147n2
technocracy: music industry consumers and,
1; "second nature" activities and, 41; systems of control, 5, 15, 39–40, 72, 98, 138;
WIPO implementation and, 90
Telecommunications Act of 1996, 1, 73, 89,
97
telegraph, 57
television, 1, 43, 48, 145n4
text-message communication, 112
theory of communicative action (TCA): adaptation to cyberliberties, 8–9, 12, 57, 138;
advantages for studying music activism,
34–35; critique of, 9–10; critique of lockdown business approach, 38; deliberative
paradigm, 14, 114, 117, 134; intellectual
sources for, 67, 146–47n3; normative expressions of resistance, 117; NSM/RM
extensions of, 110; praxis as pivotal concept for, 96; system-lifeworld dialectic
observability in, 42. *See also* Habermas,
Jürgen; McCarthy, Thomas
third media sector, 118
"This Land is Your Land," 31
Tilly, Charles, 101–2
Time Warner, 62
tinkering, 32
TiVo video recorder, 129–30
Toffler, Alvin, 108–9
TOR Project, 53–54, 146n12
Torvalds, Linus, 51
Touraine, Alain, 41–42, 102
Turner, Fred, 83–85, 106–7, 109
2600 magazine, 55

U2, 49
unconscionability doctrine, 70, 75–76
uncontrollable public sphere, 56–57
uncoupling (of lifeworld from system): fan
beliefs/expectations and, 98–99; formal
vs. informal organizations as model for,
38–39; Habermas concept of, 11; IP law
role in, 15, 17, 30; promotion of alternative media environments and, 118–19;
visibility of system-lifeworld dialectic,
42. *See also* lifeworld; system
unfuck.exe hack, 54